D0722479

500
BUTTERFLIES

500
BUTTERFLIES
Ken Preston-Mafham
Butterflies From
Around the World
FIREFLY BOOKS

A FIREFLY BOOK

Published by Firefly Books Ltd. 2007

First printing

Publisher Cataloging-in-Publication Data (U.S.)
Preston-Mafham, Ken, 1949-
500 butterflies : butterflies from around the world / Ken Preston-Mafham.
[528] p. : col. photos. ; cm.
Includes bibliographical references and index.
Summary: Introduction to butterflies, with description and illustrations of 500 species, worldwide. Includes their form, natural history and distribution.
ISBN-13: 978-1-55407-295-8
ISBN-10: 1-55407-295-6
1. Butterflies. I. Klein, Jean-Louis. II. Five hundred butterflies. III. Title.
595.789 dc22 QL542.P747 2007

Library and Archives Canada Cataloguing in Publication
Preston-Mafham, Ken
500 butterflies : butterflies from around the world / Ken Preston-Mafham.
Includes bibliographical references and index.
ISBN-13: 978-1-55407-295-8
ISBN-10: 1 -55407-295-6
1. Butterflies. I. Title. II. Title: Five hundred butterflies.
QL542.P735 2007 595.78'9
C2007-900790-2

Published in the United States by
Firefly Books (U.S.) Inc.
P.O. Box 1338, Ellicott Station
Buffalo, New York 14205

Published in Canada by
Firefly Books Ltd.
66 Leek Crescent
Richmond Hill, Ontario L4B 1H1

The Brown Reference Group plc:
(incorporating Andromeda Oxford Limited
8 Chapel Place, Rivington Street,
London EC2A 3DQ

www.brownreference.com

For the Brown Reference Group plc:
Editorial Director: Lindsey Lowe
Project Editor: Graham Bateman
Editor: Virginia Carter
Design: Steve McCurdy

All photos within the book: © Premaphotos Wildlife

Page 1 Common Pearlwing (*Scada reckia*)

Page 2-3 Giant African Swallowtail (***Papilio antimachus***) drinking with other swallowtails, Ghana

Cover Photos
Front Cover: Blue Silk Butterfly (*Morpho anaxabia*), Robert McCaw
Spine: Eastern Tiger Swallowtail (*Papilio glaucus*), Shutterstock/Jill Lang
Back cover: Comma (*Polygonia c-album*), Shutterstock/Steve McWilliam

Printed in China

Contents

CONTENTS

CONTENTS

Introduction

500 Butterflies portrays 500 species of butterflies in 14 families. Although they are drawn from all over the world, there is a very strong bias toward the tropics, where the overwhelming majority of butterflies are found. The 4,000 or so butterfly species found in Africa and Madagascar are well represented here, as are the 8,000-odd species from the American tropics. The selection from tropical Asia is smaller, partly because this area is less rich in butterflies (about 2,900 species) but also because the butterflies there tend to be much harder to see and photograph than those of Africa and tropical America. For example, when the author was in Ghana's Bobiri Forest Reserve, a visiting tour group arrived to look at the butterflies. The leader had recently taken a group to Sri Lanka, and in two weeks they had managed to see about 100 species. Within a few hours at Bobiri, their total was more than 150.

The purpose of this book is to represent butterflies you are likely to observe, which explains the species chosen. The coverage for Africa and Central and South America is fairly representative and should enable you to identify a large proportion of what you see, with the exception of the many small members of the Lycaenidae that are often on show. Also excluded are certain large species such as *Prepona* (Nymphalidae), in which the brightly colored blue upper side is normally glimpsed only briefly as the butterfly takes wing. The underside is very drab and is, alas, what you normally see if the butterfly is feeding on fallen fruit or at banana bait.

SPECIES DESCRIPTIONS

Entries in this book are arranged alphabetically by family, and within family in alphabetical sequence of the genera and species. Each entry is accompanied by a photograph. These have all been taken of butterflies in their natural habitat, showing how they look and behave in the wild. Even the use of artificial bait to attract specimens for photography has been avoided. Each entry is headed by the common name, although in many cases names have been given only recently and are far from being in general use.

Each illustration is accompanied by an overall description of the species, the type of habitat in which it lives, and other information, including a reference to the individual butterfly illustrated. There is also a data panel. This starts with the scientific name, which is generally the latest accepted name that the author has been able to track down, bearing in mind the frequent changes that are a constant source of irritation to us all. Next comes alternative common name(s) if applicable, followed by the family to which the species belongs.

The wingspan quoted is generally midway between the maximum and minimum given in other references and is intended as a very approximate guide only. Under "larval food plants" the food eaten by the caterpillar (where known) is listed. The flight period for many tropical species is given as "all year," but it should be stressed that this does not necessarily mean you will see this species on any given visit to its habitat. This is because, even in the warm tropics, butterfly numbers may drop to very low levels at certain times of the year (for example, in the dry season or at the height of the rainy season), although the species will still be on the wing somewhere. For temperate areas the months of usual emergence are given, although these times will vary according to latitude, elevation, and individual seasons. Finally, "range" lists the countries or general area in which the species has been recorded to date.

The butterfly families used in the following pages follow the "traditional" concept of retaining a larger number of smaller families. In most recent works no fewer than nine of the families used here (Acraeidae, Amathusiidae, Brassolidae, Danaidae, Heliconiidae, Ithomiidae, Libytheidae, Morphidae, and Satyridae) have been lumped into a hugely expanded and unwieldy concept of the Nymphalidae. Since this classification has not been universally accepted and because the application of smaller families makes for a much more accessible book, they have been retained here. The number of species included usually reflects the size of the family, so that in small families such as Morphidae, Brassolidae, Amathusiidae, and Libytheidae only one or two species are illustrated.

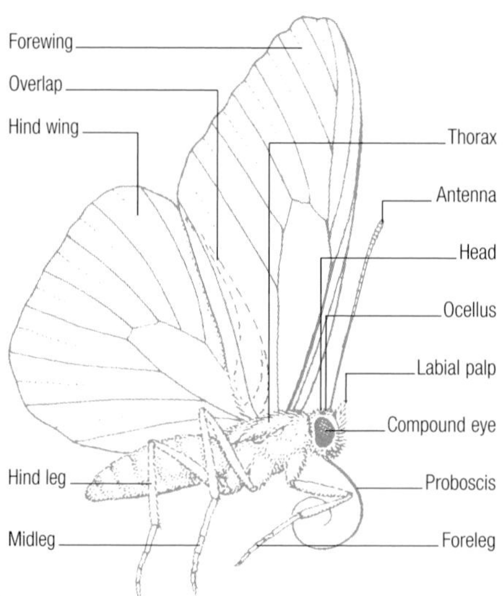

WHAT IS A BUTTERFLY?

Butterflies belong to the superfamily Papilionoidea within the large order Lepidoptera (the scale-winged insects). The most numerous members of the order Lepidoptera are the moths, and it is not always easy to distinguish a butterfly from a moth. The main difference lies in the way that the wings act together. In butterflies this is accomplished by the trailing edge of the forewing overlapping the leading edge of the hind wing, so they operate as a single unit. In moths the wings are physically coupled by a device called a frenulum.

Another difference lies in the antennae. In butterflies they are generally slender with clubbed tips, but in moths they are usually stouter and have comblike edges. However, some moths have antennae that are exactly like those of butterflies. Most moths fly at night, but some are active during the day—these are often the ones that at first glance are colorful enough to be mistaken for butterflies. Finally, the skippers (family Hesperiidae)—traditionally treated as slightly odd butterflies—have recently been found to fall somewhere between butterflies and moths and have been given their own superfamily, the Hesperioidea. This has left them stranded in something of no-man's land, and they are often excluded both from books on butterflies and from those on moths.

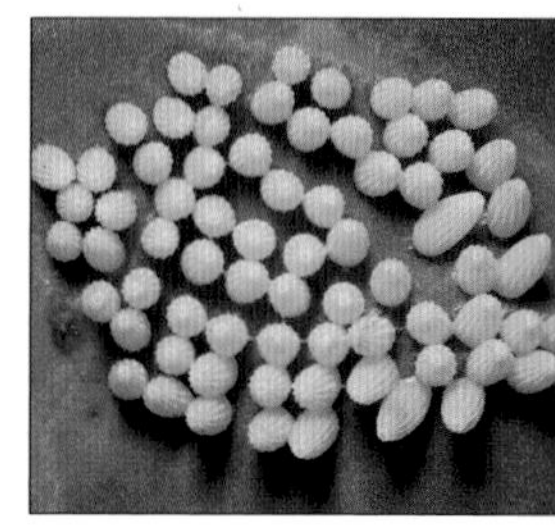

Left: Body plan of a typical butterfly.

Right: Eggs of the Large White (Pieris brassicae).

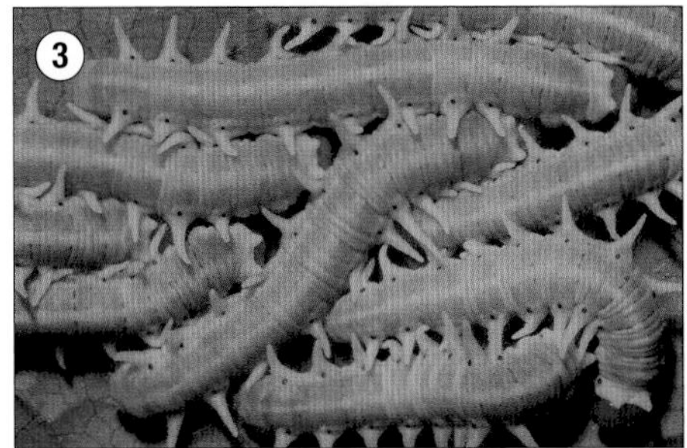

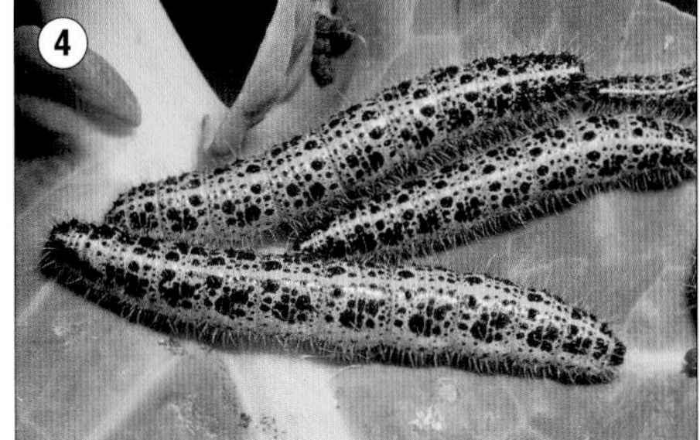

A range of caterpillars: 1 Red Daggerwing (Marpesia petreus)*; 2* Euthalia *species; 3* Mechanitis *species; 4 Large White* (Pieris brassicae).

Because most people still treat skippers as butterflies, they are included here as such.

In butterflies, as in all insects, the skeleton is on the outside (exoskeleton), with all the soft bits (heart, digestive system, and so on) inside. The adult has six legs (only four of which are fully developed in some families) and four wings. They are usually covered in numerous tiny scales, giving the butterfly its color and pattern. The head bears a pair of compound eyes made up of numerous tiny segments called facets. Below the head lies the coiled proboscis, which can be unrolled for use. It has a hollow center through which liquids can be drawn. In temperate regions the liquid most often taken is the nectar from flowers, but this is ignored by most tropical butterflies, which prefer something stronger, such as mammal dung, urine-soaked ground, rotting fruit, or fermenting sap from trees.

BUTTERFLY DEVELOPMENT

Development from egg to adult takes place in a series of stages, called metamorphosis. The eggs are laid on the food plant (or other food) singly or in clusters, sometimes containing hundreds of eggs. The egg hatches into a tiny larva, usually known as a caterpillar. The caterpillar's strong jaws are able to chew tough food such as leaves. Caterpillars need to grow as fast as possible, so they spend as much time as they safely can just filling up with food. Since their outer skin is not very elastic it has to be shed at regular intervals by molting—in this way the caterpillar can grow by expanding into a new skin while it is still soft.

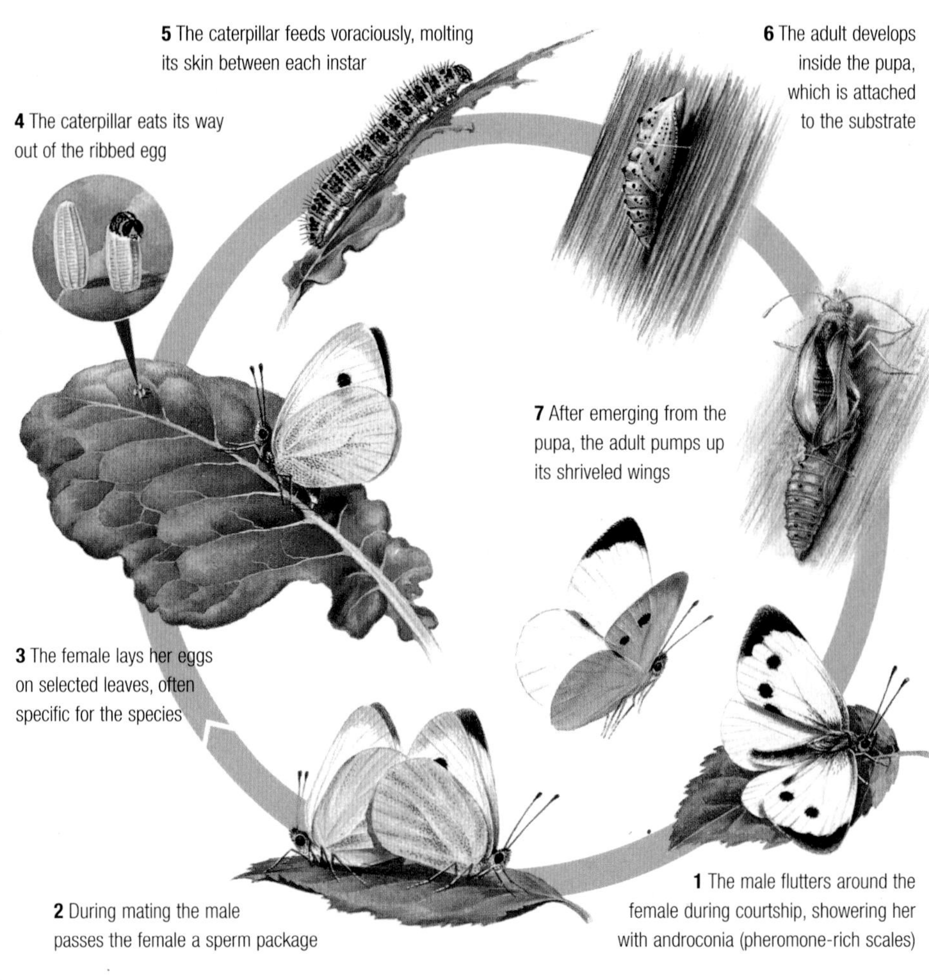
5 The caterpillar feeds voraciously, molting its skin between each instar
6 The adult develops inside the pupa, which is attached to the substrate
4 The caterpillar eats its way out of the ribbed egg
7 After emerging from the pupa, the adult pumps up its shriveled wings
3 The female lays her eggs on selected leaves, often specific for the species
2 During mating the male passes the female a sperm package
1 The male flutters around the female during courtship, showering her with androconia (pheromone-rich scales)

Most caterpillars go through five molts (known as instars) before entering the next stage of development, the pupa. Known in butterflies as a chrysalis, the pupa is an immobile stage and is attached to a leaf or other firm structure. It can be secured either by one end or with the addition of a silken loop around its middle, which is the method used by the Large White *(Pieris brassicae)*. The chrysalis is often very beautiful, perhaps covered with gold and silver spots or with a shiny, mirrorlike surface. On the other hand, it may resemble a twisted dead leaf or the head of a poisonous snake, as in *Dynastor* (Brassolidae). After about 10 days (depending on temperature) the adult butterfly forces its way out through the split skin of its chrysalis, pumps blood into its tightly folded wings to expand them, and flies off.

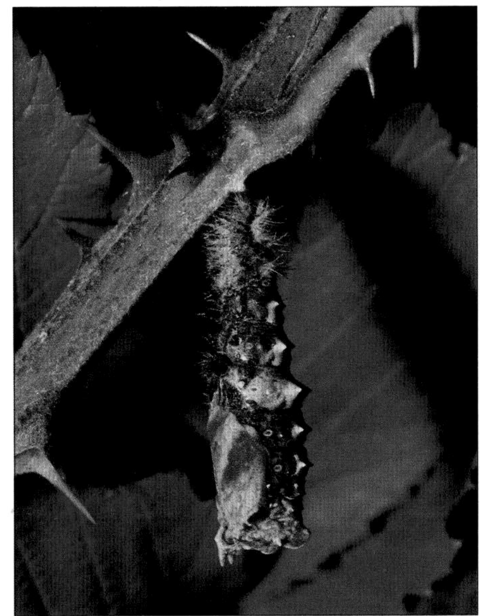

WHERE TO FIND BUTTERFLIES

The 20,000 or so species of butterflies (including skippers) currently known and named are not evenly distributed around the world. The permanently warm tropical zones hold the most species, and within them the highest species diversity is centered on Central and South America. One single area of Amazonia, such as the Rancho Grande Reserve in Rondônia, may contain 2,000 butterfly species. In Africa the richest areas can manage only about half that number, but that is still many times more than the numbers found in temperate areas.

Left: The life cycle of the butterfly is a sequence of extraordinary transformations.

Right: Types of pupae. Top: Comma (Polygonia c-album)*; Bottom: pupa from the family Nymphalidae.*

The numbers game can be misleading, however. During the author's month-long stay at Rancho Grande fewer butterflies were seen than in just five minutes in the Bobiri Forest Reserve in Ghana, a West African country not normally associated with butterfly richness. The reason so many were seen during the author's visit was because there had been heavy and unexpected rainfall at Christmas, during the dry season. By contrast, the author's visit to Rancho Grande was marked by the worst drought in living memory, and this was the cause of the disappointing absence of adult butterflies. Weather is a decisive factor in the ability to see tropical butterflies, and it pays to do some research into what is the best season before setting off.

To be sure of avoiding disappointment you may be best advised to take an organized trip, either to see butterflies exclusively or one of the more popular "butterflies and birds" itineraries. Your group leader will know the area and the best time to visit as well as the identities of most of the species. The names of specialized tour companies can be found on the Internet. If you go, do not collect specimens—leave them there for others to admire and marvel at. Living butterflies recorded on a video camera or digital still-camera will always be there for you to admire at great magnification on your computer or TV, and are far more spectacular than dead, set specimens pinned out in a box. In this enlightened age that kind of behavior is really acceptable only when done for scientific reasons.

Tropical rain forest is the richest area for butterflies, but a walk through an area of virgin forest can be a desperately unrewarding experience. For hour after hour all you may see are tree trunks, roots crossing the path, and huge quantities of dark green vegetation. You may not even see a flower, let alone the "butterfly on gaudy rain-forest blossom" so often expected by those unfamiliar with the rain forest. The experienced tropical butterfly hunter heads straight for a riverbank, logging road, or any track that lets a reasonable amount of light into the gloomy forest interior. Apart from a few specialized butterflies, such as *Caligo*, *Cithaerias*, *Haetera*, *Pierella*, and *Melanitis*, the twilight gloom of the rain-forest interior is devoid of delicate flapping wings. Damp riverside sand or muddy tracks will sometimes be covered with hordes of butterflies, as will fresh heaps of dung from mammals such as civet cats or leopards. A fig tree in fruit can be a bonanza, for butterflies that are otherwise seldom seen below the high canopy will often come down to booze on fallen fruits.

A mass of Common Grass Yellow butterflies (Eurema hecabe) *puddling in rain forest in Ghana.*

Getting the season right should not be a problem in temperate areas, where butterflies are on the wing only in specific months of summer, with a small amount of variation caused by local conditions or unusually warm or cool seasons. You know that if you visit the Rocky Mountains in January you will not see any butterflies, while in July a flowery mountain meadow should have plenty. Go south, to southern Florida or southern Texas, and it will be warm enough most years to see butterflies on the wing at Christmas time. If you have enough of the right kinds of flowers in your backyard (members of the sunflower family such as zinnias are popular) then you shouldn't even need to leave home to watch butterflies. They are found just about everywhere, even on waste lots in large cities such as Chicago and New York.

Hewitson's Glassy Legionnaire

In the normal form of this widespread butterfly the forewing of the male is red, with the upper half transparent. The hind wing is red, with a sprinkling of black spots and a black marginal border adorned with a row of large red spots. The female is slightly larger, and the red is replaced by reddish brown or gray. The male illustrated was photographed beside a track leading through a fairly open area in Bimbia Forest, Cameroon, a typical habitat for this butterfly of forests and dense bush.

DATA

Scientific name: *Acraea admatha*

Family: Acraeidae

Wingspan: 2.4 in (6 cm).

Flight period: All year.

Larval food plants: Members of the violet family (Violaceae).

Range: Over most of sub-Saharan Africa.

Small Yellow-banded Legionnaire

DATA

Scientific name: *Acraea acerata*

Family: Acraeidae

Wingspan: 1.6 in (4 cm).

Flight period: All year.

Larval food plants: Members of the morning glory family (Convolvulaceae).

Range: Throughout most of sub-Saharan Africa north of South Africa.

The ground color of the wings on this common butterfly of open bush and forest clearings varies from a rich orange brown to a rather faded shade of buff. There is a broad black border around the edges of the wings, cutting across the top third of the forewing to enclose a patch of ground color. The undersides are broadly similar. Although these butterflies are on the wing throughout the year, there are definite peaks and troughs, such that thousands may be present in one month, falling to just a handful later in the year. The caterpillars can be a pest on cultivated sweet potatoes, an important crop in tropical Africa.

Alcinoe Legionnaire

DATA

Scientific name: *Acraea alcinoe*

Family: Acraeidae

Wingspan: Male 2.8 in (7 cm); female 3.7 in (9.5 cm).

Flight period: All year.

Larval food plants: *Adenia* in the passionflower family (Passifloraceae).

Range: From West Africa to western Kenya.

One of several members of the genus *Acraea* formerly included in *Bematistes*, this is a butterfly of shady rain forests, although it copes well with degraded forests that have been logged. The male is blackish brown with orange-brown bands on all four wings. The female looks very different, being not only far larger and with much broader forewings, but marked with white instead of orange-brown bands. The female below was seen on a cool Harmattan morning in Ghana's Bobiri Forest.

Black-winged Legionnaire

Found in semiopen areas such as forest clearings, scattered woodland, and parks, this is one of the easiest members of the genus to recognize. In both sexes the forewing is black, while the hind wing is a rather attractive shade of red in the male and reddish brown in the female. In both cases there are a few black spots and a small black basal patch. The undersides are broadly similar. In the highlands of eastern Kenya there is a race in which the usually plain black forewing has a band, which is red in the male and dusky white in the female.

DATA

Scientific name: *Acraea asboloplintha*

Family: Acraeidae

Wingspan: 2.4 in (6 cm).

Flight period: All year.

Larval food plants: Passionflowers *(Passiflora).*

Range: Africa (from eastern Congo region to Uganda and Kenya).

Pink Legionnaire

DATA

Scientific name: *Acraea caecilia*

Family: Acraeidae

Wingspan: 2.2 in (5.5 cm).

Flight period: All year.

Larval food plants: Members of the turnera family (Turneraceae).

Range: West, Central, and East Africa.

Open, grassy savanna with scattered bushes and thorny trees is the main habitat for this butterfly, illustrated here in Meru National Park in Kenya. In the male (illustrated) the ground color is a distinctive shade of pinkish orange. The tips of the forewings and the extreme bases of both sets of wings are suffused with black, and there is a broad black margin to the hind wings. A smattering of black spots is fairly neatly arranged across all four wings. The female is similar, but her ground color is whitish pink. On the hind-wing undersides of both sexes there are distinct white spots in the marginal black band. Adult numbers usually peak just at the onset of the rains.

White Legionnaire

The common name of this butterfly is really relevant only for the male, seen here puddling on a muddy track in Bobiri Forest in Ghana. As can be clearly seen, he has a broad creamy white band on each hind wing, the forewings being more or less transparent. In the female the hind wings are reddish orange with a black border, although there is a rare form that is similar to the male. Occurring mainly in wet forest, this species is also sometimes found in drier forest types. Perched males will chase off anything that flies near them.

DATA

Scientific name: *Acraea circeis*

Family: Acraeidae

Wingspan: About 2 in (5 cm).

Flight period: All year.

Larval food plants: *Urera oblongifolia* in the nettle family (Urticaceae).

Range: Africa (from Sierra Leone to the Congo region and northern Angola).

White-barred Legionnaire

DATA

Scientific name: *Acraea encedon*

Family: Acraeidae

Wingspan: About 2 in (5 cm).

Flight period: All year.

Larval food plants: Members of the spiderwort family (Commelinaceae).

Range: Africa and Madagascar; subspecies *rathjensi* in the Arabian Peninsula.

The White-barred Legionnaire is one of the most widely distributed of African butterflies. It is generally found in open areas such as savanna, agricultural areas, and parks, but also occurs in large forest clearings. Its coloration is variable, and the white bar and black apex on the forewing can sometimes be absent, leaving a plain brownish orange butterfly with black spots. In some forms the ground color on the upper side is whitish. The underside ground color is normally a pale yellow. The form pictured here, feeding at a flower in Ranomafana National Park in Madagascar, is a mimic of the Common Tiger *(Danaus chrysippus).*

Jodutta Legionnaire

This is a forest butterfly, common in the rain forest of West Africa, although it is more likely to be seen in the lighter spots along a forest track or riverbank than in the denser, darker interior. In the male (illustrated, puddling on a muddy track in Bobiri Forest, Ghana) the forewing is black with a yellow bar and a slightly larger yellow patch; the hind wings have a much larger yellow area. The female is similar but marked with white rather than yellow. In both sexes the undersides are broadly similar to the upper sides, but drabber. Flight is rather slow, frequently low down near the forest floor, where females often search for plants on which to lay eggs.

DATA

Scientific name: *Acraea jodutta*

Family: Acraeidae

Wingspan: 2.2–2.4 in (5.5–6 cm).

Flight period: All year.

Larval food plants: *Urera*, *Fleurya*, *Boehmeria*, and *Pouzolzia* in the nettle family (Urticaceae).

Range: West, Central, and East Africa.

Elegant Legionnaire

DATA

Scientific name: *Acraea egina*

Family: Acraeidae

Wingspan: About 2.4 in (6 cm).

Flight period: All year.

Larval food plants: *Adenia lobata* in the passionflower family (Passifloraceae).

Range: Over most of sub-Saharan Africa.

Found in wet and dry forests, as well as Guinea-savanna and in backyards, this is a highly successful species with a powerful flight. In the male (illustrated) the upper side of the forewings is largely smoky black, with a few darker black spots and a patch of orange toward the hind edge. The hind wing is mainly orange, with a few black spots and a black border. The undersides are rather pale and washed out. This applies also to both sides of the female, which looks like a totally different species. The male illustrated was puddling on a track through Bobiri Forest, Ghana.

Common Legionnaire

DATA

Scientific name: *Acraea epaea*

Family: Acraeidae

Wingspan: 2.6 in (6.5 cm).

Flight period: All year.

Larval food plants: *Lindaeckeria dentata* and *Adenia cisampelloides* in the passionflower family (Passifloraceae).

Range: Over most of sub-Saharan Africa except for the far nontropical south.

Another former member of the genus *Bematistes*, this highly distasteful species is mimicked by the African Palmfly *(Elymniopsis bammakoo)* and the Common False Legionnaire *(Pseudacraea eurytus)*. In the female (illustrated on flowers in Bobiri Forest, Ghana) the wings are black and white, while in the male the markings are similar but with the white replaced by brownish orange. Although mainly a forest butterfly, the Common Legionnaire also seems to thrive in degraded forests and in areas of wooded Guinea-savanna. Although usually occurring as a solitary individual, at times hundreds may be seen together.

Lycoa Legionnaire

DATA

Scientific name: *Acraea lycoa*

Family: Acraeidae

Wingspan: About 2 in (5 cm).

Flight period: All year.

Larval food plants: From various families.

Range: From West Africa to Ethiopia and northern Tanzania.

A common forest species over much of Africa, this butterfly rarely occurs in large numbers and is able to tolerate a fair degree of habitat degradation. The female (illustrated in Kakamega Forest, Kenya) has four creamy white spots on each black forewing, and a yellowish hind wing, grading through brown into a blackish margin. The male is very different, being a strange, almost transparent wishy-washy glassy brown. This species is a relatively weak flier and flutters around near the forest floor, sometimes seeking out lighter spots, where it will feed on flowers.

Black-spot Legionnaire

DATA

Scientific name: *Acraea macaria*

Family: Acraeidae

Wingspan: About 3 in (7.5 cm).

Flight period: All year.

Larval food plants: *Adenia* in the passionflower family (Passifloraceae).

Range: Africa (from Senegal to Kenya).

At home even in the gloomier parts of the African rain forest, this is one of a number of rather large species that were previously included in the genus *Bematistes*. In the male the forewings are much narrower and more pointed than in the female. On the forewing he has a bright reddish brown band, just visible in the illustration; in the female this band is white, as found on the hind wings of both sexes. The butterfly illustrated is subspecies *hemileuca*, which is restricted to East Africa. This male was seen at rest in the depths of Kakamega Forest, Kenya.

Natal Legionnaire

DATA

Scientific name: *Acraea natalica*

Family: Acraeidae

Wingspan: About 2.4 in (6 cm).

Flight period: All year.

Larval food plants: *Adenia*, *Passiflora*, and *Wormskjoldia* in the passionflower family (Passifloraceae).

Range: Southern Africa.

Although its common name might imply that this attractive butterfly is restricted to the South African province of KwaZulu-Natal (from where it was first described), it is in fact widespread as far north as Zambia and Malawi. It is very much an insect of the more open kinds of habitats, such as savanna and even backyards, and generally avoids thickly forested areas. The basic color of the upper side is pinkish red, with heavy black markings at the bases and tips of the wings. The underside is also attractive, with a row of large whitish spots adorning the black edge of each hind wing.

The Wandering Donkey

Occurring mostly in open savanna, agricultural areas, and backyards, this species seems to be gradually penetrating the remaining forested areas of West Africa as they are opened up by human activities. It is seen here in Cameroon's Bimbia Forest. The butterfly's basic color is pale orange, with glassy tips to the forewings and a row of orange spots inside a black marginal band on each hind wing. The underside is similar, except that the marginal spots here are whitish. The caterpillar can be a pest on various cultivated crops, such as sweet potato and tobacco.

DATA

Scientific name: *Acraea neobule*

Family: Acraeidae

Wingspan: About 1.8 in (4.5 cm).

Flight period: All year.

Larval food plants: Very varied.

Range: Through most of sub-Saharan Africa.

Window Legionnaire

DATA

Scientific name: *Acraea oncaea*

Family: Acraeidae

Wingspan: 1.8–2 in (4.5–5 cm).

Flight period: All year.

Larval food plants: Various members of the passionflower family (Passifloraceae).

Range: Africa (from Ethiopia southward to Kwazulu-Natal in South Africa).

Sharing its open savanna home with such big game as the elephant, giraffe, and rhino, this far smaller member of the animal kingdom is still well worth our close attention. Somewhat unusually, the upper side of the wings is less attractive than the underside, being mostly a pale, rather wishy-washy shade of light red, broken by a few black spots and some black markings around the edges. The underside, as seen here in a mating pair from Kruger National Park in South Africa, is far more attractive—particularly the row of large white spots standing out clearly in the dark marginal band of the hind wing.

Orina Legionnaire

DATA

Scientific name: *Acraea orina*

Family: Acraeidae

Wingspan: About 2 in (5 cm).

Flight period: All year.

Larval food plants: Not known.

Range: Africa (from Côte d'Ivoire to Cameroon).

Undoubtedly one of the most beautiful members of the genus, this is not a common butterfly over most of its range—it is seemingly more abundant in the eastern part of its range than in the west. The male, seen here puddling on muddy ground in Ghana's Bobiri Forest, is very like that of the Yellow-veined Legionnaire *(Acraea parrhasia)*. Unlike in that species, however, there is no tendency toward translucency in any of the spots on the forewing, which in the Orina Legionnaire are all bright orange. The female is similar to that of *A. parrhasia*, but the black spots at the base of the hind wing are congealed into an almost solid mass. This butterfly's favored habitat is along forest edges and in clearings.

Yellow-veined Legionnaire

Scientific name: *Acraea parrhasia*

Family: Acraeidae

Wingspan: About 2 in (5 cm).

Flight period: All year.

Larval food plants: *Urera* in the nettle family (Urticaceae).

Range: West, Central, and East Africa.

Restricted to forested areas, this splendid butterfly is similar to the Peneleos Legionnaire *(Acraea peneleos)*. However, the male of the Yellow-veined Legionnaire is distinguished by the conspicuous yellow veins on the upper side of the forewings. These have four transparent "windows" and two that are strongly suffused with orange. Each hind wing has a broad orange band. The female (as illustrated here, puddling in Bobiri Forest, Ghana) is brown rather than orange. In both sexes the undersides are very different and a little drab, with no red at all. In subspecies *servona* the red band on the hind wing is replaced by pale yellow.

Penelope's Legionnaire

DATA

Scientific name: *Acraea penelope*

Family: Acraeidae

Wingspan: About 2 in (5 cm).

Flight period: All year.

Larval food plants: Unknown.

Range: From West Africa to Uganda and Kenya.

Rather uncommon over most of its range, this butterfly is restricted to areas of relatively undisturbed rain forest. In the male the forewing is black, with a row of transparent patches. The hind wing is bright reddish orange, with a black patch at the base and a black band around the margin. The females are generally similar, but in certain individuals the hind wings are yellow rather than red. The male illustrated was feeding on a well-trodden muddy path in Kakamega Forest in western Kenya.

Musanga Legionnaire

Considered by some specialists to consist of two species *(Acraea polis* and *A. pentapolis)*, this common butterfly is treated here as a single species. It is found in forests, often in disturbed secondary forest where its stilt-rooted host tree, *Musanga cecropioides*, is common. These trees may be stripped of their large straplike leaves by the feeding of hordes of voracious caterpillars. In the adult butterfly the wings are largely transparent, interrupted by a broad but somewhat translucent yellowish band on the hind wings and a few black spots. This butterfly is seen mostly on flowers but also basks, as seen here in Kakamega Forest, Kenya.

DATA

Scientific name: *Acraea pentapolis*

Family: Acraeidae

Wingspan: 2.8 in (7 cm).

Flight period: All year.

Larval food plants: Mainly the African Corkwood Tree *(Musanga cecropioides)* of the fig family (Moraceae).

Range: From West Africa eastward to Kenya and Tanzania and southward to Malawi.

Familiar Legionnaire

DATA

Scientific name: *Acraea pharsalus*

Family: Acraeidae

Wingspan: 2.4 in (6 cm).

Flight period: All year.

Larval food plants: Numerous and varied.

Range: From West Africa to Kenya and Mozambique.

On flowery forest roadsides or in forest clearings over much of tropical Africa, this is one of the most familiar members of the genus. It is depicted here on flowers beside a road through Kakamega Forest in Kenya. In the male (illustrated) the forewing is bright red with heavy black markings and a narrow white bar toward the apex; the hind wing is red with some black spotting and a black margin. The female is similar but a little more brown. The undersides of both sexes are much drabber, lacking the intense red coloration.

Clearwing Legionnaire

DATA

Scientific name: *Acraea rabbaiae*

Family: Acraeidae

Wingspan: About 1.8 in (4.5 cm).

Flight period: All year.

Larval food plants: *Basananthe zanzibaricum* in the passionflower family (Passifloraceae).

Range: Africa (from Kenya to Kwazulu-Natal in South Africa).

Restricted to coastal forests, this is a very local butterfly. It usually seems to occur only as the odd solitary individual, as seen here feeding on flowers along a path in Sokoke Forest in Kenya. These unique coastal forests are home to many species of plants and animals that are found nowhere else, of which this butterfly is just one example. The forewings are mainly transparent, broken by a zigzag black line about one-third of the way up from the base. The hind wings are a rather strange shade of creamy gray, with a row of grayish orange spots set in a black band along the hind margin. The underside is a little drab.

Common Glassy Legionnaire

The conspicuously large transparent areas on this butterfly's wings are similar to those of the Musanga Legionnaire *(Acraea pentapolis)*. However, the bright reddish orange, black-spotted patches on each hind wing—on which only the border is transparent—makes the Common Glassy Legionnaire a far more attractive butterfly. Males and females of this forest butterfly look alike, and the males are fond of sitting with spread wings in a shaft of sunlight beneath the trees, as seen here in Kakamega Forest in Kenya.

DATA

Scientific name: *Acraea quirina*

Family: Acraeidae

Wingspan: About 2.4 in (6 cm).

Flight period: All year.

Larval food plants: Members of the violet family (Violaceae) and the spurge family (Euphorbiaceae).

Range: From West Africa to Kenya and Tanzania.

Rogers's Large Legionnaire

DATA

Scientific name: *Acraea rogersi*

Family: Acraeidae

Wingspan: About 2.8 in (7 cm).

Flight period: All year.

Larval food plants: Mainly *Adenia lobata* (Passifloraceae); also sometimes cocoa *(Theobroma)* in the Sterculiaceae.

Range: From West Africa to Kenya.

The males of this rather large species occur in two different morphs. In the one pictured here (puddling on a muddy track in Bobiri Forest in Ghana) a large proportion of each wing is smoky brown. In the other form this is largely replaced by reddish orange, particularly on the hind wing. In both forms the wings are marked with a number of large black spots, but these are far more obvious on the hind wing of the form illustrated. The sexes are very similar, and the underside of the wings is much paler than the upper side. Both forms of this forest butterfly usually occur together, but they look like completely different species.

Small Orange Legionnaire

This small butterfly has long been known as *Acraea eponina*, but a change of name became necessary when a specimen bearing the earlier name *A. serena* came to light. This is one of the most common African butterflies, flying in disturbed areas of forest as well as in open savannas, backyards, farmland, and in waste ground in cities, where it can be abundant. The wings are bright orange brown with an orange-spotted black border, seen clearly in this male puddling on muddy ground in Bobiri Forest in Ghana.

DATA

Scientific name: *Acraea serena*

Family: Acraeidae

Wingspan: 1.6 in (4 cm).

Flight period: All year.

Larval food plants: Mainly *Triumfetta rhomboidea* in the linden family (Tiliaceae).

Range: Over most of sub-Saharan Africa.

Sotika Legionnaire

DATA

Scientific name: *Acraea sotikensis*

Family: Acraeidae

Wingspan: About 2 in (5 cm).

Flight period: All year.

Larval food plants: Members of the linden family (Tiliaceae).

Range: From West Africa to Ethiopia, southward to Angola and Zambia.

Often found feeding at flowers in open spots along forest tracks, as seen here in Kakamega Forest in Kenya, this attractive little butterfly is extremely easy to approach closely for photography. The wings are a mixture of bright orange and blackish brown, and there is a creamy yellow patch toward the tip of each forewing. *Acraea burgessi* is similar, but the area of orange is greater, and the forewing patches are orange rather than creamy yellow.

Clouded Legionnaire

Once included in the genus *Bematistes*, this beautiful species, which is seen here puddling on a muddy track after unseasonal rainfall in Bobiri Forest, Ghana, is found mainly in forested areas. In the male (illustrated) the wings are a mixture of black and brownish orange. The female is similar but rather drabber and with broader forewings. In subspecies *carpenteri* a band of white cuts across the female's forewing.

DATA

Scientific name: *Acraea umbra*

Family: Acraeidae

Wingspan: 3 in (7.5 cm).

Flight period: All year.

Larval food plants: *Adenia* species in the passionflower family (Passifloraceae).

Range: From West Africa to Uganda.

Smoky Legionnaire

DATA

Scientific name: *Acraea vestalis*

Family: Acraeidae

Wingspan: About 2.6 in (6.5 cm).

Flight period: All year.

Larval food plants: *Adenia cisampelloides* in the passionflower family (Passifloraceae).

Range: From West Africa to western Tanzania.

As with the Clouded Legionnaire *(Acraea umbra)*, this member of the genus was once included in the genus *Bematistes*. As can be seen here, the Smoky Legionnaire is very similar to the previous species, but it lacks the orange band on the forewing. Although primarily a forest butterfly, to a certain extent it is able to cope with the degradation caused by human activities seen in so many forests throughout the region. It is usually seen feeding at flowers along the edges of forests, as depicted here in Bobiri Forest in Ghana.

Fiery Legionnaire

Found in marshy areas, especially rain-forest swamps, throughout the whole of the large island of Madagascar, the Fiery Legionnaire is usually seen only as the odd solitary individual. The one illustrated here was photographed feeding on a tiny orange flower on a roadside through rain forest in the Périnet Reserve. This was the only specimen of this small but beautiful butterfly seen by the author during six months in Madagascar. As can be seen here, the upper side is a rich fiery orange with black borders; the underside is much less spectacular.

DATA

Scientific name: *Acraea zitja*

Family: Acraeidae

Wingspan: About 1.2 in (3 cm).

Flight period: All year.

Larval food plants: Unknown.

Range: Madagascar.

Carmine Trooper

The 50 or so members of the genus *Actinote* are the Latin American equivalents of *Acraea* in Africa and Asia. The species illustrated (subspecies *salmonea*), seen puddling on a muddy track through rain forest in Tingo Maria National Park in Peru, is probably one of the most attractive members of a generally drab genus. There are two large carmine patches on each forewing, and the hind wings are black; the undersides are similar. Note the bright orange body, which serves as further visual reinforcement that this highly distasteful, warningly colored butterfly should be left alone by its enemies.

DATA

Scientific name: *Actinote alcione*

Family: Acraeidae

Wingspan: About 2.4 in (6 cm).

Flight period: All year.

Larval food plants: Members of the sunflower family (Asteraceae).

Range: Colombia, Ecuador, Peru, and Bolivia.

Rusty Trooper

Photographed puddling on the same rain-forest track at Tingo Maria as the previous species, this butterfly (of which subspecies *sobrina* is illustrated) is another attractive member of the genus. Its forewings and hind wings have striking rust-colored patches; the pattern on the upper side is similar to the underside shown here. Members of this genus lay their eggs in very large batches on the undersides of the leaves of their food plant. The resulting hordes of rather spiky caterpillars feed voraciously and often strip the plant entirely of its leaves.

DATA

Scientific name: *Actinote negra*

Family: Acraeidae

Wingspan: About 2.4 in (6 cm).

Flight period: All year.

Larval food plants: Members of the sunflower family (Asteraceae).

Range: Colombia, Ecuador, Peru, and Bolivia.

Polka Dot Butterfly

DATA

Scientific name: *Pardopsis punctatissima*

Family: Acraeidae

Wingspan: 1.8 in (4.5 cm).

Flight period: All year.

Larval food plants: *Hybanthus capensis* of the violet family (Violaceae).

Range: Throughout sub-Saharan Africa.

This tiny member of the family is restricted to dry bush country, savanna, and open woodland, avoiding the dense, humid rain forests in which so many other butterflies thrive. The orange wings are peppered above and below with a neat array of black spots. As well as giving the butterfly its common name, these spots form a pattern that is unique in the family. Colonies tend to be widespread but localized, and in the more temperate parts of its range, such as South Africa, the Polka Dot Butterfly is on the wing only during the warmer months of the year. The specimen illustrated was photographed in a backyard on the coast near Mombasa in Kenya.

Argus Butterfly

The most notable feature of members of this genus is the very large rounded hind wing, which is out of all proportion to the much smaller, triangular, and fairly pointed forewing. Both above and below, the wings are white with smoky black borders, and the hind wing has two large eyespots. These butterflies tend to keep to the understory of gloomy forest, perching on shrubs a few feet above the ground, as seen here in a patch of forest in the Botanical Gardens at Lae in Papua New Guinea. The caterpillars feed in large groups and may strip their food plant of its leaves.

DATA

Scientific name: *Taenaris myops*

Family: Amathusiidae

Wingspan: About 3.7 in (9.5 cm).

Flight period: All year.

Larval food plants: Palms (Arecaceae).

Range: New Guinea.

Bronze Owlet

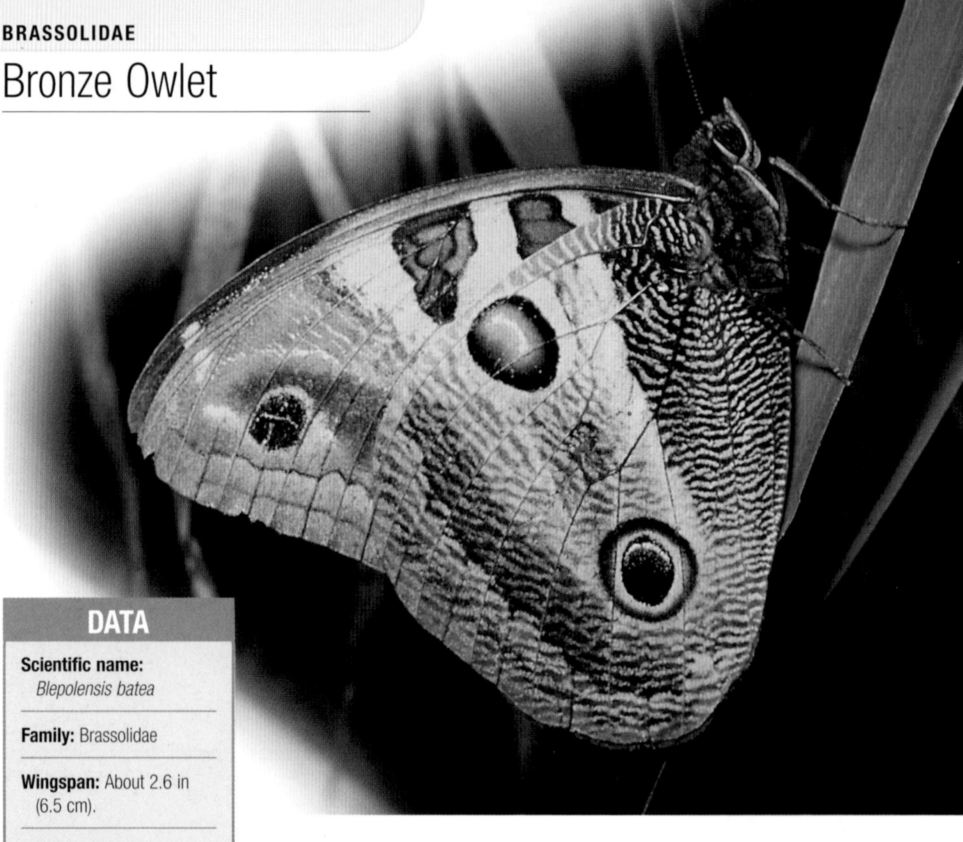

DATA

Scientific name: *Blepolensis batea*

Family: Brassolidae

Wingspan: About 2.6 in (6.5 cm).

Flight period: All year.

Larval food plants: Grasses (Poaceae).

Range: Southern Brazil and Paraguay.

The members of this genus are among the smaller representatives of the family, dwarfed by their huge *Caligo* relatives, although they are still far larger than most European or North American butterflies. The upper side of the forewing is orange in the inner half and dark brown on the rest, with two pale spots near the wing tip. The hind wing is similar but without the pale spots. On the underside, as seen here, there are three smallish eyespots. This Owlet was one of several examples of this species fluttering around among long grass in the Caraça National Park in the State of Minas Gerais in Brazil.

Magnificent Owl

The upper side of the forewings on this spectacularly large butterfly are blackish brown with a large purple patch. This is absent on the hind wings, which have a broad yellowish band instead. However, these showy colors are normally seen only briefly when the butterfly takes wing—it is the striking underside that is normally on show as the butterfly perches on a tree trunk in the shady rain forest, as seen here in Guatopo National Park in Venezuela. The single large eyespot on the hind wing is found in several other species, but it is the pale creamy yellow band running across both wings that characterizes this species.

DATA

Scientific name: *Caligo atreus*

Family: Brassolidae

Wingspan: About 4.7 in (12 cm).

Flight period: All year.

Larval food plant: Crab's claws *(Heliconia)* in the family Strelitziaceae and banana *(Musa)* in the family Musaceae.

Range: From Mexico to Peru.

Common Giant Owl

DATA

Science name: *Caligo eurilochus*

Family: Brassolidae

Wingspan: About 5.1 in (13 cm).

Flight period: All year.

Larval food plants: Crab's claws *(Heliconia)* in the family Strelitziaceae, *Calathea* in the arrowroot family (Marantaceae), and banana *(Musa)* in the family Musaceae.

Range: From Guatemala to the Amazon Basin.

As far as the upper sides are concerned this is probably the drabbest member of the genus, blackish brown being the main color, with just a hint of a shimmer of blue. The underside, as seen here in rain forest at Finca La Selva in Costa Rica, is fairly typical for the genus, having a single large eyespot on the hind wing set in a fairly plain background. This is subspecies *sulanus*, found from Guatemala to Panama; in some of the South American subspecies the hind wing is even plainer, apart from the eyespot.

Cream-striped Owl Butterfly

DATA

Scientific name: *Caligo teucer*

Other common name: Cocoa Mort-bleu (in Trinidad).

Family: Brassolidae

Wingspan: About 4.3 in (11 cm).

Flight period: All year.

Larval food plants: Crab's claws *(Heliconia)* in the family Strelitziaceae and banana *(Musa)* in the family Musaceae.

Range: Over much of tropical South America.

The form illustrated here is subspecies *insulanus*, found in Trinidad and photographed in typical pose on a tree trunk in an abandoned semi-forested cocoa plantation. The topside of the forewing is mainly brown with a pale creamy stripe running up the middle. The hind wing is also brown, but there is a purplish blue shimmer on the inner half. Owl butterflies are mainly active in the evening and soon perch again after being provoked into flight during the day when resting, which is almost always carried out on a tree trunk in deep shade.

Common Bamboo Owlet

DATA

Scientific name: *Eryphanis polyxena*

Other common name: Purple Mort-bleu (in Trinidad).

Family: Brassolidae

Wingspan: About 3 in (7.5 cm).

Flight period: All year.

Larval food plants: Bamboo (Poaceae).

Range: From Guatemala to the Amazon Basin.

The truly spectacular nature of the brilliant purple topside coloration is rather teasingly revealed by the tiny patch of purple visible in the illustration, just above the point where the forewings and hind wings meet. As with all members of the Brassolidae, the upper surfaces of these rain-forest butterflies are revealed only when the butterfly is on the wing. When perching—as here on a tree in an old forested cocoa plantation at Simla in Trinidad—the much drabber yet still very interesting underside is all that is on show. Compared with *Caligo*, the eyespot on the hind wing is very much reduced and far less like a real eye.

Reeves's Bamboo Owlet

DATA

Scientific name: *Eryphanis reevesii*

Family: Brassolidae

Wingspan: About 3 in (7.5 cm).

Flight period: All year.

Larval food plants: Bamboo (Poaceae).

Range: Over much of tropical South America.

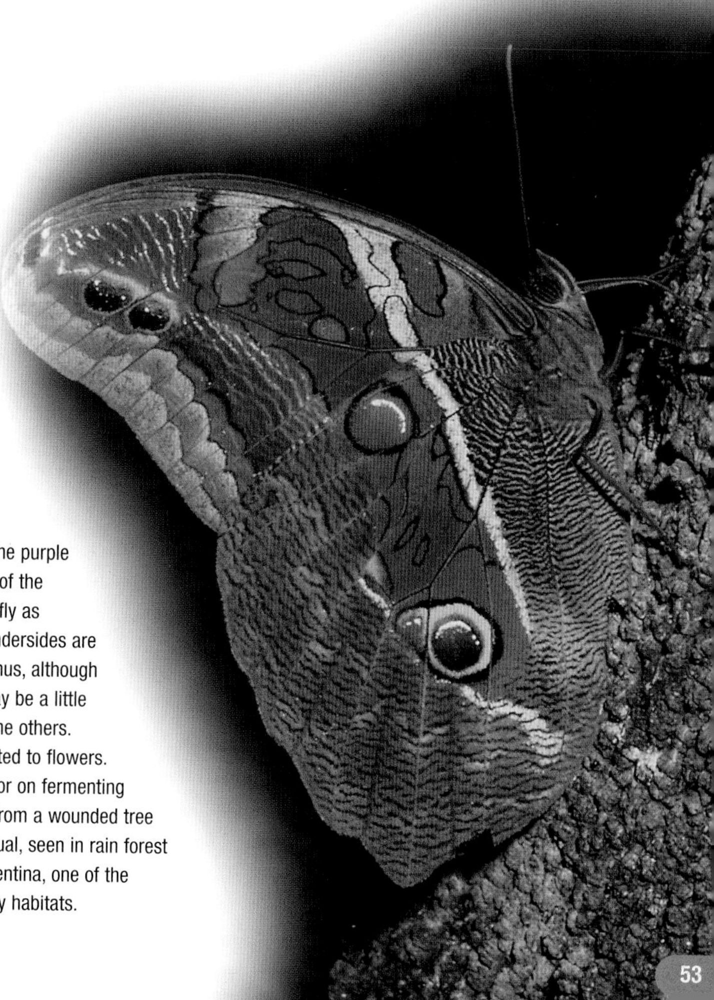

As with the previous species the purple glint on the upper surfaces of the wings can be glimpsed only briefly as the butterfly flashes past. The undersides are similar in all members of the genus, although the eyespot on the hind wing may be a little larger in this species than in some others. Brassolid adults are never attracted to flowers. They feed instead on fallen fruit or on fermenting and highly aromatic sap oozing from a wounded tree trunk, exemplified by this individual, seen in rain forest at the mighty Iguaçu Falls in Argentina, one of the world's most spectacular butterfly habitats.

The Small Monk

DATA

Scientific name: *Amauris damocles*

Family: Danaidae

Wingspan: About 3 in (7.5 cm).

Flight period: All year.

Larval food plants: Milkweeds (family Asclepiadaceae).

Range: From West Africa to Tanzania.

The Small Monk is one of several similar poisonous and distasteful species exhibiting a conspicuous black-and-white "warning" pattern. This species is most commonly found in dry forest and Guinea-savanna, but it also occurs in open disturbed areas in rain forest, as seen here at Bobiri in Ghana. With a scattering of white patches, both the upper and undersides of the black forewings are broadly similar in several species, but in this species the hind wing is much paler, with a large area of pale creamy yellow. The caterpillar is black with yellow spots.

The Novice

DATA

Scientific name: *Amauris ochlea*

Family: Danaidae

Wingspan: About 3.2 in (8 cm).

Flight period: All year.

Larval food plants: Milkweeds (family Asclepiadaceae)

Range: From Somalia through East Africa to KwaZulu-Natal in South Africa.

The large unbroken white band on the forewing is characteristic of this species, which is generally found in open forest and shady places, and is seen here in a small remnant patch of forest near Mombasa in Kenya. The white patch on the hind wing covers most of its area and is at least 10 percent larger than that of the Monk *(Amauris tartarea)*, whose white forewing band is broken into three sections. As in all *Amauris* species, the pattern on both sides of the wings is broadly similar.

The Friar

DATA

Scientific name: *Amauris niavius*

Family: Danaidae

Wingspan: About 3.7 in (9.5 cm).

Flight period: All year.

Larval food plants: Milkweeds (family Asclepiadaceae).

Range: Throughout almost the whole of sub-Saharan Africa.

Noticeably larger than the previous species, even on the wing, this extremely widespread butterfly is mimicked by the female Mocker Swallowtail *(Papilio dardanus)* form illustrated on page 394. Unlike the other black-and-white species shown here, the Friar has no white spots in the black margin of the hind wing, making it easily recognizable. The underside of the hind wing is almost pure white, with just a small area of blackish margin. Both sexes feed on flowers, while males often puddle on muddy paths, as seen here in Bobiri Forest in Ghana.

The Monk

This species is similar to The Novice *(Amauris ochlea)*, but the white patch on its forewings is broken into three and the white patch on the hind wings is noticeably smaller. The Monk is most often found in open forest but also does well in some of the more closed rain forests and in agricultural areas wherever its food plants occur. Both sexes come frequently to flowers, but the males also drink from muddy ground, as seen here near the village of Konda in Togo. As with many danaids, the males are also attracted to the withered stems of certain plants, especially heliotropes, from which they imbibe pyrrolizidine alkaloids.

DATA

Scientific name: *Amauris tartarea*

Family: Danaidae

Wingspan: About 3.2 in (8 cm).

Flight period: All year.

Larval food plants: Milkweeds (family Asclepiadaceae).

Range: West, Central, and East Africa.

Common Tiger

DATA

Scientific name: *Danaus chrysippus*

Family: Danaidae

Wingspan: About 3.2 in (8 cm).

Flight period: All year.

Larval food plants: Milkweeds (family Asclepiadaceae).

Range: Over the whole of Africa and much of Asia; recently also found in southern Europe.

Found in virtually every kind of habitat—from backyards and cultivated areas to semidesert and open forests—this species is easily recognized by its slow, sailing flight. Various forms occur, of which the most attractive is probably forma *alcippus*. Its hind wings are almost completely white, as illustrated here in Bimbia Forest in Cameroon. This is the only form found in West Africa. Populations farther east usually have pale orange hind wings, as in the forewings, which may or may not have a large white-spotted black area at the tips .The Common Tiger is mimicked by a number of other African butterflies, such as the female Diadem (*Hypolimnas misippus*).

The Soldier

DATA

Scientific name: *Danaus eresimus*

Family: Danaidae

Wingspan: About 2.6 in (6.5 cm).

Flight period: All year.

Larval food plants: Mostly milkweeds (family Asclepiadaceae).

Range: From the United States (Florida and Texas) to Brazil.

In the tropical part of its huge range this species is on the wing throughout the year, but in Florida it is found mostly from February through October, and in Texas from August through January. Like the Queen *(Danaus gilippus)* and the Monarch *(D. plexippus)*, its basic color is yellowish orange, with blackish borders to the wings and a series of silvery whitish spots. The absence of any white border to some of the black veins on the hind wings is the easiest way to distinguish this species from the next. The Soldier is usually found in disturbed forests; the specimen illustrated was photographed on the edge of a coffee plantation near Jalapa in Veracruz State, Mexico.

The Queen

DATA

Scientific name: *Danaus gilippus*

Family: Danaidae

Wingspan: About 2.8 in (7 cm).

Flight period: All year in south; April–November in California and Nevada.

Larval food plants: Milkweeds (family Asclepiadaceae).

Range: From the southern United States to the Amazon Basin.

For differences from the Soldier *(Danaus eresimus)* see the previous page. The Queen is found in open woodland and fields as well as in desert, as seen here in Arizona in August. It flies almost always with the Monarch *(D. plexippus)*. Like all members of the Danaidae, the Queen is toxic when eaten by most birds or other animals, so is generally avoided by them. In summer a migration takes place northward as far as Wyoming and Illinois. The pale green eggs are laid singly on flower buds, stems, and leaves of the host plant.

Monarch

DATA

Scientific name: *Danaus plexippus*

Family: Danaidae

Wingspan: About 3 in (7.5 cm).

Flight period: All year in south; summer in north.

Larval food plants: Milkweeds (family Asclepiadaceae).

Range: Throughout the Americas; also in Australia and parts of Asia.

Larger than the two species—the Soldier *(Danaus eresimus)* and the Queen *(D. gilippus)*—with which it often occurs, the Monarch is easily distinguished by its much more pronounced black veining and by the large silver spots on the underside of the forewing. It is found in every kind of habitat except for dense forest, often being very common in backyards, as seen here in South Carolina. It is a noted migrant, and the large overwintering populations found in California and especially in the mountains of central Mexico are world-famous tourist attractions.

Common Crow

DATA

Scientific name: *Euploea core*

Family: Danaidae

Wingspan: About 3.8 in (9.6 cm).

Flight period: All year.

Larval food plants: Varied, including oleander, fig, mandivillea, and hoya.

Range: Over much of Asia and Australia.

With such a large range it is not surprising that this is a variable butterfly and that several subspecies have been described. The general coloration of the upper side is dark brown, sometimes with whitish tips to the wings. There are always a few whitish spots on the forewings and a close-set row of much larger white spots near the rear edge of the hind wing. The underside is paler and more liberally marked with white spots. The Common Crow is found in a variety of habitats, including backyards, as seen here in Nepal.

Lacy Tree Nymph

These large butterflies have a very lazy style of flight and spend much of their time floating around gently on their broad, pale whitish, lace-patterned wings, which are heavily sprinkled with large black spots. In this species the wings are noticeably narrower than in *Idea leuconoe*, while in the very similar *I. lynceus* and *I. stolli* the outer edge of the forewing is clearly indented. All four species can often be found on flowers, sometimes in backyards, but more frequently in clearings in forest, as seen here in an open swampy area in Pasoh Forest Reserve, Malaysia. The caterpillars are black and white with some red spots.

DATA

Scientific name: *Idea hypermnestra*

Family: Danaidae

Wingspan: About 5.9 in (15 cm).

Larval food plants: Milkweeds (family Asclepiadaceae).

Flight period: All year.

Range: From Myanmar (Burma) to Indonesia.

Jupiter Tiger

DATA

Scientific name: *Ideopsis juventa*

Family: Danaidae

Wingspan: About 3.5 in (9 cm).

Flight period: All year.

Larval food plants: Milkweeds (family Asclepiadaceae).

Range: From Malaysia through Indonesia to the Philippines.

The Jupiter Tiger is one of a number of very similar Asian danaids in which the ground color is a beautiful shade of pale blue. In this species a triple band of black around the margins of the wings encloses a distinctive series of blue dots. The dots are small around the wing margins, but larger between the next two bands farther in. As with many danaids, the adult butterflies often visit flowers, one of their favorites being the naturalized and highly invasive weed *Lantana camara*, as seen here in Bako National Park in Borneo.

Blue Glassy Tiger

This is another blue danaid from Asia. Its upper side is broadly similar to that of the Jupiter Tiger *(Ideopsis juventa)*. However, the blue area on the Blue Glassy Tiger is restricted by a larger area of black veining and is rather less attractive. As can be seen here, the blue on the underside of the forewing is much brighter than on the blacker hind wing. This species is fond of puddling on muddy ground, as seen here in Thale Ban National Park in southern Thailand, alongside a specimen of the Five-bar Swordtail *(Graphium agetes)*.

DATA

Scientific name: *Ideopsis similis*

Family: Danaidae

Wingspan: About 3.3 in (8.5 cm).

Flight period: All year.

Larval food plants: Milkweeds (family Asclepiadaceae).

Range: From India and Sri Lanka to Malaysia and China.

Tiger Mimic Queen

DATA

Scientific name: *Lycorea cleobaea*

Family: Danaidae

Wingspan: About 3.9 in (10 cm).

Flight period: All year.

Larval food plants: Papaya *(Carica)* in the Caricaceae, figs *(Ficus)* in the Moraceae, and milkweeds *(Asclepias)* in the Asclepiadaceae.

Range: From Mexico to Argentina; a rare vagrant to Florida and Texas.

With their relatively long narrow wings the members of this genus are unlike other members of the family and form mimicry complexes with other similarly marked slender-winged members of the families Ithomiidae and Heliconiidae. For an idea of the general appearance of the upper side, see the Sweet-oil Butterfly *(Mechanitis isthmia)* on page 113. Although widespread, the Tiger Mimic Queen is uncommon, usually appearing as singletons among much more abundant ithomiids. It is found in fairly open habitats such as cocoa plantations, wooded roadsides, and disturbed areas of rain forest, as pictured here in Brazil.

Clearwing Mimic Queen

While the Tiger Mimic Queen *(Lycorea cleobaea)* is part of the so-called tiger-striped mimicry grouping, this species is part of a similar grouping of butterflies, mostly ithomiids such as *Olyras*, which have semitransparent wings. Formerly included in a separate genus, *Ituna*, this species is found in rain forest, open woodland, and even in city parks. As with other members of *Lycorea*, it tends to occur mainly as the odd solitary individual, as seen here in Peru's Tingo Maria National Park, where a male is drinking from mineral-rich water seeping across a rock in rain forest.

DATA

Scientific name: *Lycorea ilione*

Family: Danaidae

Wingspan: About 4.3 in (11 cm).

Flight period: All year.

Larval food plants: Figs *(Ficus)* in the Moraceae.

Range: From Mexico to Brazil and Peru.

African Blue Tiger

Seen here in the early morning basking on a leaf in disturbed rain forest near Kpalimé in Togo, this species can be mistaken for no other African butterfly, although it is similar to the Common Forest Queen *(Euxanthe eurinome)*, which is probably a mimic. The intricate array of pale bluish spots set against a blackish brown background is found in both sexes, the undersides being dressed in a similar scheme. The African Blue Tiger is widespread in dry forest, but in rain forest it prefers disturbed areas, such as where logging has taken place.

DATA

Scientific name: *Tirumala petiverana*

Family: Danaidae

Wingspan: 3.2 in (8 cm).

Flight period: All year.

Larval food plants: Milkweeds (family Asclepiadaceae).

Range: Over most of tropical Africa.

Gulf Fritillary

DATA

Scientific name: *Agraulis vanillae*

Family: Heliconiidae

Wingspan: About 2.8 in (7 cm).

Flight period: All year in south; in summer farther north.

Larval food plants: Passionflowers *(Passiflora)* in the family Passifloraceae.

Range: From the United States to Brazil and Argentina.

Equally at home in open forest, fields, scrublands, and city suburbs, in the United States this lovely butterfly is only permanently resident in the southern parts of the states of Texas, Florida, and California. In summer it migrates northward, almost reaching the Canadian border. The butterfly illustrated here was photographed in August, perching on a shrub in a backyard in South Carolina. With its array of large silvery spots the underside is particularly striking, but the upper side is also attractive, being mainly orange with a few black markings, especially along the borders of the hind wings. Both sexes are often found on flowers.

Orange-banded Longwing

DATA

Scientific name: *Dryadula phaetusa*

Family: Heliconiidae

Wingspan: About 3 in (7.5 cm).

Flight period: All year.

Larval food plants: Passionflowers *(Passiflora)* in the family Passifloraceae.

Range: From Mexico to Brazil and Argentina.

Not a great deal is known about this scarce species, which haunts rather open habitats such as forest edges, scrubbed-up fields, and wooded roadsides. As can be seen, the upper side is a fairly bright orange brown, with a series of blackish bars cutting across each wing. The underside is similar but generally paler, especially on the hind wings, on which two yellowish orange lines join up to form a large "U" against a brown background. The specimen illustrated here was busily feeding at flowers in Finca El Rey National Park in Salta province, Argentina.

Small Orange Longwing

DATA

Scientific name: *Eueides aliphera*

Other common name: in Trinidad known as Small Flambeau.

Family: Heliconiidae

Wingspan: About 2 in (5 cm).

Flight period: All year.

Larval food plants: Passionflowers *(Passiflora)* in the Passifloraceae and members of the Turneraceae.

Range: Mexico to Brazil.

Often included in *Heliconius*, this small butterfly is relatively common in forest, both in undisturbed high-canopy primary rain forest and in disturbed areas such as along flower-rich forested roadsides. This mating pair was seen beside a road winding up through forest in Trinidad's Northern Range. The upper side of the wings is basically orange with narrow blackish borders. The Julia Longwing *(Dryas julia)*, with which this species often flies, is very similar but very much larger, with a wingspan of about 2.8 in (7 cm).

Isabella Longwing

DATA

Scientific name: *Eueides isabella*

Family: Heliconiidae

Wingspan: About 3.2 in (8 cm).

Flight period: All year.

Larval food plants: Passionflowers *(Passiflora)* in the family Passifloraceae.

Range: From Mexico to the Amazon Basin.

Often listed in *Heliconius*, this tropical species occasionally migrates into southern Texas, where small colonies may become briefly established. It is a forest species and is most often seen along roadsides and in light gaps, as shown here in Trinidad. With its pattern of black, yellow, and orange (the underside is similar but paler), it is a typical distasteful member of the tiger-striped mimicry ring. Included in this group are Muellerian co-mimics such as the danaid Tiger Mimic Queen *(Lycorea cleobaea)* and the ithomiid Sweet-oil Butterfly *(Mechanitis isthmia),* and palatable Batesian mimics such as the Two-banded Tiger Crescent *(Eresia eunice)* and the pierid *Dismorphia amphione.*

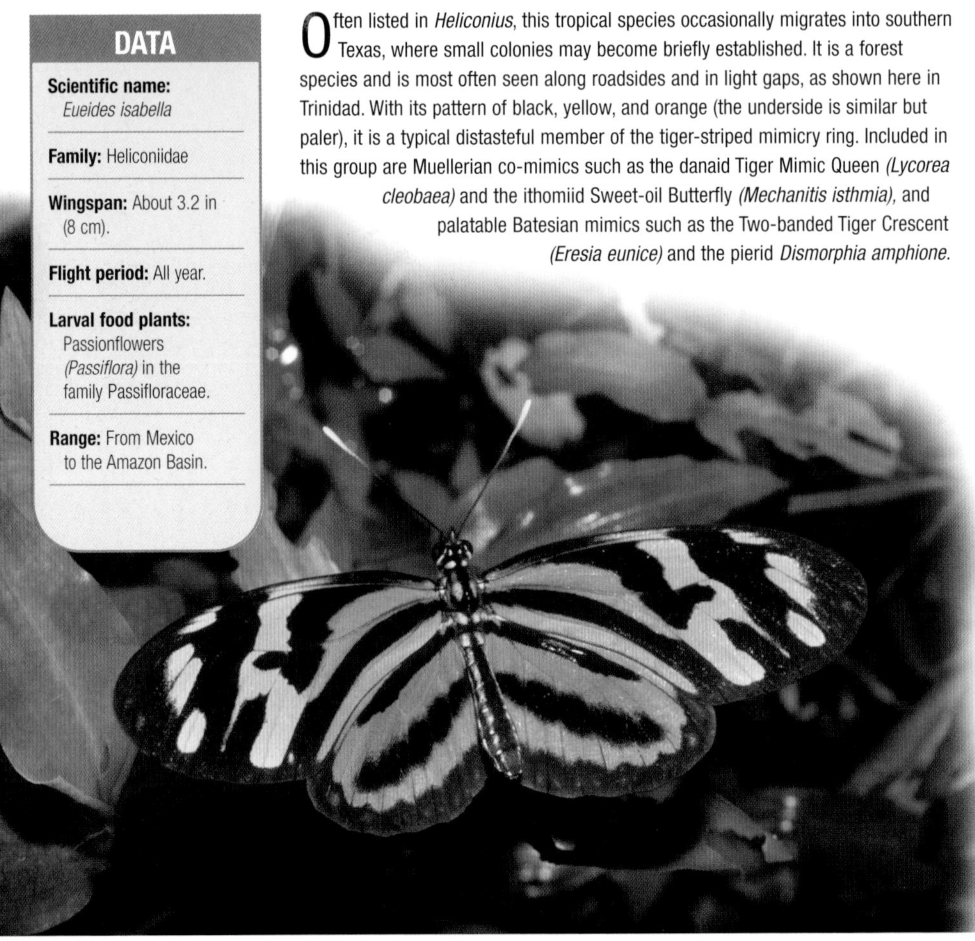

Zebra Longwing

DATA

Scientific name: *Heliconius charitonius*

Family: Heliconiidae

Wingspan: About 3.2 in (8 cm).

Flight period: All year.

Larval food plants: Passionflowers *(Passiflora)* in the family Passifloraceae.

Range: Southern United States, Central and South America, West Indies.

Found on the wing throughout the year in its tropical range as well as in Florida, this distinctive and unmistakable brown and yellow striped butterfly (the underside is similar but paler than the upper side) is seen only from April through November in Texas and in high summer farther north, where it occasionally migrates as far as Nebraska. Like all heliconiids, the adults feed on protein-rich pollen, which can extend their lives to as much as nine months in nature. This species often comes to flowers in backyards, as seen here in Florida. As with many heliconiids, the adults often sleep in groups, returning to the same roost night after night.

Doris Longwing

Although the color of the forewing varies little, being black with yellow patches, the hind wing is highly variable, ranging from blue to greenish yellow to orange to blackish brown—and various subtle combinations of these. Numerous subspecies' names have been applied to these variations, but it now seems that they can all arise from a single batch of eggs, and they are now generally listed for convenience as forms. This forest butterfly is often found on flowers or puddling on muddy tracks, as seen here in Peru's Tingo Maria National Park.

DATA

Scientific name: *Heliconius doris*

Family: Heliconiidae

Wingspan: About 3.2 in (8 cm).

Flight period: All year.

Larval food plants: Passionflowers *(Passiflora)* in the family Passifloraceae.

Range: From Mexico to the Amazon Basin.

Red Postman

DATA

Scientific name: *Heliconius erato*

Family: Heliconiidae

Wingspan: About 2.8 in (7 cm).

Flight period: All year.

Larval food plants: Passionflowers *(Passiflora)* in the family Passifloraceae.

Range: From Mexico to the Amazon Basin; a rare stray into Texas.

The Red Postman has very variable coloration, which is often linked to distinct geographical regions, giving rise to numerous named subspecies. The illustration below is subspecies *favorinus*, seen dry-puddling on a stone in Tingo Maria National Park in Peru. In some other subspecies there is no red at all, the forewing being plain blue. It is impossible to begin to describe here the numerous variations that occur over the large range of this butterfly. It is a common species, found in all types of forest, in agricultural lands and on flowers in backyards.

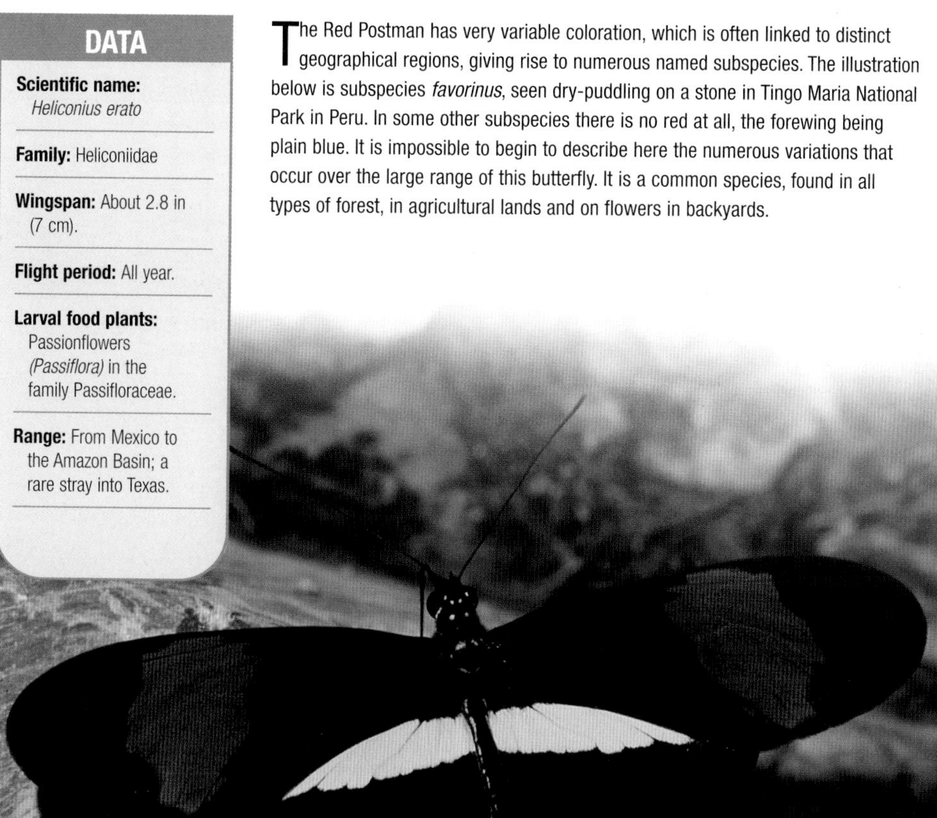

Wallace's Blue Longwing

DATA

Scientific name: *Heliconius wallacei*

Family: Heliconiidae

Wingspan: About 3 in (7.5 cm).

Flight period: All year.

Larval food plants: Passionflowers *(Passiflora)* in the family Passifloraceae.

Range: Over much of tropical South America; Trinidad.

Variation in this species is less extreme than in the Red Postman *(Heliconius erato)* and the Doris Longwing *(H. doris)*, but a number of forms are still recognized. Forma *flavescens* is pictured below, puddling on damp ground in the rain forest at Tingo Maria, Peru. Note the very long thin antennae, typical of members of the Heliconiidae. In some forms the yellow patches on the forewings are replaced by bluish white. In all forms the underside is similar to the upper side, but much paler.

Malachite Longwing

Green is not a common color in butterflies, and this is one of the most beautiful examples in the world. Its pattern of green and brown is broadly similar on both the upper and the lower wing surfaces. This rain-forest inhabitant is seldom seen near ground level, spending much of its time high in the canopy, so the author was fortunate to find this solitary individual puddling on a track through Tingo Maria National Park in Peru. In a more recent encounter a male was observed diving and swooping above a female in a lengthy courtship in Brazil's Atlantic coast rain forest.

DATA

Scientific name: *Philaethria dido*

Family: Heliconiidae

Wingspan: About 3.2 in (8 cm).

Flight period: All year.

Larval food plants: Passionflowers *(Passiflora)* in the family Passifloraceae.

Range: From Mexico to the Amazon Basin.

Streaked Paradise Skipper

DATA

Scientific name: *Abantis leucogaster*

Family: Hesperiidae

Wingspan: 1.4 in (3.5 cm).

Flight period: All year.

Larval food plants: Not known.

Range: From West Africa to Tanzania.

Seen here feeding on flowers alongside a track running through Bobiri Forest in Ghana, this charming skipper can also sometimes be found drinking on muddy ground. The forewing is blackish gray, with long glassy streaks following the veins, while the hind wing is shining white with a black margin. This rain-forest skipper is not a common sight, so the author was fortunate to see several specimens at Bobiri in January of 2005. The form found in East Africa is smaller and has fewer black markings on the hind wing.

Golden-banded Skipper

With its brown wings and the broad golden band on its forewing, this is unlike any other butterfly in the United States, with the exception of the Arizona Banded Skipper *(Autochton pseudocellus)*. The latter is a very rare species, restricted to a small area of southern Arizona (although it is also found in Mexico). It has a white ring at the base of the antennal club, which is lacking in the Golden-banded Skipper. This is a butterfly of open woodland, as illustrated here in Arizona. The males spend much of their time perched, awaiting passing females.

DATA

Scientific name: *Autochton cellus*

Family: Hesperiidae

Wingspan: About 1.6 in (4 cm).

Flight period: May–June in north; May–August or longer in south.

Larval food plants: Various members of the pea family (Fabaceae).

Range: United States (Arizona and southern Texas in the west; New York to Florida in the east); Mexico.

Common Orange Sprite

DATA

Scientific name: *Celaenorrhinus galenus*

Family: Hesperiidae

Wingspan: About 1.4 in (3.5 cm).

Flight period: All year.

Larval food plants: Acanthus (family Acanthaceae) and vervain (family Verbenaceae).

Range: West, Central, and East Africa.

Several similar but much more local species differ only in minor details of pattern from the butterfly illustrated here, and the only sure way to tell some of them apart is by dissecting out the male genital organs. This is a very common butterfly in forests throughout its range, and in the early morning males will be seen flying rapidly around their display grounds, sometimes after spending the night in the tightly closed flowers of morning glories *(Ipomoea)*. Although they are often found feeding at flowers, the adults also spend a considerable amount of time basking, as here in Kenya's Kakamega Forest.

Common Black Sprite

With its basic ground color of blackish brown this rain-forest skipper is far less attractive than the Common Orange Sprite *(Celaenorrhinus galenus)*, with which it often flies. Yet the large silver patch on the forewing gives this common little butterfly a certain air of distinction. The undersides are grayish black with little in the way of silver markings. The adults spend much of their time out of sight with their wings spread flat beneath some rain-forest leaf, but they also emerge to feed on flowers and bask, as seen here in Kakamega Forest in Kenya.

DATA

Scientific name: *Celaenorrhinus proxima*

Family: Hesperiidae

Wingspan: About 1.4 in (3.5 cm).

Flight period: All year.

Larval food plants: *Mimulopsis* (family Acanthaceae).

Range: From West Africa to Tanzania.

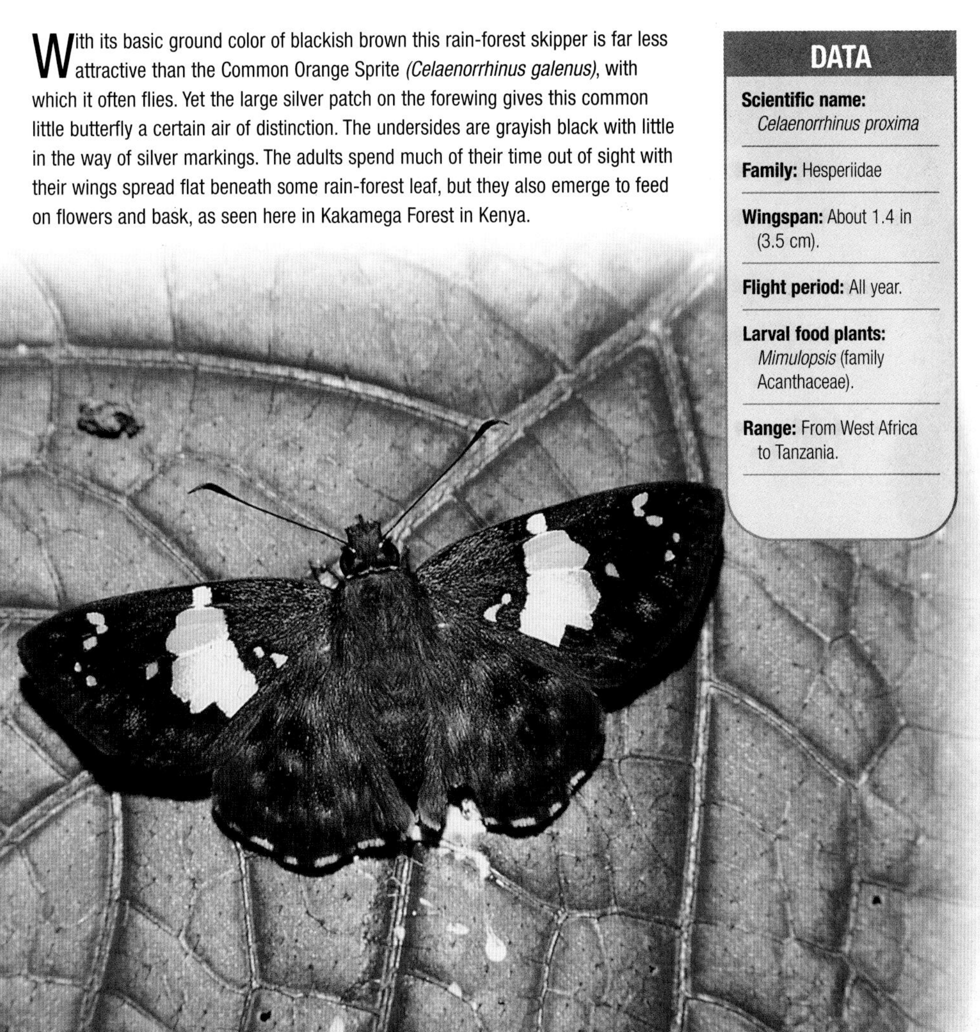

Brown Forest Sylph

DATA

Scientific name: *Ceratrichia brunnea*

Family: Hesperiidae

Wingspan: About 1.2 in (3 cm).

Flight period: All year.

Larval food plants: Grasses (Poaceae).

Range: Central Africa and eastward to extreme western Kenya.

The forest sylphs can be distinguished from other African skippers at a glance by their very long antennae. In this species the upper side of the wings is mainly brown and a little drab, but the underside is much brighter, especially the hind wing, which has a large white patch. The Brown Forest Sylph is particularly fond of feeding at the flowers that usually spring up in large numbers in open, disturbed areas of rain forests, such as natural clearings, or along roads and broad tracks, as seen here in Kenya's Kakamega Forest.

Two-pip Policeman

The smoky brown upper sides typical of this species are found in several other members of the genus, and it is the white band on the underside of the hind wing that is the key to telling three common similar species apart. In the Two-pip Policeman there are two black dots on this band. In the One-pip Policeman *(Coeliades anchisus)* there is only one, while in the Policeman *(C. forestan)* there is none. Members of this genus all have a fast and powerful flight and inhabit forest margins, wooded areas, savanna, and backyards. They often come to flowers, as seen here in the Drakensberg Mountains in KwaZulu-Natal, South Africa.

DATA

Scientific name: *Coeliades pisistratus*

Family: Hesperiidae

Wingspan: About 2 in (5 cm).

Flight period: All year.

Larval food plants: From various families.

Range: Over most of sub-Saharan Africa.

Silver Flat

Scientific name: *Eagris lucetia*

Family: Hesperiidae

Wingspan: About 1.2 in (3 cm).

Flight period: All year.

Larval food plants: *Allophylus* (family Sapindaceae) and *Rhus* (family Anacardiaceae).

Range: Central and East Africa.

As the common name suggests, the skippers in this genus spend much of their time with their wings spread out flat against a leaf. This silvery gray and white species gives the distinct impression, at least from a few paces away, of a large white bird dropping that has splashed onto a leaf, as depicted here in Kenya's Kakamega Forest. Like a number of skippers, males will feed from genuine bird droppings as well as flowers, although females prefer the latter. Most common in rain forest, the Silver Flat is also found in disturbed areas, as long as a few trees are still present.

Silver-spotted Skipper

DATA

Scientific name: *Epargyreus clarus*

Family: Hesperiidae

Wingspan: About 2 in (5 cm).

Flight period: May–June in mountains and the north; May–September in the south; more or less all year in Florida.

Larval food plants: Many members of the pea family (Fabaceae).

Range: United States, Canada, and extreme northern Mexico.

One of the most widespread butterflies in the continental United States, this skipper is found mainly in open woodland, prairie valleys, and wooded canyons, especially where these run though desert. Thistles, as pictured here in Arizona, are a frequent attraction for the adult butterflies, but many other flowers are also visited. The upper side of the forewing is dark brown with several pale golden spots. These are also visible on the undersides, with the addition of a large silver patch on the hind wing that is missing from the upper side.

Dingy Skipper

DATA

Scientific name: *Erynnis tages*

Family: Hesperiidae

Wingspan: About 1 in (2.5 cm).

Flight period: Mainly May–June.

Larval food plants: Various.

Range: Over much of Europe, eastward to Russia and China.

As seen here in the typical habitat of a grassy hillside in England, the Dingy Skipper has the habit of going to roost in late evening on a dead brown plant, in this case the old dried-up seed head of a knapweed flower *(Centaurea)*. With its wings spread widely, or sometimes just partly opened, as here, the butterfly is always very hard to spot when asleep, even though it may be in full view. The wings are basically brown, with a number of paler areas and a row of whitish dots along the edges.

Blood-red Skipper

DATA

Scientific name: *Haemactis sanguinalis*

Family: Hesperiidae

Wingspan: About 1.6 in (4 cm).

Flight period: All year.

Larval food plants: Not known.

Range: South America (Ecuador, Bolivia, and Peru).

This is one of the most spectacular of the vast array of brilliantly colored skippers found in the rain forests of Central and South America, a region that holds about 90 percent of the world's most beautiful hesperiids. One can only wonder why this should be, and why the species found in Europe and North America should be so drab by comparison. The black-and-red "sunburst" pattern on the upper side of the Blood-red Skipper is found on no other species, making this butterfly instantly recognizable. It often puddles on muddy ground and also basks on leaves, as seen here at Tingo Maria in Peru.

Fiery Skipper

The Fiery Skipper is found in grassy places throughout much of the Americas and is common in suburban backyards, where its caterpillars can be a pest on lawns. Flying throughout the year in south Florida and south Texas, summer migration may take breeding females as far north as Ontario and Prince Edward Island by August. The main points of identification are the shortish antennae and the yellowish underside to the hind wing, which also has several dark patches.

DATA

Scientific name: *Hylephila phyleus*

Family: Hesperiidae

Wingspan: About 1.2 in (3 cm).

Flight period: During summer in the north; all year farther south.

Larval food plants: Grasses (Poaceae).

Range: From Canada to Argentina.

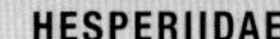

Malagasy Red and Gold Skipper

DATA

Scientific name: *Malaza empyreus*

Family: Hesperiidae

Wingspan: About 1.2 in (3 cm).

Flight period: All year.

Larval food plants: Not known.

Range: Madagascar.

Madagascar is home to many species of plants and animals that are found nowhere else in the world. This is one of them and it is also one of the rarest. So seldom has this lovely skipper been glimpsed in its rain-forest home that some of the world's largest museums hold only a handful of specimens rather than the hundreds usually held of most butterfly species. The author was therefore exceptionally fortunate to spot this individual hanging upside down beneath a leaf on a roadside in the Périnet Reserve. Its combination of red, gold, and black spots makes it instantly recognizable.

Black-veined Mylon

DATA

Scientific name: *Mylon maimon*

Family: Hesperiidae

Wingspan: About 1.6 in (4 cm).

Flight period: All year.

Larval food plants: *Hiraea fagifolia* and *Stigmatophyllon convolvulifolium* (family Malphigiaceae).

Range: From Mexico south through the west of South America to Argentina; also Paraguay.

With numerous species that are confusingly similar, *Mylon* is a difficult genus, and the specimen illustrated here—photographed puddling on damp ground in Peru's Tingo Maria National Park—is allocated to this species only provisionally. It was formerly known as *M. menippus*. As in most members of the genus, the basic color of the wings is whitish cream with a network of heavily marked blackish veins and the odd smoky zigzag mark here and there.

Common Firetip Skipper

DATA

Scientific name: *Myscelus amystis*

Family: Hesperiidae

Wingspan: About 1.8 in (4.5 cm).

Flight period: All year.

Larval food plants: *Guarea* (family Meliaceae).

Range: Mexico to Argentina.

With nine mirrorlike silvery spots on each forewing, reduced to just one on each hind wing, this is quite a beautiful species. Its basic color is a warm rusty brown. As with many tropical skippers, the wings are held out flat while the butterfly is feeding—in this case on a boneset *(Eupatorium)* flower on a roadside through forest in southern Trinidad. These flowers, members of the aster family (Asteraceae), are renowned for attracting large numbers of butterflies, especially various skippers.

Buff-tipped Skipper

DATA

Scientific name: *Netrobalane canopus*

Family: Hesperiidae

Wingspan: Male about 1.2 in (3 cm); female 1.4 in (3.5 cm).

Flight period: All year.

Larval food plants: In various families.

Range: Africa (mainly in the south and east).

Although mainly a butterfly of more open habitats such as savanna and bush country, the Buff-tipped Skipper is also found in open forest, as seen here on the coast of KwaZulu-Natal in South Africa. The males have the habit of perching all day in a prominent position, usually at the tip of a twig, chasing off any butterflies that trespass nearby. The rounded brown patch at the apex of each forewing is unique among African skippers and makes this species instantly recognizable. The underside is mainly a wishy-washy glassy whitish color, shading to brownish at the tips of the forewings.

Woodland Skipper

This species is plain orange on the upper side with no white spots, but with several elongate dark patches and a toothed dark margin. The undersides are usually pale orange with a few even paler patches. There are several subspecies, showing variations on this overall theme. The Woodland Skipper is found in chaparral, sagebrush desert, and woodland, as seen here in Utah. The males spend most of the day perched, waiting for females to fly past. Both sexes visit flowers for nectar.

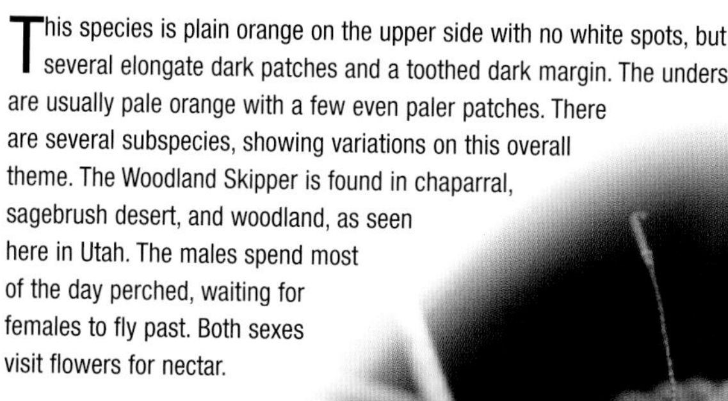

DATA

Scientific name: *Ochlodes sylvanoides*

Other common name: Western Skipper

Family: Hesperiidae

Wingspan: About 1.2 in (3 cm).

Flight period: Late summer and fall.

Larval food plants: Grasses (Poaceae).

Range: Western North America (from British Columbia to California, east to Colorado).

Large Skipper

DATA

Scientific name: *Ochlodes venatus*

Family: Hesperiidae

Wingspan: About 1.2 in (3 cm).

Flight period: June–August.

Larval food plants: Grasses (Poaceae).

Range: Widespread in Europe, eastward to China and Japan.

The upper side of the forewings in this very common butterfly is brownish orange. In the male there is a black sex brand. In the female (illustrated above) there is a scattering of pale patches on all four wings. The undersides are light orange, with a few pale patches. The Large Skipper is found in all kinds of open habitats, from grassy hillsides and mountain slopes to backyards, roadsides, patches of waste ground, and open woodland rides.

Blue-glossed Skipper

A dense coat of hairlike scales thickly covering the body is typical of most skippers, but this is never more beautifully illustrated than in this species, with its wonderful blue gloss. The wings are somewhat less spectacular, being pale sandy brown. The skipper illustrated was one of a pair mating on a forested roadside in Trinidad's Northern Range. During an eight-week stay, this was the only time the author saw this species, illustrating how scarce even supposedly common species can be at certain times of the year.

DATA

Scientific name: *Onophas columbaria*

Family: Hesperiidae

Wingspan: About 1.2 in (3 cm).

Flight period: All year.

Larval food plants: Grasses (Poaceae).

Range: From Mexico to Brazil.

Javelin Skipper

With its plump, heavy, torpedo-like body and blue-tinted translucent wings, this is a distinctive species. Not all forms are as attractive as the one illustrated, however, which was seen puddling on damp ground in Peru's Tingo Maria National Park. From its pristine condition it would appear to have emerged from its pupa only recently, and this may have been the first time it had fed as an adult. Note the orange band across the rear of the abdomen and the small white patches near the tips of the hind wings.

DATA

Scientific name: *Oxynetra semihyalina*

Family: Hesperiidae

Wingspan: About 2 in (5 cm).

Flight period: All year.

Larval food plants: Not known.

Range: Widespread in the South American tropics.

Shining Blue Skipper

DATA

Scientific name: *Paches loxus*

Family: Hesperiidae

Wingspan: About 1.6 in (4 cm).

Flight period: All year.

Larval food plants: *Byttneria aculeata* (family Sterculiaceae).

Range: Mexico to Panama.

With its iridescent blue wings held out to the sides, this magnificent skipper could at first glance easily be mistaken for a member of the Lycaenidae. A close look at the head, however, reveals that it is much broader than in any lycaenid, and the body is much more densely hairy. Close examination of the specimen illustrated (in lowland rain forest at Finca La Selva in Costa Rica) reveals a certain amount of wing damage, confirming that this is a not a pristine specimen and that it must be at least a few weeks old. In the tropics adult butterflies probably live longer than they do in temperate areas.

Musical Ghost Skipper

DATA

Scientific name: *Phanus vitreus*

Family: Hesperiidae

Wingspan: About 1.8 in (4.5 cm).

Flight period: All year.

Larval food plants: *Inga longispica* in the pea family (Fabaceae).

Range: Mexico to Argentina.

With its attention deeply held by the sweet nectar in a *Eupatorium* flower on a roadside through rain forest in southern Trinidad, the specimen illustrated failed to notice the photographer at first, but quickly took flight after this single picture was taken. This is a perfect example of how frustrating butterfly photography can be. Even so, this picture of a Musical Ghost Skipper serves to illustrate the magnificent array of glasslike markings on all four of the deep brown wings. These markings are arranged in hooklike shapes on the forewings. As with most skippers, the larva lives in a shelter made of leaves.

Draco Skipper

DATA

Scientific name: *Polites draco*

Other common name: Rocky Mountain Skipper

Family: Hesperiidae

Wingspan: About 1 in (2.5 cm).

Flight period: June–July.

Larval food plants: Grasses (Poaceae).

Range: United States and Canada (Rocky Mountains).

Found in grassy meadows at high elevations, this skipper is fond of coming to thistle flowers, as seen here in the Rockies in Wyoming. In the male the upper side is dark brownish orange with a large black stigma and a few pale patches. The female is paler and lacks the stigma. In both sexes the underside of the hind wing is pale greenish orange with contrasting cream spots and no pale veins. In the similar Sand Hill Skipper *(Polites sabuleti)* there are obvious yellow veins.

Checkered Skipper

Frequenting open grasslands, grassy woodland edges (as seen here in Georgia), and backyards, this very widespread species is similar to a number of others. The males are fairly easy to distinguish because they lack the hair plumes seen on the hind legs of all other members of the genus. The marks along the underside edge of the hind wing are rounded in this species but triangular in similar species, but the general brown and white checkered pattern is confusingly similar in several species.

DATA

Scientific name: *Pyrgus communis*

Family: Hesperiidae

Wingspan: About 1.2 in (3 cm).

Flight period: June–October in north; all year in south.

Larval food plants: Herbs of the mallow family (Malvaceae).

Range: From Canada to Argentina.

European Grizzled Skipper

This Old World species is not dissimilar to the American Checkered Skipper *(Pyrgus communis)*, illustrating the general high degree of uniformity in the genus. In the European Grizzled Skipper the upper sides are brown with numerous white spots, especially along the wing margins. The underside of the forewing is broadly similar but paler, while the hind-wing underside is greenish with rows of large pale whitish patches. Found in flowery grasslands, bogs, and woodland glades, this butterfly seldom occurs in large numbers.

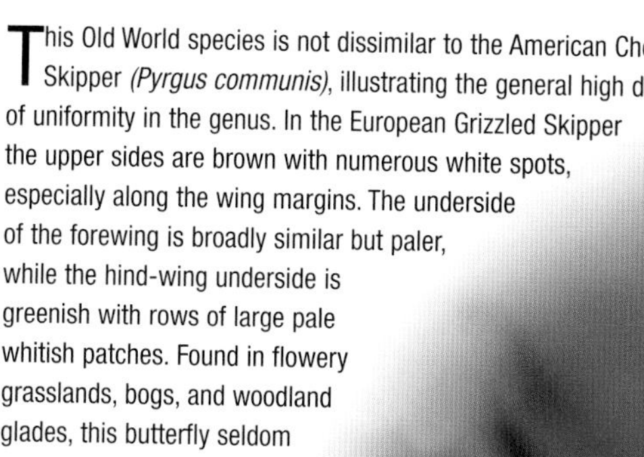

DATA

Scientific name: *Pyrgus malvae*

Family: Hesperiidae

Wingspan: About 1 in (2.5 cm).

Flight period: April–June and July–August; single-brooded in the north, May–June.

Larval food plants: Various.

Range: Widespread in Europe and east to China.

Tropical Checkered Skipper

DATA

Scientific name: *Pyrgus oileus*

Family: Hesperiidae

Wingspan: About 1.2 in (3 cm).

Flight period: All year.

Larval food plants: Mallows (Malvaceae).

Range: From Texas and Florida southward to Argentina and in much of the West Indies.

This mating pair, photographed on a forested roadside in Trinidad's Northern Range, perfectly illustrates the differences between the sexes of this very widespread little skipper. The male, which is smaller than the female, has very large areas of white spots on the upper side, covering a large proportion of the wings. In the female the situation is reversed, the darker brown area of the wings being far larger than the area occupied by the numerous small white spots. Found mainly in open forest, the permanent populations of this butterfly in the United States are restricted to southern Texas and Florida, with occasional migrations northward to northern Texas and Arkansas.

Blue-studded Skipper

DATA

Scientific name: *Sostrata festiva*

Family: Hesperiidae

Wingspan: About 1.2 in (3 cm).

Flight period: All year.

Larval food plants: Not known.

Range: Through much of the South American tropics.

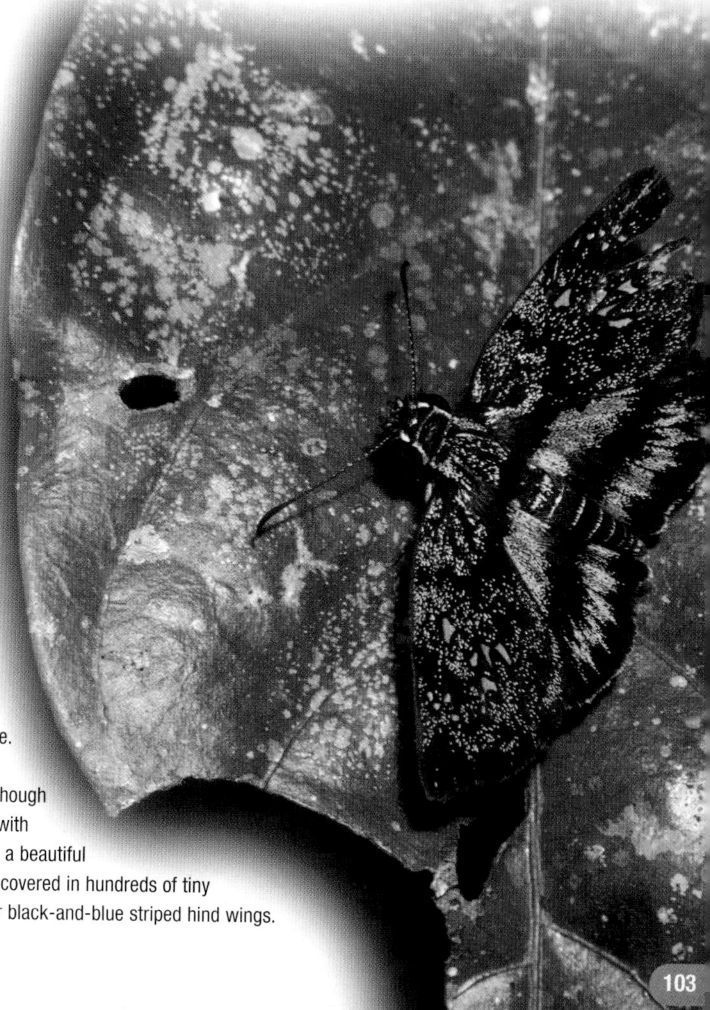

It is always frustrating when an otherwise perfect specimen is seen to have damaged wings, as is the case with the right-hand wings of this individual, photographed in rain forest in Trinidad's Northern Range. Often the wings will have been damaged by an attacking bird, although in males the cause can be fights with rivals. Despite the damage, this is a beautiful butterfly; its brown forewings are covered in hundreds of tiny bluish dots, and it has spectacular black-and-blue striped hind wings.

Forest Grizzled Skipper

DATA

Scientific name: *Spialia ploetzi*

Family: Hesperiidae

Wingspan: About 1 in (2.5 cm).

Flight period: All year.

Larval food plants: *Triumfetta rhomboidea* in the linden family (Tiliaceae).

Range: From West Africa to Kenya and Tanzania.

With its brown topside liberally spotted with white, the Forest Grizzled Skipper is similar to three other members of the same genus. It differs, however, in the underside, in which the white markings are very subdued compared with the other three species. The preferred habitat is also different—this species is found mainly in forests, as seen here in Kenya's Kakamega Forest, but it prefers more open areas, such as along roads and riverbanks, and even backyards. The three other species are restricted to open savanna.

Small Skipper

The upper side of both sexes is plain brownish orange, with a black sex brand in the male. The underside is generally paler and lacks any distinct markings. The clubbed tip of the antennae is brownish on the underside, which serves to distinguish this species from the otherwise very similar Essex Skipper *(Thymelicus lineola)*. The Small Skipper is an abundant butterfly in grassy places. It often visits flowers in some numbers—three or four individuals may crowd onto a single thistle head. Knapweed is also popular, as seen attracting this specimen in England.

DATA

Scientific name: *Thymelicus sylvestris*

Family: Hesperiidae

Wingspan: About 1.2 in (3 cm).

Flight period: June–July.

Larval food plants: Grasses (Poaceae).

Range: Over most of Europe, eastward to Iran and southward to Morocco.

Long-tailed Skipper

DATA

Scientific name: *Urbanus proteus*

Family: Hesperiidae

Wingspan: About 1.8 in (4.5 cm).

Flight period: All year.

Larval food plants: Various members of the pea family (Fabaceae).

Range: From the southern United States to Argentina.

In the United States this skipper can easily be distinguished from all others by the prominent long tails on its hind wings, its green body, and the green areas in the wing bases on its upper side. During summertime there is a strong migration northward from the permanent populations in the far south, which sometimes reach as far north as Michigan and Connecticut. The Long-tailed Skipper's preferred habitat consists of open places, such as grassy roadsides, as seen here in Florida. Its caterpillar, known as the Bean-leaf Roller, lives in a tent of rolled-up leaves.

Neso Filmywing

DATA

Scientific name: *Ceratinia neso*

Family: Ithomiidae

Wingspan: About 2.2 in (5.5 cm).

Flight period: All year.

Larval food plants: *Solanum* species in the potato family (Solanaceae).

Range: Widespread in tropical South America.

This is a rain-forest butterfly. Here a female is seen carefully fixing one egg at a time to the underside of a leaf in forest near Satipo in Peru. Butterflies in the genus *Ceratinia* all have semitransparent wings, with a variety of color patterns on the remaining areas. In a number of species, as seen here, there is a large yellow band on the forewing, but in this species there is also a slightly more glassy yellow elongate band on the hind wing. The silver spots along the edge of the hind wing are common to a number of species. The topside is very similar to the underside.

Big-bordered Dircenna

The butterflies in this genus can be distinguished by a combination of their transparent amber-colored, distinctively veined wings and yellow antennae. This species can be separated from other similar butterflies by the broad black borders on all wings, the black spot in the elongate forewing cell, and the absence of any black markings on the inner margin of the forewing. Both sexes visit flowers, but are most often found as solitary individuals perched on a leaf in the partial shade of the rain forest understory, as seen here at Tingo Maria in Peru.

DATA

Scientific name: *Dircenna dero*

Family: Ithomiidae

Wingspan: About 2.8 in (7 cm).

Flight period: All year.

Larval food plants: *Solanum* species in the potato family (Solanaceae).

Range: From Mexico to Brazil.

Curvy-veined Greta

Most of the butterflies in this genus have transparent wings and can be distinguished from members of related genera by details of the venation on the hind wing. The pupae have a silvery mirrorlike surface and often hang in groups from the underside of a broad rain-forest leaf. In this species the adult is distinguished mainly by the broad white bar that runs across the upper part of the forewing. Like most ithomiids, it is most often found perched on a leaf in the deep shade of the rain forest, as seen here in Guatopo National Park in Venezuela.

DATA

Scientific name: *Greta andromica*

Family: Ithomiidae

Wingspan: About 2.2 in (5.5 cm).

Flight period: All year.

Larval food plants: *Cestrum* species in the potato family (Solanaceae).

Range: From Guatemala to Peru.

White-barred Sheerwing

Frequenting the shady depths of the rain-forest understory, the transparent butterflies in this genus can be recognized by the very sparse venation in the hind wing—the most reduced venation of any of the ithomiiids. In some ways this species resembles the Curvy-veined Greta *(Greta andromica)*, but the white bar on the forewing is much reduced in size, as is the hind wing, which is very small compared to the forewing. The butterfly illustrated has managed to locate some tiny and very inconspicuous flowers in the deep shade of the rain forest at Tambopata in Peru.

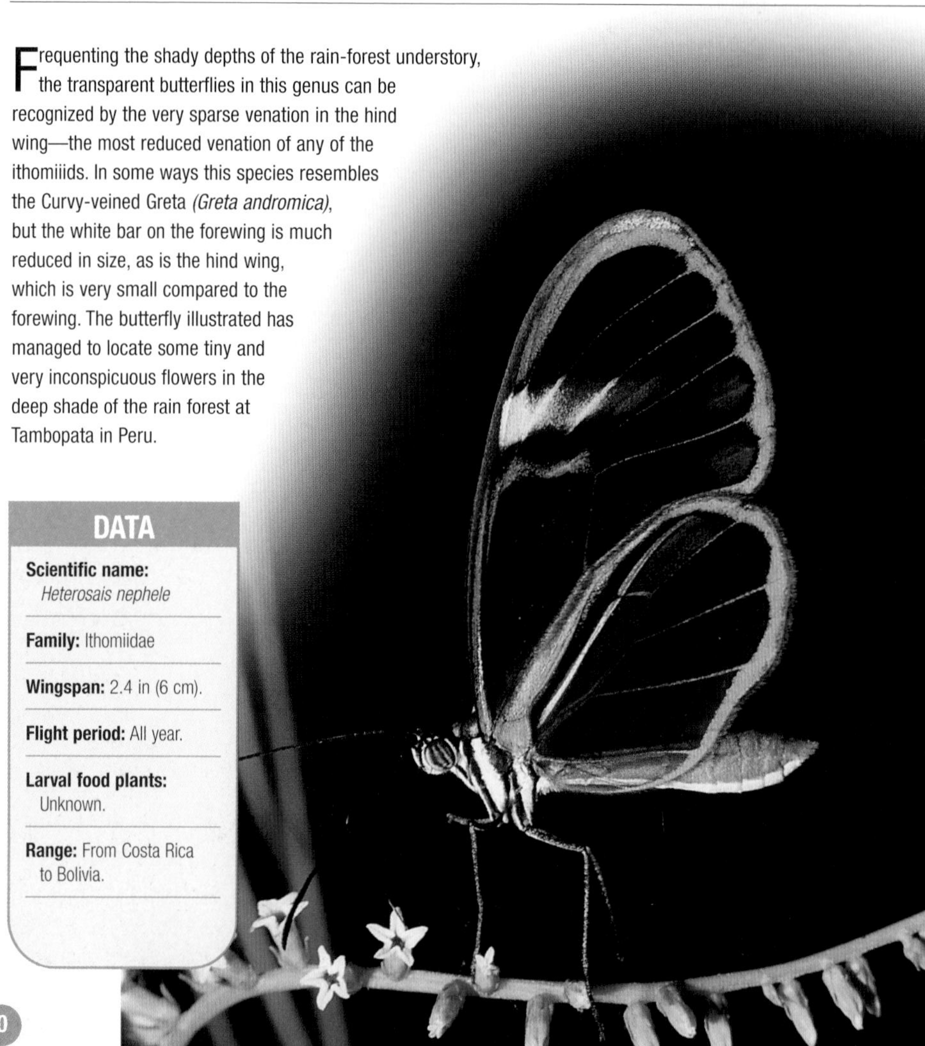

DATA

Scientific name: *Heterosais nephele*

Family: Ithomiidae

Wingspan: 2.4 in (6 cm).

Flight period: All year.

Larval food plants: Unknown.

Range: From Costa Rica to Bolivia.

Blue Transparent

With its glinting bluish transparent wings this rather delicate species flits around in the shady understory of the tropical rain forest, seeking out tiny flowers on which to sip nectar, as illustrated here at the Simla research facility in Trinidad's Northern Range. The border of the wings is an attractive pale orange, and there are a few white markings at the tips of the forewings. The elongate black patch on the yellow bar on the hind-wing margin is an androconial blister, indicating that this is a male.

DATA

Scientific name: *Ithomia pellucida*

Family: Ithomiidae

Wingspan: About 2.2 in (5.5 cm).

Flight period: All year.

Larval food plants: Members of the potato family (Solanaceae).

Range: Widespread in tropical South America; Trinidad.

Saffron-patched Blisterwing

The members of this genus range from transparent to tiger-striped. This species is a kind of intermediate form, with broad orange margins to wings that are heavily marked with a rather glassy shade of yellow, interspersed with small areas of wing that are completely transparent. Photographed in rain forest at Tingo Maria in Peru, this individual is feeding on a bird dropping, a common habit in this family of butterflies. Some species are known as ant butterflies because they follow ant birds (which, in turn, follow swarms of army ants) to feed on their droppings.

DATA

Scientific name: *Ithomia salapia*

Family: Ithomiidae

Wingspan: About 2.2 in (5.5 cm).

Flight period: All year.

Larval food plants: Members of the potato family (Solanaceae).

Range: Widespread in tropical South America.

Sweet-oil Butterfly

DATA

Scientific name: *Mechanitis isthmia*

Family: Ithomiidae

Wingspan: About 2.8 in (7 cm).

Flight period: All year.

Larval food plants: *Solanum* species in the potato family (Solanaceae).

Range: Widespread in tropical areas of South America; also Trinidad.

Along with the next three species this is a member of the tiger-striped mimicry grouping, which also includes the Two-banded Tiger Crescent *Eresia eunice* (family Nymphalidae) and the arctiid moth *Dysschema irene*. In all of these the basic wing color is brownish orange. In the Sweet-oil Butterfly the pattern is variable, but there is usually a zigzag yellow band toward the apex of the forewing, which is tipped with a series of yellowish spots. On the underside there are two yellow bands on each forewing and a row of silver spots around all four wing margins. This is a very successful species, able to adapt to major disturbance of its normal rain-forest home and often found in cocoa plantations, as seen here in Trinidad.

Confused Tigerwing

DATA

Scientific name: *Mechanitis lysimnia*

Family: Ithomiidae

Wingspan: About 2.8 in (7 cm).

Flight period: All year.

Larval food plants: *Solanum* species in the potato family (Solanaceae).

Distribution: From Mexico to Brazil.

As with the Sweet-oil Butterfly *(Mechanitis isthmia)*, the Confused Tigerwing is a very variable butterfly, and numerous subspecies have been named. There are usually either one or two silver or silvery yellowish marks on the black outer third of each forewing, and a band of pale glassy yellow along the upper half of the hind wing, which is bordered with black. The undersides are broadly similar. This is another very successful species, found in virtually every kind of habitat, including backyards and even city streets. It is pictured here in streamside gallery forest in Brazil's savanna-like *campo cerrado* near Brasilia.

Disturbed Tigerwing

DATA

Scientific name: *Mechanitis polymnia*

Family: Ithomiidae

Wingspan: About 2.8 in (7 cm).

Flight period: All year.

Larval food plants: *Solanum* species in the potato family (Solanaceae).

Range: From Mexico to the Amazon region.

One of the commonest butterflies of the region, this species is frequently seen in mixed groups containing several members of the tiger-striped mimicry complex. This very adaptable species is at home in a wide variety of habitats, from steamy rain forests to city parks and streets. The pattern on the upper side is extremely variable but often resembles that of the Sweet-oil Butterfly *(Mechanitis isthmia)*. The underside, as depicted in this mating pair in Venezuela's Guatopo National Park, is similar to the upper side, being a mixture of brownish orange, yellow, and black.

Common Streakwing

Members of this forest-dwelling genus are frequently mistaken for species of *Heliconius* in the field and are sometimes even placed in the *Heliconius* section of collections. The most obvious distinction is the much smaller head and eyes in the nine species of *Melinaea*, most of which are found on the eastern slopes of the Andes (although three species penetrate northward into Central America). The pattern of yellow, orange, black, and white on the upper side of this species (formerly known as *M. egina*) is broadly similar to that on the underside, as seen here in gallery forest in the *campo cerrado* near Brazil's capital city, Brasilia.

DATA

Scientific name: *Melinaea ludovica*

Family: Ithomiidae

Wingspan: About 3.5 in (9 cm).

Flight period: All year.

Larval food plants: Members of the potato family (Solanaceae).

Range: Over much of tropical South America.

Orange-patch Streakwing

DATA

Scientific name: *Melinaea marsaeus*

Family: Ithomiidae

Wingspan: About 3.5 in (9 cm).

Flight period: All year.

Larval food plants: Members of the potato family (Solanaceae).

Range: Colombia, Ecuador, and Peru.

Most ithomiids are inhabitants of the gloomy understory of the tropical rain forest, but this species seems to prefer the shadiest spots of all. In the half light beneath the dense leafy canopy the large areas of black on the wings of this rather skulking butterfly become almost invisible. As a result, the bright orange patches stand out with particular prominence. These patches serve as a warning sign to any potential enemies to keep away and not try to make a meal out of this extremely unpalatable species, seen here in Tingo Maria National Park in Peru.

Cloud-forest Skulker

The genus *Oleria* is a group of smallish ithomiids that attains its greatest diversity in the Amazon Basin. *Oleria vicina* is one of four species found in Costa Rica, all of which are forest butterflies. The individual seen here was feeding on an orchid on the edge of cloud forest at Monteverde, although *Senecio megaphylla*, a member of the aster family, is probably the plant most commonly visited for nectar. Not all members of the genus have the mainly transparent wings with prominent orange borders seen here.

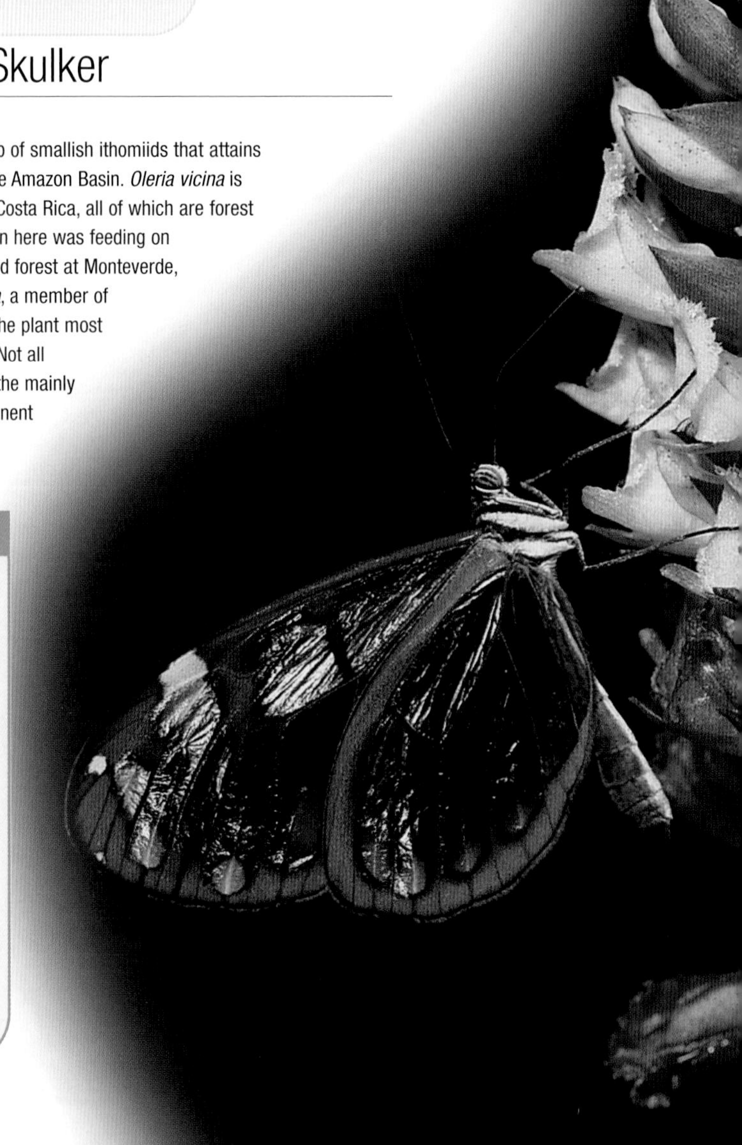

DATA

Scientific name: *Oleria vicina*

Family: Ithomiidae

Wingspan: About 2.2 in (5.5 cm).

Flight period: All year.

Larval food plants: *Solanum trizygum* and *Lycianthes multiflora* of the potato family (Solanaceae).

Range: Costa Rica and northern Panama.

Rusty Ticlear

This rather little-known genus of butterflies contains just three species, all of which are restricted to Central America. They are mainly inhabitants of rain forest but can also be found in areas that have been seriously disturbed by humans. The butterfly illustrated here was one of several feeding on flowers in bright sunshine on the edge of a tree-shaded coffee plantation near Jalapa in Veracruz State, Mexico. The forewings are heavily barred with black against a semitransparent tawny background, but the hind wings are mainly tawny, with a row of elongate white spots around the margins.

DATA

Scientific name: *Olyras theon*

Family: Ithomiidae

Wingspan: About 3.7 in (9.5 cm).

Larval food plants: Members of the potato family (Solanaceae).

Range: Mexico to Honduras.

White-barred Crystalwing

The members of the genus *Pseudoscada* are among the smallest of the ithomiids, and little seems to be known of their habits. There is even some dispute about the true number of species—18 are listed, but possibly far fewer are genuine species rather than variations on a theme. In this species the wings are mainly transparent, with orange borders and a white bar on each forewing. As with many ithomiids, this is a butterfly of the gloomy rain-forest understory, as seen here in Peru's Tingo Maria National Park, where a typically small drab rain-forest flower is providing a source of nectar.

DATA

Scientific name: *Pseudoscada timna*

Family: Ithomiidae

Wingspan: About 1.6 in (4 cm).

Flight period: All year.

Larval food plants: Members of the potato family (Solanaceae).

Range: Over much of tropical South America.

Cream-patch Clearwing

There is a great deal of variation in wing pattern among the species in this genus. Some have almost completely transparent wings, while in others there are no transparent areas at all. The species illustrated here (in rain forest in Venezuela's Guatopo National Park) lies somewhere between these two extremes. The central area of each wing is semitransparent, while on each forewing there is a broad creamy white patch. The wing borders are orange and contain three silvery spots at the tip of each forewing and six around each hind wing.

DATA

Scientific name: *Pteronymia veia*

Family: Ithomiidae

Wingspan: About 2.4 in (6 cm).

Flight period: All year.

Larval food plants: Probably members of the potato family (Solanaceae).

Range: South America (Amazonia).

Common Pearlwing

DATA

Scientific name: *Scada reckia*

Family: Ithomiidae

Wingspan: About 1.8 in (4.5 cm).

Flight period: All year.

Larval food plants: *Solanum* species in the potato family (Solanaceae).

Range: Over much of tropical South America.

The 14 or so species of rather small butterflies in the genus *Scada* can be found in forests through much of the tropical zone of South and Central America, southward to the Amazon Basin and northward to Nicaragua. They are all semitranslucent and characterized by a slightly feeble flight, seldom straying far from the gloomier parts of the rain-forest understory. In the species illustrated here, photographed at Tambopata in Peru, the wings are mainly a semitransparent white bordered with black and with a black band across the forewing. There are a few silver spots near each wing tip.

Atlantic Pearlwing

Unlike in *Scada reckia*, in this species about half of each wing is transparent (the other half being pale creamy yellow), and there are no dark borders or any other markings. As with many members of this family, these butterflies spend a large part of each day perched on a leaf in the shady interior of the rain forest, as seen here in Atlantic coast rain forest at Montes Claros in Minas Gerais State, Brazil. In contrast to some of the tiger-striped members of the family, which often throng in some numbers, this little butterfly usually occurs as the odd lone individual.

DATA

Scientific name: *Scada karschina*

Family: Ithomiidae

Wingspan: About 1.8 in (4.5 cm).

Flight period: All year.

Larval food plants: Members of the potato family (Solanaceae).

Range: Brazil (Pará to Rio de Janeiro).

Black-fronted Prestonian

DATA

Scientific name: *Tithorea harmonia*

Family: Ithomiidae

Wingspan: About 3 in (7.5 cm).

Flight period: All year.

Larval food plant: *Prestonia* in the dogbane family (Apocynaceae).

Range: From Mexico to Brazil.

Over its wide range this species varies somewhat and has been split into a number of subspecies, of which this is *martina*, photographed in shady rain forest in Peru's Tingo Maria National Park. Its coloration is very similar to that of several heliconiids, such as *Heliconius isabella*. Both are members of the tiger-striped mimicry complex that is such a conspicuous element of the butterfly fauna of South and Central America. In this species the pattern is similar on both sides of the wings, being the typical tiger-striped combination of yellow, orange, and black, with silver spots in the black borders.

Snout Butterfly

The Libytheidae is a small family in which the palpi extend forward to form a "snout." This resembles a leaf stalk when the butterfly is at rest with its leaflike wings closed, as shown in the accompanying photograph, taken in Santa Rosa National Park in Costa Rica. This is subspecies *mexicana*, found in lowland Mexico and Central America. Subspecies *larvata* occurs on the Mexican Plateau and in the southwestern United States, while subspecies *bachmanii* ranges from Kansas and south Texas to the Eastern Seaboard, sometimes migrating in summer as far north as Maine and Ontario.

DATA

Scientific name: *Libytheana carinenta*

Family: Libytheidae

Wingspan: About 1.6 in (4 cm).

Flight period: All year in south; summer in north.

Larval food plants: Members of the elm family (Ulmaceae).

Range: From the southern United States to Brazil.

African Copper

The common name of this little butterfly of dry bush country is not particularly suitable, since this is one of the few "coppers" in which the upper side is not a rich coppery orange but a somewhat dull shade of brown, even in the males. The only element of brightness is a row of whitish marks along the margins of the wings. The underside of the hind wing, as seen here, is also a little dull. This is not true of the forewing, which exhibits a series of black-bordered white dots on an orange background. When at rest on stony ground, as seen here, this species is very hard to spot.

DATA

Scientific name: *Aloeides taikosama*

Family: Lycaenidae

Wingspan: About 1 in (2.5 cm).

Flight period: Mainly summer (September–March).

Larval food plants: Unknown.

Range: South Africa (KwaZulu-Natal and Transvaal); Lesotho.

Common Silver Spot

In the male of this forest species, seen here puddling on damp ground in Ghana's Bobiri Forest, the upper side is mainly bright greenish blue with broad black borders. The underside bears a striking pattern of silvery white elongate spots against a brownish background. It is this pattern that is seen when the butterfly is at rest or feeding at flowers (a frequent activity), when the wings are usually closed. In the female the upper side is brown to almost black, with a red patch at the tip of the hind wings (also seen in the male) and a few pale spots on the forewings.

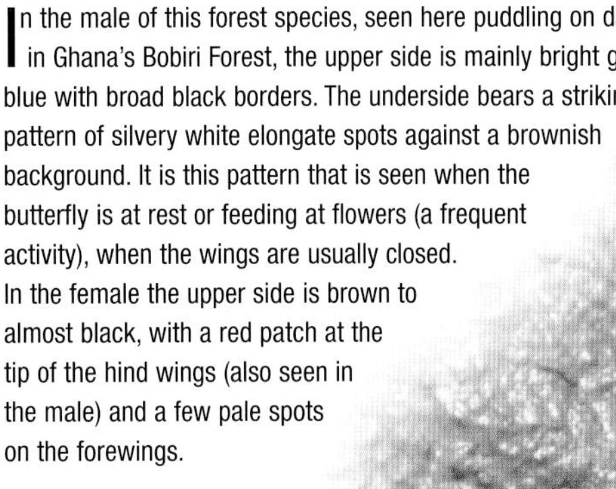

DATA

Scientific name: *Aphnaeus orcas*

Family: Lycaenidae

Wingspan: About 1.2 in (3 cm).

Flight period: All year.

Larval food plants: Wide-ranging, in several families.

Range: Africa (Gambia to western Kenya).

Aetolus Stripestreak

Members of this genus are classic examples of false-head mimicry and have been much studied. The pattern of broad blackish brown stripes on the underside directs the observer's eye away from the genuine head (seen here on the left) and toward the tip of the hind wings, with their antenna-like tails and dark, headlike markings. The orange bands on the borders of the hind wing also direct the eye to the false head and away from the real head. To maximize the effect, the wings are constantly shuffled up and down, making the tails twitch in an antenna-like fashion. The upper side of this rain-forest species, seen here at Finca La Selva in Costa Rica, is mainly whitish with broad brown borders.

DATA

Scientific name: *Arawacus aetolus*

Family: Lycaenidae

Wingspan: About 1 in (2.5 cm).

Flight period: All year.

Larval food plants: *Solanum lancaeifolium* in the potato family (Solanaceae).

Range: From Central America to Brazil.

Brown Argus

In both sexes of this little butterfly the upper side of the wings is brown, with a row of bright orange dots along the outer wing margins. The underside is pale gray or light gray brown, with a scattering of white-ringed black spots and usually a row of orange spots along the margins, although the latter are sometimes virtually absent. When feeding at flowers, as seen here in England, the wings are often held wide open, especially if the weather is cool and the butterfly needs to absorb some warmth. The favored habitats are always open, such as heaths and grassy slopes.

DATA

Scientific name: *Aricia agestis*

Family: Lycaenidae

Wingspan: About 1 in (2.5 cm).

Flight period: April–August. Usually two broods in the north; three in the south.

Larval food plants: Rock roses (Cistaceae) and various stork's-bills (Geraniaceae).

Range: From western Europe (excluding Spain and Portugal) eastward to Iran and Siberia.

Great Blue Hairstreak

On the wing throughout the year in Florida, southern Texas, and much of Mexico, this splendid butterfly is found farther north only in the summer months, in several broods. In the male the upper side of each wing is a brilliant iridescent blue with a broad black border. The female is similar but slightly duller. The underside of both wings is mainly black, with a narrow blue band on the forewing. Both wings bear a few red spots near their bases, and there are some gold spots near the tips of the hind wings. This species is found in a wide range of habitats, the butterfly illustrated was photographed on a semidesert roadside in Tamaulipas State, Mexico.

DATA

Scientific name: *Atlides halesus*

Family: Lycaenidae

Wingspan: About 1.5 in (3.7 cm).

Flight period: March–November.

Larval food plants: Mistletoes *(Phoradendron)* in the Loranthaceae.

Range: United States (northward to Oregon and New York); Mexico.

Bush Scarlet

As its common name suggests, the color of the upper side of this wide-ranging butterfly is predominantly a bright fiery scarlet, although there are considerable areas of black on the forewings. Both sexes are similar, although the female is slightly less vivid. The underside is very like a dead leaf, particularly the hind wing, which is coppery brown with a short tail. On the underside of the forewings there is a sprinkling of black-edged white spots. This is a butterfly of open savannas, photographed here in typical habitat in Kruger National Park, South Africa.

DATA

Scientific name: *Axiocerses amanga*

Family: Lycaenidae

Wingspan: About 1.1 in (2.8 cm).

Flight period: All year.

Larval food plants: Sour-plum trees *(Ximenia)* in the family Olacaceae.

Range: From West Africa across the continent to South Africa.

Coast Scarlet

Seasonally dry forest and scrub along the coast of East Africa are the main habitats for this rather local little butterfly, pictured here in a remnant of coastal scrub among increasing housing development north of Mombasa in Kenya. Compared with the Bush Scarlet *(Axiocerses amanga)*, the underside is far less like a dead leaf, being well sprinkled with elongate silver and blue spots, ringed in black. The ground color of the hind wings is pale brown on the outer half, grading into rich orange on the rear half, while the hind wing is a vivid shade of red. The upper side is scarlet with black wing tips.

DATA

Scientific name: *Axiocerses styx*

Family: Lycaenidae

Wingspan: About 1.2 in (3 cm).

Flight period: All year.

Larval food plants: *Brachystegia* in the pea family (Fabaceae).

Range: Africa (from Malawi and Mozambique to Tanzania and Kenya).

Pygmy Blue

DATA

Scientific name: *Brephidium exilis*

Family: Lycaenidae

Wingspan: 0.5–0.75 in (1.2–1.9 cm).

Flight period: All year in south; summer in north.

Larval food plants: Mainly members of the saltbush family (Chenopodiaceae).

Range: From the United States (eastern Oregon and Nebraska) southward to Venezuela.

One of the world's smallest butterflies, the Pygmy Blue is found mainly in rather dry, open habitats where its food plants abound, such as desert, prairie, and salt marsh. It is also found in habitats altered by humans, such as vacant lots (as seen here in Farmington, New Mexico), weedy fields, roadsides, and farmyards. It occurs mostly along the coast in the southeastern United States, but inland farther west. In both sexes the upper side is coppery brown, with dull blue wing bases and a row of small dark spots on the outer margin of the forewing. The underside is brown, dappled with white, and a row of black spots around the margin of the hind wing.

European Green Hairstreak

Differing only in minor details of pattern from several of its North American cousins, such as the Western Green Hairstreak *(Callophrys affinis)* the European Green Hairstreak is found on rough open ground from sea level to high in the mountains. It is in such places, often on nutrient-deficient soils, that its main food plants abound. This butterfly rarely rests with its wings open, allowing its plain brown upper sides to be seen. When the wings are closed, the green underside, with its line of white spots on each wing, blends in with the vegetation on which the butterflies usually sit (except when visiting flowers, as seen here in England).

DATA

Scientific name: *Callophrys rubi*

Family: Lycaenidae

Wingspan: About 1 in (2.5 cm).

Flight period: In summer (usually May–July) in a single brood.

Larval food plants: Various, e.g., gorse *(Ulex)* in the pea family (Fabaceae) and ling *(Calluna)* in the heather family (Ericaceae).

Range: From western Europe and North Africa to Siberia.

Dusty-blue Hairstreak

With its dusty-blue upper sides this species is similar to the Red-banded Hairstreak *(Calycopis cecrops)*, which is widespread in the eastern United States. Both species exhibit the silvery gray underside seen here, with a zigzagging red line on forewing and hind wing. In *C. cecrops*, however, the red line on the hind wing is broader and the black eyespots larger. The upper side is mainly blue in the male and brown in the female. The Dusty-blue Hairstreak is found in a variety of open habitats, often in semidesert, as seen here on a roadside near Ciudad Victoria in Tamaulipas State, Mexico.

DATA

Scientific name: *Calycopis isobeon*

Family: Lycaenidae

Wingspan: About 1 in (2.5 cm).

Flight period: All year.

Larval food plants: Dead leaves and fruits of many plants and even seeds on the ground.

Range: From Panama to Mexico and south Texas, occasionally straying into Kansas.

Spring Azure

Seen here feeding on the flowers of a roadside plant of white bryony *(Bryonia dioica)* in England, where it is known as the Holly Blue, this little butterfly is often seen in backyards as well as in a wide range of other habitats, from forests to brushlands and mountainsides. In the male the upper side is sky blue to violet, with a whitish border to each wing. The female is similar but a little duller. Both sexes tend to spend most of their time with closed wings, revealing only the unspectacular whitish undersides with their sprinkling of black dots.

DATA

Scientific name: *Celastrina argiolus*

Family: Lycaenidae

Wingspan: About 1.2 in (3 cm).

Flight period: Mainly April–July; longer in the south of its range.

Larval food plants: In many different families.

Range: Over most of North America, Europe, and Asia; also in North Africa.

Tailed Green-banded Blue

As with many members of the Lycaenidae, the caterpillars of this forest species have an obligatory association with ants—in this case those belonging to the genus *Anonychomyrma*. The caterpillar provides the ants with secretions from special glands, and in return the ants act as bodyguards, fiercely attacking any intruders that might threaten the caterpillar. The butterfly pictured here was photographed in rain forest near the coast of Queensland, Australia. The male's upper side is blue with brown borders. The female is very different, being mainly whitish on the lower half of each wing and brown on the upper half.

DATA

Scientific name: *Danis cyanea*

Family: Lycaenidae

Wingspan: 1.2 in (3 cm).

Flight period: All year.

Larval food plants: Matchbox bean *(Entada phaseoloides)* in the pea family (Fabaceae).

Range: Northeastern Australia and New Guinea.

Common Posy

Found mainly in forests, from monsoon forests that are only seasonally wet to permanently humid rain forests, this little butterfly is also often seen in backyards in cities, as long as some trees are present. In both sexes the upper side of the forewings is reddish orange, with broad bluish black tips. In the male the hind wing is brownish, grading into bluish near the edges, while in the female the hind wing is coppery. In both sexes the hind wing bears two prominent white tails. As can be seen here on an individual photographed in gloomy coastal mangrove forest at Pangandaran in Java, the undersides are paler, with a scattering of black lines.

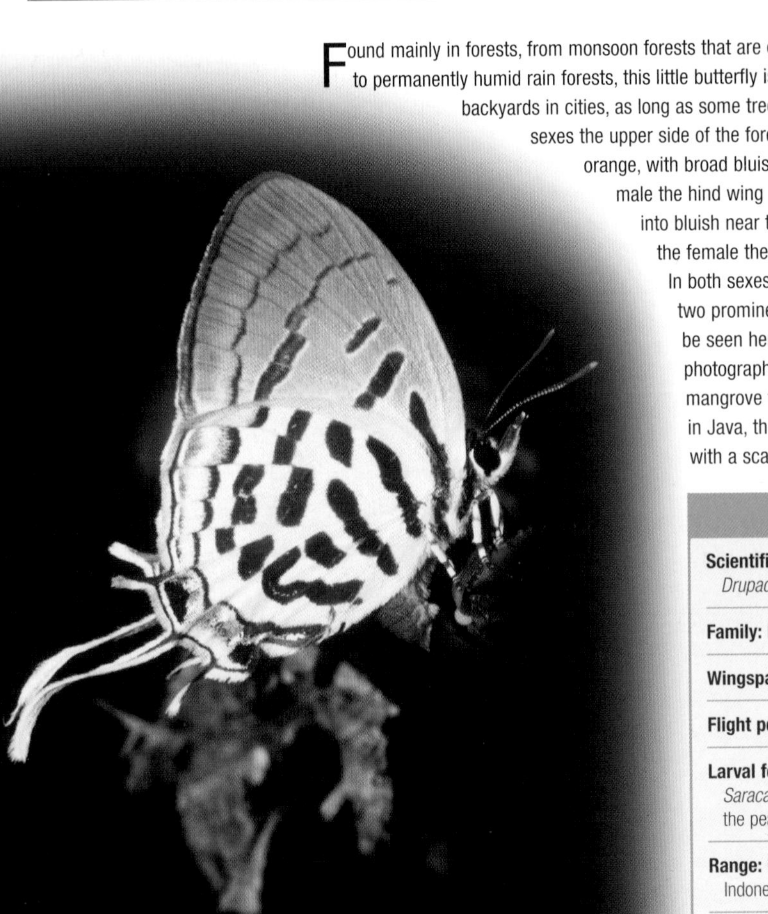

DATA

Scientific name: *Drupadia ravindra*

Family: Lycaenidae

Wingspan: About 1 in (2.5 cm).

Flight period: All year.

Larval food plants: *Saraca thaipingensis* in the pea family (Fabaceae).

Range: Myanmar (Burma) to Indonesia and the Philippines.

Fulvous Hairstreak

This West Indian species has relatively recently become established as a breeding species in the United States, where it is found in southern Florida. The upper side of the wings is brownish orange, with broad black borders. The underside is pale brownish gray, and there is a black line across both forewing and hind wing, although only the latter also has a row of white dashes and a brownish red mark near the hind margin. The antennae, banded in black and white, have orange tips. The Fulvous Hairstreak can be common on some of the West Indian islands, such as Cuba, where the accompanying photograph was taken in a tree-filled hotel garden, a typical habitat for this butterfly.

DATA

Scientific name: *Electrostrymon angelia*

Family: Lycaenidae

Wingspan: About 0.8 in (2 cm).

Flight period: All year.

Larval food plants: *Schinus terebinthifolius* in the cashew family (Anacardiaceae).

Range: On various West Indian islands and in southern Florida.

Reakirt's Blue

Although only permanently resident in the south of its range in the United States, summertime migratory flights may take this small butterfly as far north as Saskatchewan. Its habitat covers open woodland, prairie, mountainsides, lush meadows, creek sides, and semidesert, as here in Arizona's Chiricahua Mountains. The male's upper side is light blue with slightly darker wing veins and a dark border blending into the blue of the wing. The female is similar but darker. The underside, depicted here, is light gray, with a row of white-ringed black spots on the forewing and three black-and-blue spots near the hind-wing margin.

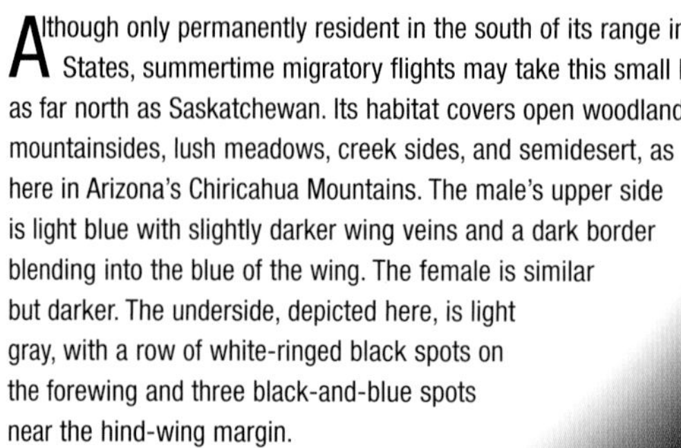

DATA

Scientific name: *Hemiargus isola*

Other common name: Mexican Blue

Family: Lycaenidae

Wingspan: About 0.9 in (2.3 cm).

Flight period: April–October.

Larval food plants: Many legumes (Fabaceae), including mesquite *(Prosopis juliflora)* and rattleweeds *(Astragalus)*.

Range: Southwest United States to Costa Rica.

Scarce Copper

Tramping up a flowery mountain valley after a heavy rainstorm and suddenly coming upon dozens of shimmering copper butterflies opening their wings to bask in the sun is a memory to treasure. This is exactly how the accompanying photograph came to be taken, on a dripping wet mountainside in the French Alps. Also found in open flowery habitats in the lowlands, the Scare Copper is one of the prettiest European lycaenids, especially the male (pictured), which is usually unspotted. The female is far less attractive, being heavily marked with black spots. In both sexes the underside is light brown with a smattering of black spots.

DATA

Scientific name: *Heodes virgaureae*

Family: Lycaenidae

Wingspan: About 1.2 in (3 cm).

Flight period: July–August in a single brood.

Larval food plants: Docks *(Rumex)* in the Polygonaceae.

Range: From Europe eastward to Mongolia.

Common Fairy Hairstreak

DATA

Scientific name: *Hypolycaena hatita*

Family: Lycaenidae

Wingspan: About 1.2 in (3 cm).

Flight period: All year.

Larval food plants: *Syzygium* in the myrtle family (Myrtaceae).

Range: Over much of tropical Africa, south to Zambia and Malawi.

The males of this forest butterfly are exceptionally beautiful and are fond of feeding on bird droppings, although they will also puddle on muddy tracks, as seen here in Ghana's Bobiri Forest. They seldom spend much time with their wings spread wide, so the author was fortunate to snatch the accompanying picture, showing the sumptuous brilliant blue-violet of the forewings, with their broad black tips, and the broad white margins of the hind wings. The female is much drabber, being mainly brownish, with white tips to the hind wings. In both sexes the undersides are whitish gray with a pair of orange lines on each wing.

Black-patch Hairstreak

The long streamerlike hind-wing tails typical of the butterflies in this forest-loving genus are very evident in this photograph, taken in Budongo Forest in Uganda. As with all lycaenids that have so-called false heads, the wings are constantly shuffled so that the long "antennae" move in a lifelike manner. In this species the upper-side coloration is mainly blackish brown in the male, with some blue scaling on the basal half of each wing. The female is similar, but paler. As can be seen, the underside is silvery whitish, with a red band across each wing and a red-and-black eyelike marking near the tip of the hind wing.

DATA

Scientific name: *Hypolycaena liara*

Family: Lycaenidae

Wingspan: About 1.2 in (3 cm).

Flight period: All year.

Larval food plants: *Vitex* in the mint family (Lamiaceae).

Range: Africa (from Guinea to Kenya and Tanzania).

Giant Sapphire

DATA

Scientific name: *Iolaus alcibiades*

Family: Lycaenidae

Wingspan: About 1.6 in (4 cm).

Flight period: All year.

Larval food plants: Unknown.

Range: Africa (from Guinea to the Congo region).

The male of this forest butterfly is a lovely creature. It is seen here basking on a leaf in Ghana's Bobiri Forest on an early morning cooled drastically by the seasonal Harmattan wind blowing from the north. The basic color of the upper side is sapphire blue, with black on the outer half of the forewings and a very narrow black border to the hind wings. In the female the forewings are similar to those of the male but paler. The hind wing is different, however, with a zigzagging black line a little way in from the margin, enclosing two large red spots. In both sexes the underside is white, with a dotted red line near the outer margin of each wing.

Long-tailed Blue

The Long-tailed Blue is one of the most widespread butterflies in the world but it has never managed to colonize the Americas. It occurs mainly in open flowery places in warmer regions. The specimen illustrated was photographed in seasonally wet monsoon forest in India during the dry season, when butterflies are generally scarce. In the male the upper side has a rather hairy appearance and is violet blue with narrow dark borders to the wings. The female is brown, except for the bluish violet wing bases. In both sexes the underside is pale brown, with numerous wavy white lines and a pair of very eyelike spots near the tip of the hind wing.

DATA

Scientific name: *Lampides boeticus*

Family: Lycaenidae

Wingspan: About 1.2 in (3 cm).

Flight period: All year in tropics; in summer in temperate regions.

Larval food plants: Legumes (Fabaceae).

Range: From southern Europe and Africa eastward to Japan, Australia, and Hawaii (introduced).

Marine Blue

On the wing throughout the year in the tropical southern part of its range, in the United States this species is more seasonal. It flies all year around in southern California and Texas and migrates northward in summer, sometimes reaching as far north as Minnesota, where it is likely to be seen between June and October. It flies in a variety of habitats, from desert (as seen here in Arizona) and thorn scrub to parks and backyards. The male's upper side is pale lavender blue, with a narrow dark border and white fringes. The female is similar, but larger and less blue. In both sexes the underside is pale brown with numerous wavy whitish bands and two eyespots near the tip of the hind wing.

DATA

Scientific name: *Leptotes marina*

Other common name: Striped Blue

Family: Lycaenidae

Wingspan: About 1 in (2.5 cm).

Flight period: All year.

Larval food plants: Legumes (Fabaceae).

Range: North America, south to Central America.

Malagasy Marine Blue

The large island of Madagascar, lying off the east coast of Africa, is renowned for the number of animal species that are found there and nowhere else. This wealth of endemic species includes the little butterfly pictured here, puddling on damp ground in the spectacular forest that can be found near Morondava, with its great stands of fat-stemmed baobab trees. As with many species in the genus *Leptotes*, the upper side of the male is mainly purplish blue, while the female is similar but with more brown than blue. The underside is white with numerous wavy-edged brownish markings, and there are two very eyelike spots near the tip of the hind wing.

DATA

Scientific name: *Leptotes rabenafer*

Family: Lycaenidae

Wingspan: About 1 in (2.5 cm).

Flight period: All year.

Larval food plants: Unknown.

Range: Madagascar.

Small Copper

DATA

Scientific name: *Lycaena phlaeas*

Family: Lycaenidae

Wingspan: About 1.2 in (3 cm).

Flight period: In summer.

Larval food plants: Mostly docks *(Rumex)* in the Polygonaceae.

Range: Europe, North Africa, temperate Asia, and North America.

Found in a variety of open habitats, ranging from urban waste lots to flowery mountainsides, this butterfly usually has several broods each year, although there is only a single brood in the arctic populations. Adults visit a wide range of flowers for nectar, but also spend time basking with partly open wings, as seen here in England. On the upper side the forewings are coppery orange with a few black dots and a broad black border. The hind wing is mostly black, with an orange band near the hind margin. Below, the forewing is pale orange with a scattering of black spots and a gray border, while the hind wing is pale gray with some small black spots and a row of slightly bigger orange spots along the lower margin.

Adonis Blue

Having decreased markedly in numbers in Europe over the last 30 years, this lovely butterfly now seems to be making something of a comeback, at least in England. It frequents warm, grassy slopes with plenty of flowers, particularly those of the pea and aster families, as seen here in England. The male upper side (pictured) is a beautiful bright blue, with narrow white wing borders through which the black wing veins can be seen to protrude. The female is brown, and in both sexes the underside is pale gray brown with a scattering of black dots and some red dots near the hind-wing margin. Several North American "blues" look very similar, especially the male of the Northern Blue *(Plebejus idas)*.

DATA

Scientific name: *Lysandra bellargus*

Family: Lycaenidae

Wingspan: About 1.2 in (3 cm).

Flight period: In summer.

Larval food plants: Small legumes (Fabaceae), mainly horseshoe vetch *(Hippocrepis comosa)*.

Range: From Europe to Russia, Iraq, and Iran.

Krause's Legionnaire Mimic

Looking quite unlike the more conventional members of the family Lycaenidae, the butterflies in this purely African genus all mimic other distasteful butterflies, in this case legionnaires such as the Sotika Legionnaire *(Acraea sotikensis)*. The similarity to their models is notable. The topside of this forest butterfly is a combination of orange and brown, while the underside is much paler and lacks the vibrant colors seen in this male, perched briefly on a leaf in Uganda's Kibale Forest National Park. The female is similar but paler.

DATA

Scientific name: *Mimacraea krausei*

Family: Lycaenidae

Wingspan: About 2.2 in (5.5. cm).

Flight period: All year.

Larval food: Algae.

Range: From Central Africa to Sudan, Kenya, and Uganda.

Common Harlequin

DATA

Scientific name: *Mimeresia libentina*

Family: Lycaenidae

Wingspan: About 1.4 in (3.5 cm).

Flight period: All year.

Larval food: Algae.

Range: Africa (Sierra Leone to Gabon).

This is the commonest member of the genus, able to survive in various forest types, including those severely degraded by humans. It is typically seen fluttering around in the gloomy understory of the forest or, as here (at Boabeng-Fiema in Ghana), perched in the half light on a slender stem. In the male the upper side of the forewing is mainly black, with a large red patch near the rear margin. The hind wing is red, with very broad black margins. The female has much more extensive red markings, although they tend toward orange rather than the blood red of the male. The underside of the hind wing is as seen here, the forewing being mainly blackish with a pale orange tip.

Silver-studded Blue

Open grassy banks, heaths, and coastal sand dunes are the kinds of places to look for this butterfly. It is scarce in parts of its range, for example, in the British Isles, but in favorable spots it can occur in huge numbers. Certain popular flowers such as wild carrot *(Daucus carota)* may be laden down with 30 or more busily feeding adults. The male, as seen here on heathland in England, is blue, with black borders and a white fringe. The female is brown with extensive blue on the wing bases, particularly on the hind wings. The underside of both sexes is pale smoky gray, with a few white-ringed black dots and a series of orange spots around the wing margins.

DATA

Scientific name: *Plebejus argus*

Family: Lycaenidae

Wingspan: About 1.1 in (2.8 cm).

Flight period: May onward, often in two broods.

Larval food plants: Mainly legumes (Fabaceae), but also ling *(Calluna vulgaris)* in the Ericaceae.

Range: Throughout Europe and temperate Asia to Japan.

Melissa Blue

DATA

Scientific name: *Plebejus melissa*

Other common name: Orange-margined Blue

Family: Lycaenidae

Wingspan: About 1 in (2.5 cm).

Larval food plants: Many different legumes (Fabaceae).

Flight period: Several flights; April–October in south; May–September in north.

Range: From central Canada to Mexico.

You could encounter this little butterfly in a wide range of habitats from mountain meadows, marshes, weedy fields, and roadsides to waste lots in desert towns, as seen here in Farmington, New Mexico. In the male the upper side does not differ much from that of the Silver-studded Blue *(Plebejus argus)*, although it has more lilac in the blue. The female is brown with a line of orange U-shaped marks near the wing borders. The underside is similar in both sexes, being grayish white with a few white-ringed black dots and a row of orange spots near the edge of both wings. On the hind wings the outer part of each orange dot is iridescent blue.

Common Blue

DATA

Scientific name: *Polyommatus icarus*

Family: Lycaenidae

Wingspan: About 1.2 in (3 cm).

Flight period: April–September, in 2 to 3 broods; 1 brood in north.

Larval food plants: Small legumes (Fabaceae).

Range: Canary Islands, North Africa, Europe, and temperate Asia.

This is the most common and successful of the blue lycaenids in Europe, found in most kinds of habitats, from road verges in large cities to grassy banks, open woodland, mountainsides, and sea cliffs. The male, seen here basking in the sun in England, is a beautiful azure blue, with narrow black wing borders and white fringes. The female is brown, often heavily flushed with blue, this being variable. In both sexes the underside is pale grayish fawn, with a scattering of white-ringed black dots and a row of orange dots near the wing margins.

Mother-of-pearl Hairstreak

The entire pattern on the underside of this forest butterfly is dedicated to persuading the observer that its tail is really its head. The tip of the hind wings bears two antenna-like tails that arise from just above a dark eyelike spot. Several brownish lines on the hind wing lead the gaze directly toward this feature and away from the inconspicuous real head (on the left in this picture, taken on the edge of a coffee plantation in Veracruz State, Mexico). The author can testify to the efficacy of the deception, only identifying the true head after a kind of visual double take. The upper side is pale blue with black borders, broadening out to form a black tip to the forewing.

DATA

Scientific name: *Rekoa meton*

Family: Lycaenidae

Wingspan: About 1.4 in (3.5 cm).

Flight period: All year.

Larval food plants: Various legumes (Fabaceae).

Range: From Mexico to Paraguay; also Trinidad.

Sylvan Hairstreak

Occurring in open forest, creekside willow thickets, and wooded desert canyons (as seen here in Utah), this species is very much a western butterfly and is found no farther east than eastern New Mexico. There is only a single flight, during May in the warm lowlands of California, in June in the coastal ranges of that state, and in July and August farther north and in the mountains. Both sexes are similar. The upper side is light brown with a single tail at the tip of each hind wing. The underside is pale gray with a single row of black spots on each wing. There are several much larger orange spots and a bluish patch toward the tip of the hind wing.

DATA

Scientific name: *Satyrium sylvinum*

Other common name: Western Willow Hairstreak

Family: Lycaenidae

Wingspan: About 1.1 in (3.2 cm).

Flight period: May–July.

Larval food plants: Various willows *(Salix)* in the Salicaceae.

Range: Western United States (Washington and Oregon to California), and in Mexico (Baja California).

Ella's Barred Blue

This fast-flying little butterfly is found mainly in thornbush country and savanna—as seen here, sipping nectar from one of the many colorful flowers that had sprung up after abundant rains in the Timbavati Reserve in Transvaal Province, South Africa. Above, the basal third of the forewings is pale blue, while the rest is a blackish brown, in which are set four large yellow dots. The hind wings are more extensively blue, grading to blackish near the margins, and there are two white-tipped black tails on each hind wing. Below, the wings are pale cream, crossed by a number of reddish brown bars, each with a gold stripe running up its center.

DATA

Scientific name: *Spindasis ella*

Family: Lycaenidae

Wingspan: About 1 in (2.5 cm).

Flight period: Mainly in summer (September–April).

Larval food plants: Acacias in the pea family (Fabaceae).

Range: From South Africa and Namibia to Mozambique and Kenya.

Gray Hairstreak

DATA

Scientific name: *Strymon melinus*

Family: Lycaenidae

Wingspan: About 1 in (2.5 cm).

Flight period: Many flights, from spring to fall.

Larval food plants: Very varied, in many families; includes yucca, hop, beans, and mallow.

Range: From southern Canada to Venezuela.

Found in a huge variety of habitats, from sea level to 10,000 feet (3,050 m), and pictured here in open woodland in the Rockies in Utah, the Gray Hairstreak is one of the commonest and most widespread of North American butterflies. The upper side is blackish brown with a red spot near the tip of the hind wing, from which two short tails arise. The underside can be dark gray to silvery white, depending on the subspecies, and is always darker in males than in females. A red line zigzags across all four wings, and there is a red spot near the hind-wing tails. The male's abdomen is orange.

Dotted Blue

These charming little butterflies have one of the prettiest undersides of any African lycaenid—silvery gray with a neat pattern of black spots. The upper side varies according to sex. In males it is violet blue with dark brown outer margins. The female is dark brown with a blue sheen near the wing bases and a whitish central area to the forewing. When the Dotted Blue feeds at flowers, the wings are normally kept shut, as seen here in Transvaal Province, South Africa. Grassy, tree-dotted savanna is its typical habitat, but it is also found in semidesert scrublands and grassy mountainsides.

DATA

Scientific name: *Tarucus sybaris*

Family: Lycaenidae

Wingspan: About 1 in (2.5 cm).

Flight period: All year, but most abundant September–April.

Larval food plants: Buffalo thorn *(Zizyphus mucronata)* in the family Rhamnaceae

Range: Africa (from the Congo region to South Africa, Angola, and Namibia).

Lesser Fiery Copper

DATA

Scientific name: *Thersamonia thersamon*

Family: Lycaenidae

Wingspan: About 1.6 in (4 cm).

Flight period: April–May and July–August, in two broods.

Larval food plants: Docks *(Rumex)* in the Polygonaceae and broom *(Cytisus)* in the Fabaceae.

Range: From Italy across western Asia to Iraq and Iran.

Photographed here in flowery scrublands beside the Mediterranean Sea in Israel—a typical habitat—this attractive butterfly is a member of the subfamily Lycaeninae, known as coppers. In the male the upper side of the forewings is gleaming coppery gold with black borders. The hind wings are sometimes flushed faintly with violet and partially suffused with black, and they have black borders. In the female (pictured) all wings bear a smattering of black spots and the hind wings are heavily suffused with black. In both sexes the underside is similar, being pale orange with black spots on the forewing and pale gray brown with black spots on the hind wing, which has a broad orange band near its outer margin.

Fluffy Tit

Usually found as a single individual, this amazingly long-tailed little butterfly is at home in a variety of warm tropical habitats, including rain forest, monsoon forest, and shady backyards with plenty of trees. It also occurs in semiflooded swamp forest, as seen here in Malaysia not far from the capital, Kuala Lumpur, with the occasional roar of jets overhead on their way to the international airport. In the male (pictured) the upper side of the forewings is black, with pale gray blue bases. The hind wings are whitish gray flushed with blue; there is a black patch near the outer margin. The female is mainly brown. In both sexes the underside is as seen here, but the female has much shorter tails.

DATA

Scientific name: *Zeltus amasa*

Family: Lycaenidae

Wingspan: About 1 in (2.5 cm).

Flight period: All year.

Larval food plants: Various.

Range: From India to Thailand and Indonesia.

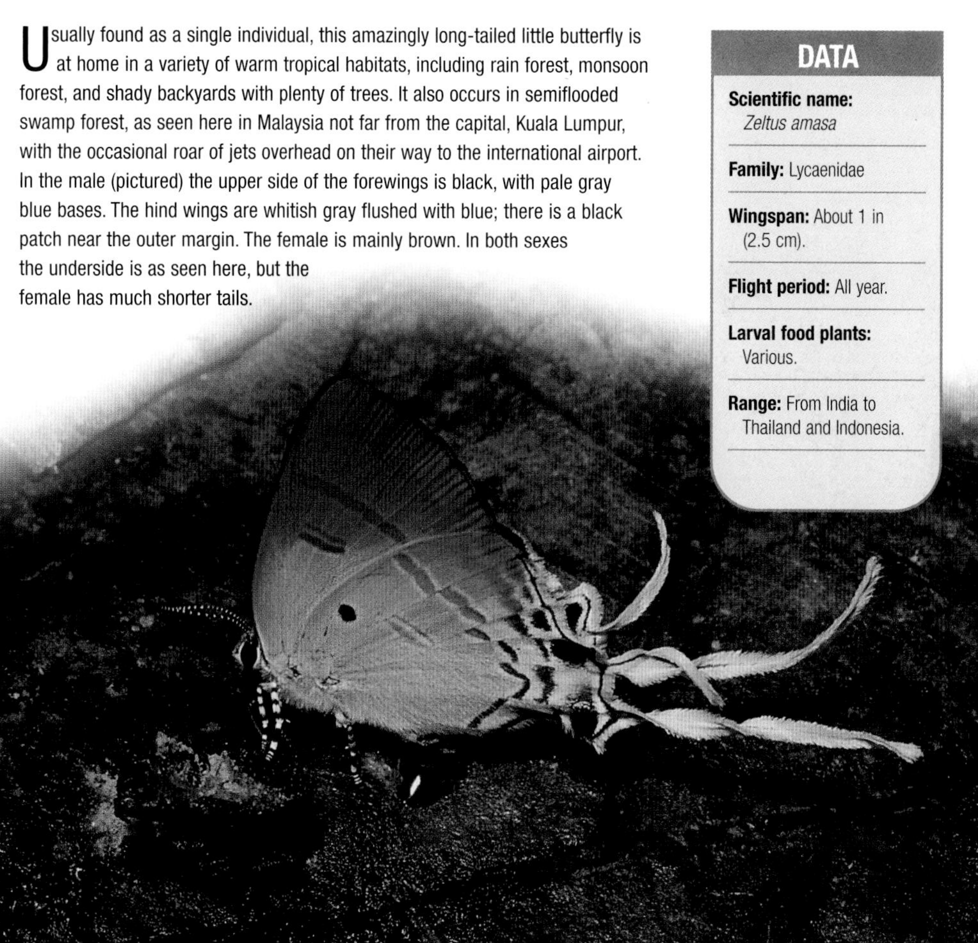

Blue Morpho

If you walk through any rain forest in Central or South America it is usually not long before the first morpho comes dancing along on its flashing blue wings. Unfortunately, as soon as the butterfly settles, as it often does, it closes its wings, making itself far more inconspicuous and difficult to spot. Many of the published photographs of morphos apparently sitting happily with wings spread wide are of dead specimens or captured specimens that have been refrigerated to force them to bask open-winged. In this species, photographed in Peru's Tingo Maria National Park, the upper side is mainly brilliant metallic blue, with black wing bases and margins. The row of eyespots on the underside, as seen here, is typical of most morphos.

DATA

Scientific name: *Morpho deidamia*

Family: Morphidae

Wingspan: About 5 in (13 cm).

Flight period: All year.

Larval food plants: *Machaerium seemani* lianas (Fabaceae).

Range: Over much of the South American tropics.

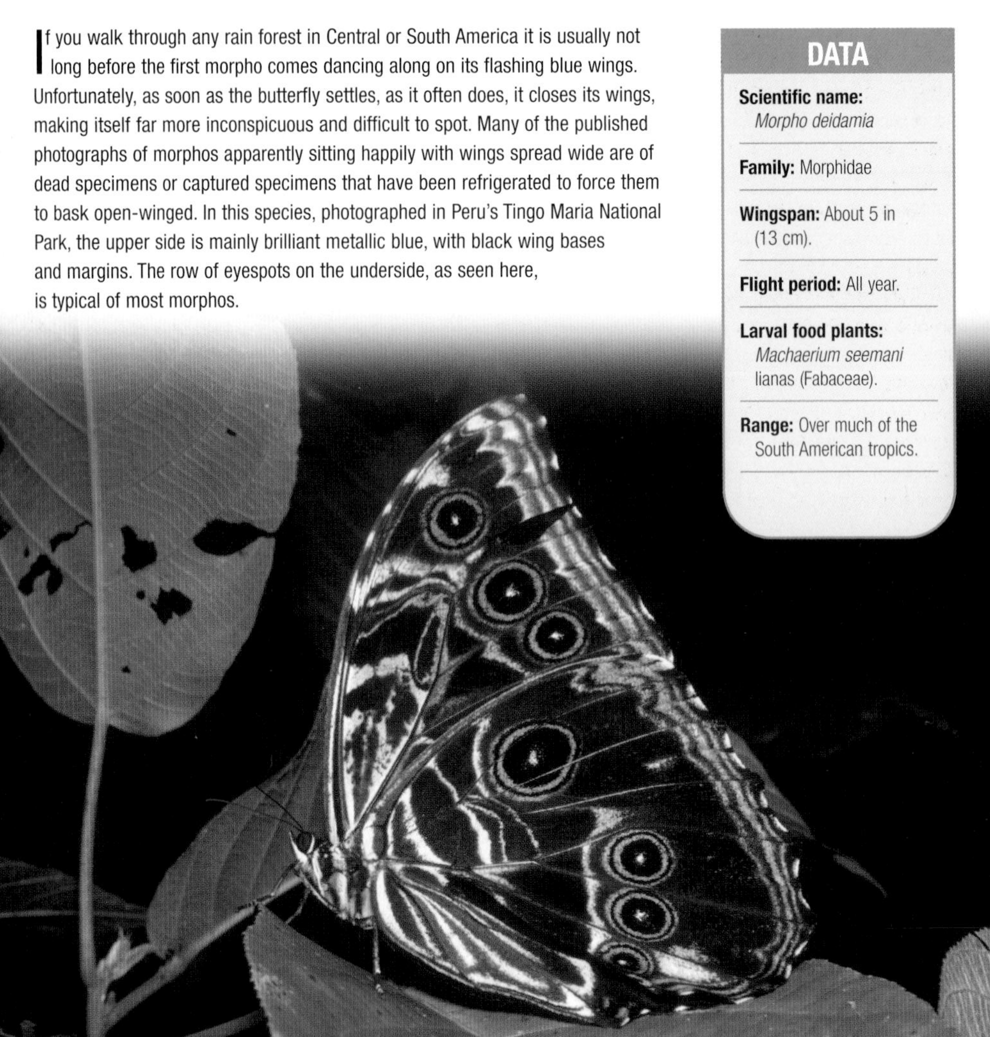

White Morpho

It is rare to find a newly emerged butterfly hanging on its empty chrysalis, its wings newly formed, but this is exactly what happened to the author in rain forest near Nueva Friburgo in Brazil, and this picture was the result. It would have been nice to use available light rather than flash, but it was too gloomy and windy at the time. Unlike in most of the blue species, the underside of this morpho does not bear the prominent row of ocelli (eyespots), but the hind wing has a single row of very narrow elongated "eyespots." On the forewing there are a few small spots and a curved dark band. The upper side is mainly white with a row of black spots near each wing margin.

DATA

Scientific name: *Morpho laertes*

Family: Morphidae

Wingspan: About 5.5 in (14 cm).

Flight period: All year.

Larval food plants: Unknown.

Range: Southeastern Brazil.

Blue Morpho

This is one of several species in which the sexes are completely different. In the male the upper side is brilliant metallic blue, with thin black tips to each forewing, containing a small white flash. The female is white and brown with black wing margins. As can be seen in the accompanying illustration, taken in rain forest in Peru's Tingo Maria National Park, the brown underside bears the typical row of eyespots found in many different species, although here they are particularly attractive. Each has a reddish outer ring enclosing a dark center with a white dash in it. Note also the flush of red near the wing bases and on the face.

DATA

Scientific name: *Morpho menelaus*

Family: Morphidae

Wingspan: About 5.5 in (14 cm).

Flight period: All year.

Larval food plants: Unknown.

Range: Widespread in the South American tropics.

Sister

DATA

Scientific name: *Adelpha bredowii*

Family: Nymphalidae

Wingspan: About 2.8 in (7 cm).

Flight period: April–October, in several flights; June–October in north.

Larval food plants: Mostly oaks *(Quercus)* in the Fagaceae.

Range: United States (Oregon and California to Colorado, Arizona, and Texas) south to Honduras.

The Sister is typically found in semidesert mountains, near oaks. The specimen illustrated here was puddling beside a stream running though a gulch in the Chiricahua Mountains in southern Arizona, a typical kind of habitat. The orange patch on the tip of the forewings is characteristic and is found in no other North American butterfly. The most similar is Lorquin's Admiral *(Basilarchia lorquini)*, which has a rather wishy-washy broad orange border to the tip of the forewing. Both species share the lines of white patches on forewing and hind wing, although they are more disjointed on the Sister's forewing. The underside pattern is very complex, containing shades of lavender blue.

Erotia Sister

DATA

Scientific name: *Adelpha erotia*

Family: Nymphalidae

Wingspan: About 2.4 in (6 cm).

Flight period: All year.

Larval food plants: Unknown.

Range: Costa Rica to Colombia, Venezuela, and Brazil.

For many years the taxonomy of this butterfly has been confused, and it has been listed under the names *Adelpha delinita* and *A. aeolia*. It is one of the largest and most robust members of the genus, and the author was fortunate to come across what is evidently a fresh specimen in fine condition, dry-puddling on a forested roadside in the Chapada de Guimarães, Brazil. Note how the broad white band on the hind wing lines up with the white band, which then turns to orange, on the forewing. There are two smaller orange spots near the tip of the forewing and a very small orange spot (larger in most other species) near the tip of the hind wing. The underside bears a complex pattern, mostly white mixed with red and pale brown.

Mesentina Sister

Members of this genus are most often found puddling on damp ground, and this species is no exception, being seen here drinking from a film of water seeping across a rock face in rain forest in Tingo Maria National Park, Peru. This is one of a number of species in which there are no white bands on the upper side of the wings. The hind wings are a rather somber shade of plain brown, while the forewings, with their large orange patches, are a little more colorful. The underside is a complex mosaic of brownish orange and silvery white.

DATA

Scientific name: *Adelpha mesentina*

Family: Nymphalidae

Wingspan: About 2 in (5 cm).

Flight period: All year.

Larval food plants: Unknown.

Range: Amazon region of South America.

Small Tortoiseshell

One of the most familiar butterflies in European backyards, this species spends the winter as a hibernating adult. Overwintered specimens are often seen on the wing as early as March, feeding on spring flowers such as willow catkins. Once eggs have been laid, the adults die off, and the new generation appears in late summer. The accompanying illustration is somewhat unusual, since it shows a rarely seen courtship ritual—the male sits behind a female and repeatedly strikes her with his antennae. Milbert's Tortoiseshell *(Aglais milberti)*, which is widespread in North America, looks similar, and both species have rather cryptic black and pale orange undersides.

DATA

Scientific name: *Aglais urticae*

Family: Nymphalidae

Wingspan: About 1.8 in (4.5 cm).

Flight period: April–June, August–September.

Larval food plants: Stinging nettles *(Urtica)* in the Urticaceae.

Range: From western Europe across Russia and temperate Asia to the Pacific coast.

Tiger-with-tails

The butterfly illustrated here made a nuisance of itself. It constantly landed on the author's camera bag to feed on the sweat with which it was soaked, thanks to the hothouse atmosphere of the rain forest on the Argentinian side of the Iguaçu Falls. Finally, after being driven away repeatedly, the persistent intruder landed on a nearby log, enabling this picture to be taken, showing the very leaflike underside, with the tail on each hind wing resembling a leaf stalk. The upper side of this rain-forest species (often included in *Consul)* displays a fairly typical tiger-striped pattern, similar to that of the Isabella Longwing *(Eueides isabella)*.

DATA

Scientific name: *Anaea fabius*

Family: Nymphalidae

Wingspan: About 3 in (7.5 cm).

Flight period: All year.

Larval food plants: Pepper *(Piper)* in the family Piperaceae.

Range: Mexico to northern Argentina.

Amazonian Blue Leafwing

Often listed these days in the genus *Memphis*, this is another species in which the underside strongly resembles a dead leaf. In the accompanying illustration the blue and black upper side is on show, which is unusual, because the wings are usually snapped shut as soon as the butterfly perches. This one certainly had no need of basking, since it was photographed on a punishingly hot and humid afternoon in the private reserve at Rancho Grande near Porto Velho, Brazil. With its excellent visitor facilities, this reserve has received intense attention from visiting lepidopterists and currently boasts nearly 2,000 butterfly species. Alas, because of a sustained drought, few of them were seen by the author during a month-long visit.

DATA

Scientific name: *Anaea glaucone*

Family: Nymphalidae

Wingspan: About 2.2 in (5 cm).

Flight period: All year.

Larval food plants: Unknown.

Range: Amazon region of South America.

Skeletonized Leafwing

DATA

Scientific name: *Anaea itys*

Family: Nymphalidae

Wingspan: About 2.8 in (7 cm).

Flight period: All year.

Larval food plants: *Casearia, Ryanea, Laetia* (Flacourtiaceae).

Range: Southern Mexico to northern Argentina.

This species, often now included in *Zaretis*, is one of the most leaflike of butterflies. The specimen featured here was feeding on fermenting sap that oozed from a fallen tree in rain forest at Iguaçu Falls in Argentina, which is about as far south as this species is likely to be found. The forewing upper side is orange near the base, yellowish near the middle, and black at the tip. The hind wing is basically orange all over. In the genera *Consul*, *Memphis*, and *Zaretis* as well as in *Anaea*, the part-grown caterpillar makes a chain of its own frass (waste) and hangs on it, suspended from the tip of a leaf of the food plant.

Coolie

Although often found on the edge of primary rain forest, this lovely butterfly is seldom found within the forest itself, preferring the edges of forest roads, areas of secondary growth, coffee and cocoa plantations, and backyards. The male's upper side, as displayed so vividly here at the Simla research facility in Trinidad, is a rich mixture of black, white, and red, on which there is a definite purple shimmer when viewed from a certain angle. The female is much less splendid, being largely black with numerous white spots and with a broad orange band down the middle of each wing. She has two distinctive blue patches near the front margin of the forewing. In both sexes the underside is pale brownish with white markings.

DATA

Scientific name: *Anartia amathea*

Family: Nymphalidae

Wingspan: About 2.4 in (6 cm).

Flight period: All year.

Larval food plants: Acanthus family (Acanthaceae).

Range: Trinidad and much of tropical South America.

Brown Peacock

DATA

Scientific name: *Anartia fatima*

Family: Nymphalidae

Wingspan: About 2.2 in (5.5 cm).

Flight period: All year.

Larval food plants: *Blechum*, *Justicia*, *Dicliptera*, and *Ruellia* (Acanthaceae).

Range: From the southern United States to Panama.

Despite having only a tiny toehold in the United States, in southern Texas, the Brown Peacock can be quite abundant there, flying throughout the year. In the tropical part of its range this is a butterfly of weedy second-growth areas, backyards, and roadsides. You will not find it in undisturbed rain forest, but it will often abound in an area that has been cleared and colonized by grasses and weeds, as seen here at the OTS research facility at Finca La Selva in Costa Rica. The rich deep chocolate-brown upper side, with its pale cream stripes and red hind-wing patches, makes this an instantly recognizable species. The underside is similar but much paler.

White Peacock

DATA

Scientific name: *Anartia jatrophae*

Family: Nymphalidae

Wingspan: About 2.2 in (5.5 cm).

Flight period: All year in south; summer in north.

Larval food plants: Acanthaceae, Verbenaceae, and Scrophulariaceae.

Range: From the southern United States to South America and the West Indies.

Like the Coolie *(Anartia amathea)* and the Brown Peacock *(A. fatima)*, the White Peacock is a butterfly of open weedy places where its food plants, which are intolerant of the heavy shade found in dense undisturbed forest, can thrive in the sun. Most of its habitats are created as a result of forest destruction and include semiforested roadsides, as seen here near Jalapa in Veracruz State, Mexico. However, it does fly in natural openings in the forest such as occur with landslides caused by earthquakes. In the United States it is far more widespread than the previously mentioned species, being resident and common in the south of Florida and Texas and migrating northward in summer, sometimes as far as Iowa. The white upper side is diagnostic, and the underside is similar.

Forest Admiral

DATA

Scientific name: *Antanartia delius*

Family: Nymphalidae

Wingspan: About 2.4 in (6 cm).

Flight period: All year.

Larval food plants: *Musanga* in the fig family (Moraceae).

Range: From West Africa to Kenya and Tanzania.

Found in disturbed secondary forest or clearings, this species is seldom abundant. For example, the individual pictured here sipping nectar from flowers beside the main track through Bobiri Forest in Ghana was the only one seen by the author during a three-month stay in West Africa. This specimen kept its wings half closed as it fed, opening them fully only for a few moments to reveal the rather dirty orange lower half and black outer half of the forewings, and the orange hind wings with their broad black margins. The underside is a cryptic mixture of blackish gray and pale orange. The long hind wing tails are very characteristic.

Painted Empress

The Painted Empress is one of the smaller nymphalids that you are likely to encounter in Africa. It is not a species that is seen very often, however, since it seems to spend most of its time high up in the rain-forest canopy where it lives. The author was fortunate to come across this specimen, which had been tempted down out of the canopy to drink from a muddy track in Ghana's Bobiri Forest. On very rare occasions collectors may also lure this species to traps baited with fruit. The upper side of the forewings, as seen here, is mainly a mixture of deep orange and black, while the hind wing is predominantly deep orange. The underside is similarly patterned but very pale.

DATA

Scientific name: *Apaturopsis cleochares*

Family: Nymphalidae

Wingspan: About 1.6 in (4 cm).

Flight period: All year.

Larval food plants: Unknown.

Range: From West Africa to Kenya, Tanzania, and Zimbabwe.

Map Butterfly

DATA

Scientific name: *Araschnia levana*

Family: Nymphalidae

Wingspan: About 1.4 in (3.5 cm).

Flight period: Mainly May–June and again August–September.

Larval food plants: Stinging nettles *(Urtica)* in the family Urticaceae.

Range: From France across Russia and temperate Asia to Japan.

The flowers of hemp agrimony *(Eupatorium cannabinum)*, a member of the sunflower family, are very attractive to butterflies. Pictured here on a roadside in France, these flowers are receiving the attention of a Map Butterfly. This widespread species of open forest and wooded roadsides seems to be extending its range northward at present, perhaps as a result of global warming. The mainly brown and cream butterfly pictured is from the second brood, which occurs from August to September. Adults of the first brood (May–June) look different—they are much smaller and have orange as the ground color. Both sexes look similar, the underside being a complex mosaic of white, brown, orange, and pale purple.

Dark Green Fritillary

DATA

Scientific name: *Argynnis aglaja*

Family: Nymphalidae

Wingspan: About 2.2 in (5.5 cm).

Flight period: June–July.

Larval food plants: Mostly violets *(Viola)* in the family Violaceae.

Range: From western Europe and Morocco across Asia to Japan.

Once included in the genus *Mesoacidalia*, this species is now included in an expanded concept of *Argynnis*. The specimen pictured here was puddling on a damp roadside in the French Alps, this being an activity that is relatively rare in European butterflies but seen frequently in the tropics, where feeding at flowers is often a minority activity. The Dark Green Fritillary is a species of open habitats such as moorland, flowery mountainsides, and coastal sand dunes. The upper side is basically brownish orange with numerous black markings. The underside, as seen here, is light brown flushed with green, and there is a scattering of large silvery spots on the hind wing.

Silver-washed Fritillary

DATA

Scientific name: *Argynnis paphia*

Family: Nymphalidae

Wingspan: About 2.4 in (6 cm).

Flight period: July–August.

Larval food plants: Mostly violets *(Viola)* in the family Violaceae.

Range: From western Europe and Algeria across temperate Asia to Japan.

A grassy woodland track with plenty of flowering thistles and brambles is the place to see this stately butterfly, photographed here in exactly that kind of habitat in an ancient oak wood in southwest England. While feeding, the butterfly usually keeps its wings spread, revealing the tawny orange upper side with its numerous black markings—the general appearance being very similar to that of the Dark Green Fritillary *(Argynnis aglaja)*. A form in which the ground color is silvery yellow is common in some areas. The underside of the hind wing lacks the silver spots seen in *A. aglaja*, bearing instead some broad and rather dull silvery lines.

African Castor

This was the first butterfly the author saw on his trip to West Africa in 2004. It was one of the few butterflies still to be seen on the wing at the start of the dry season in Aburi Botanic Gardens near Ghana's capital, Accra. The disturbed forest habitat found here is typical for this species, which is also common in farmlands around villages. However, it was to be two more months before this very flighty butterfly was finally captured on camera, as seen here in the butterfly paradise of Bobiri Forest. Captured in typical pose, with wings spread out on a leaf, this fresh specimen shows clearly how the brown upper surfaces of the wings are overlaid with a patina of silvery scales. The sexes are very similar, and both have more or less plain brown undersides.

DATA

Scientific name: *Ariadne enotrea*

Family: Nymphalidae

Wingspan: About 2 in (5 cm).

Flight period: All year.

Larval food plants: *Tragia* and *Dalechampia* in the spurge family (Euphorbiaceae).

Range: From West Africa to Kenya and Tanzania.

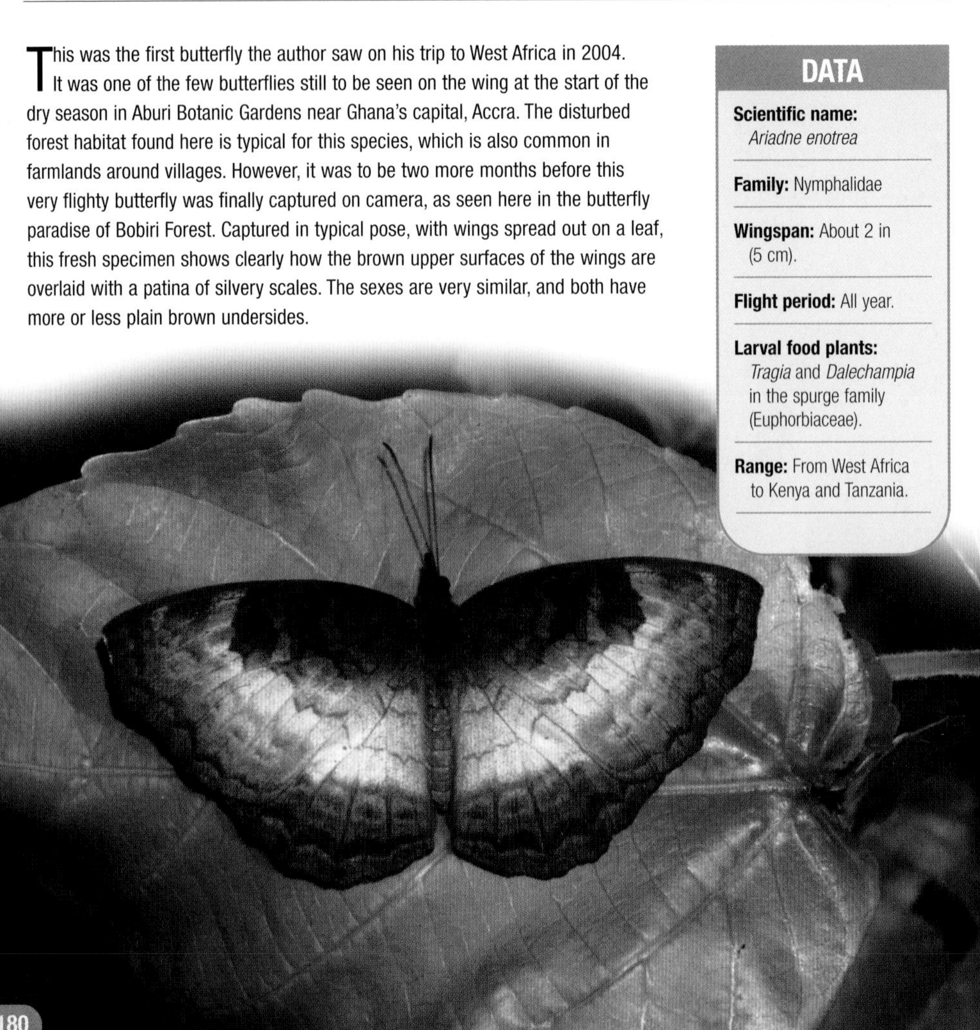

Hackberry Butterfly

DATA

Scientific name: *Asterocampa celtis*

Family: Nymphalidae

Wingspan: About 1.4 in (3.5 cm).

Flight period: March–November in south; May–August in north.

Larval food plants: Various species of *Celtis* (Ulmaceae).

Range: Over much of the United States except for northwestern areas and much of the Southwest; south to Mexico.

As seen here in Florida, the males of this species spend much of the day perched on tree trunks, often of their hackberry food plants *(Celtis)*, waiting for females to show up. As clearly shown, the underside is a very pale grayish brown, and there are two rows of yellow, black, and blue eyespots—three on the forewing and seven on the hind wing. The upper side is basically similar but is a slightly deeper shade of brownish orange, and the eyespots are much smaller and less numerous. This is a butterfly of open woodland, replaced in the desert Southwest by the very similar Desert Hackberry Butterfly *(Asterocampa leilia)*.

Forest Glade Nymph

Being one of the commonest and most widespread butterflies of the African tropics, this is often the first butterfly to be seen on a visit there. It is very much a species of the shady forest floor, fluttering down low above the ground and settling to feed on fallen fruits such as figs. It will also puddle on mud, especially when this is scarce during the dry season. The sexes differ somewhat in coloration. In the slightly larger female, seen here resting briefly on a leaf in Ghana's Bobiri Forest, the black forewing bears a number of white spots and the hind wing is brown with a white (sometimes yellow orange) basal patch. In the male the forewing spots are pale yellow, as is the hind-wing patch. In both sexes the underside is like a washed-out upper side.

DATA

Scientific name: *Aterica galene*

Family: Nymphalidae

Wingspan: About 2 in (5 cm).

Flight period: All year.

Larval food plants: Mainly *Quiscalis*, *Combretum*, and *Terminalia* (family Combretaceae); *Scotellia* (family Flacourtiaceae).

Range: Over most of tropical Africa.

Malagasy Nymph

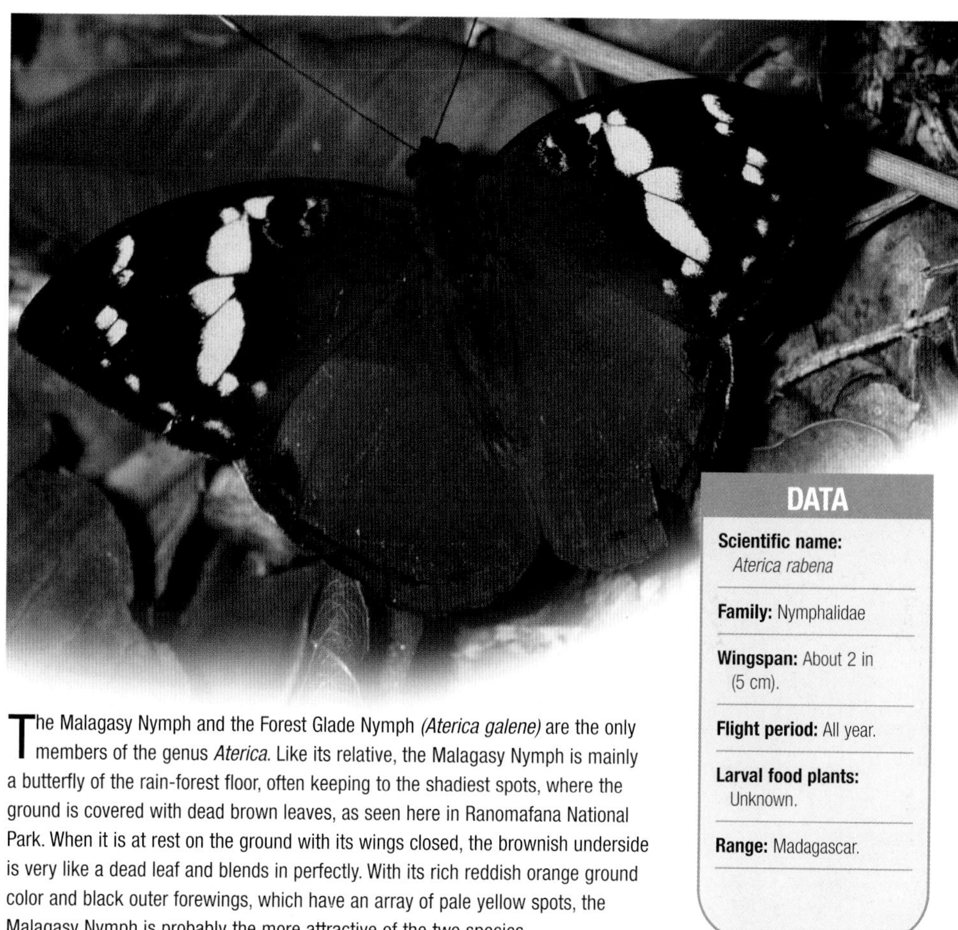

DATA

Scientific name: *Aterica rabena*

Family: Nymphalidae

Wingspan: About 2 in (5 cm).

Flight period: All year.

Larval food plants: Unknown.

Range: Madagascar.

The Malagasy Nymph and the Forest Glade Nymph *(Aterica galene)* are the only members of the genus *Aterica*. Like its relative, the Malagasy Nymph is mainly a butterfly of the rain-forest floor, often keeping to the shadiest spots, where the ground is covered with dead brown leaves, as seen here in Ranomafana National Park. When it is at rest on the ground with its wings closed, the brownish underside is very like a dead leaf and blends in perfectly. With its rich reddish orange ground color and black outer forewings, which have an array of pale yellow spots, the Malagasy Nymph is probably the more attractive of the two species.

Sulawesi Sergeant

DATA

Scientific name: *Athyma eulimene*

Family: Nymphalidae

Wingspan: About 1.6 in (4 cm).

Flight period: All year.

Larval food plants: Unknown.

Range: Indonesia (islands of Sulawesi, Sula, and Banggai).

The white band clearly visible across the abdomen, not far below its base, is nearly always present in butterflies of this genus, whose larvae generally feed on members of the plant families Rubiaceae and Euphorbiaceae. Pictured here in rain forest in Tangkoko Batuangus National Park, Sulawesi, this specimen clearly shows the brown wings marked with a pattern of pale orange bands and blotches. The underside is different, being paler brown and marked with silver rather than orange bands. The caterpillars in this genus are interesting because they construct imitations of their own likeness out of droppings combined with silk, which are intended to fool their enemies.

Red-spotted Purple

DATA

Scientific name: *Basilarchia arthemis astyanax*

Family: Nymphalidae

Wingspan: About 3 in (7.5 cm).

Flight period: Many flights all summer in south; one or two in north.

Larval food plants: Trees of many different families.

Range: Eastern United States.

This butterfly was formerly treated as a species in its own right but is now regarded as one of several subspecies of *Basilarchia arthemis*. It is typically a species of open forest, sometimes coming down to puddle on forest tracks, as seen here in the Great Smoky Mountain National Park in Tennessee. With its blue-black forewing, which grades into a shimmering grayish blue hind wing, it is (along with subspecies *arizonensis*) a mimic of the poisonous Pipevine Swallowtail *(Battus philenor)*. The underside is also mimetic, being blackish with a row of orange spots near the wing margins and a few more near the wing bases, where there are also some blue spots.

Weidermeyer's Admiral

Very much a western butterfly, this species is found in city suburbs, along stream sides, and in wooded mountain canyons, as seen here in the Rockies in Utah. The adults feed on a variety of natural products. These include sap runs on trees, mud, carrion, flowers, and, as here, animal droppings. In this case the dropping is full of vegetable fibers, indicating that it probably came from a herbivore. The upper side of the wings is dark brown, with a broad white band down each wing and a few white spots near the tip of the forewing. The underside is largely white, the most prominent feature being the row of red spots near the hind-wing margin.

DATA

Scientific name: *Basilarchia weidermeyeri*

Family: Nymphalidae

Wingspan: About 2.8 in (7 cm).

Flight period: June–August.

Larval food plants: Aspens, cottonwoods, and willows (Salicaceae); cherries and other trees in the Rosaceae.

Range: North America (from southern British Columbia to California, North Dakota, and New Mexico).

Common Palm Forester

Seen here basking in Bobiri Forest in Ghana, *Bebearia cocalia* is a common butterfly in all types of forest, from undisturbed rain forest to small remnant patches of forest in farmland, and even palm-fringed beaches on the coast. The fact that palms are the larval food plant is the reason for the acceptability of the latter habitat. The male is brown, with a superb purple sheen that is visible only from certain angles. The female (illustrated) is much larger. She is basically brownish red, with the black outer half of the forewing being speckled with large white spots. In both sexes the underside resembles a dead leaf.

DATA

Scientific name: *Bebearia cocalia*

Family: Nymphalidae

Wingspan: About 2.4 in (6 cm).

Flight period: All year.

Larval food plants: Palms (Arecaceae).

Range: From West Africa to Kenya.

Cutter's Forester

DATA

Scientific name: *Bebearia cutteri*

Family: Nymphalidae

Wingspan: About 2.4 in (6 cm).

Flight period: All year.

Larval food plants: Unknown.

Range: West Africa.

This species is likely to be found only in relatively wet forest of good quality, as seen here in Bobiri Forest in Ghana. Spending most of its time flying low down among dense undergrowth, it is not usually an easy butterfly to see unless it is tempted out of cover to feed on fruits or, as here, to puddle on wet muddy ground. In the male (pictured) the upper side is an iridescent greenish blue, with black at the apex of the forewing and black borders on the hind wing. There is a large yellow patch near the tip of the forewing. The female is similar but slightly larger, and in both sexes the underside is greenish gold, with some black spots forming a row around the hind-wing margin and others grouped near the wing bases.

Gray Forester

This is one of those butterflies in which the males and females are so totally different that you could easily take them for different species. The male is a rather drab blackish brown creature with a gray sheen. The much larger female is a superb butterfly, as can be seen here in a pristine newly hatched specimen puddling on damp ground in Ghana's Bobiri Forest. Her wings are brownish red, with a large yellow patch on the forewings, and a lovely iridescent blue band on the hind wings, which continues to the rear of the forewing. The underside is pale greenish. This is a generally scarce butterfly of good-quality wet forest.

DATA

Scientific name: *Bebearia demetra*

Family: Nymphalidae

Wingspan: About 2.4 in (6 cm).

Flight period: All year.

Larval food plants: Unknown.

Range: Africa (Sierra Leone to Central African Republic).

Western Fantasia

This is another species in which the male and female are very different. The male is a rather drab shade of brown with a narrow yellow band near the tip of each forewing. The female is much larger; a very fresh specimen is seen here puddling in Ghana's Bobiri Forest. She is a much livelier shade of brown, with a broad blue band on the hind wing that continues to the rear of the forewing, which has a large yellow band near its apex. In both sexes the underside is greenish with a white band across the forewing, below its tip. This is a relatively common butterfly in many types of forest as well as in dense secondary growth.

DATA

Scientific name: *Bebearia phantasina*

Family: Nymphalidae

Wingspan: About 2.4 in (6 cm).

Flight period: All year.

Larval food plants: Unknown.

Range: West Africa.

Sophus Forester

One of the most common and widespread members of the genus, this is another species in which the sexes are very different, the female being the more colorful. This time we are illustrating a handsome fresh male, seen puddling on damp ground in Ghana's Bobiri Forest. His basic color is brown, mottled with black and with a yellow band near the tip of the forewing. The much bigger female is metallic blue. The outer part of the forewing is black and has a broad yellow band. This very adaptable butterfly is found in all kinds of forested habitats, including those that are severely degraded, and even in city backyards where trees are present.

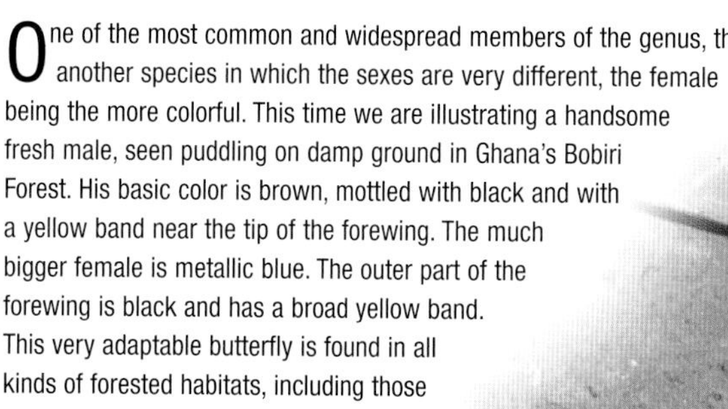

DATA

Scientific name: *Bebearia sophus*

Family: Nymphalidae

Wingspan: About 2.4 in (6 cm).

Flight period: All year.

Larval food plants: *Landolphia* in the dogbane family (Apocynaceae) and *Chrysophyllum* (Sapotaceae).

Range: Over much of tropical Africa.

Hewitson's Forester

DATA

Scientific name: *Bebearia tentyris*

Family: Nymphalidae

Wingspan: About 1.8 in (4.5 cm).

Flight period: All year.

Larval food plants: *Hypselodelphys* in the arrowroot family (Marantaceae).

Range: Africa (Côte d'Ivoire to Congo region).

Able to survive in severely degraded forests, this species can be extremely abundant in high-quality rain-forest habitats, as seen here in Bobiri Forest in Ghana. It was one of the most abundant butterfly species seen during the author's visit to Ghana in December and January, after unseasonal rains had produced some very attractive muddy areas. This male is evidently newly emerged, as evidenced by the superbly rich purple grading into the basic brown of his upper side. This purple sheen is only visible from certain angles on older specimens, which generally appear brown, the normal color of the underside. By contrast, the female looks like a different species, being brown with a yellow band on each wing and a pale yellow and brown underside.

Light Brown Forester

Looking like a version of Hewitson's Forester *(Bebearia tentyris)* but without the superb purple sheen, the male of this species is a lighter, brighter shade of orange brown than the very similar Absolon Forester *(B. absolon)*. The female, pictured puddling in Bobiri Forest, Ghana, is similar to that of Hewitson's Forester, but lacks the pale yellow band on the forewing upper side. The Light Brown Forester is a common butterfly in a variety of disturbed habitats and in forests, but is scarce or absent in the really wet areas of rain forest.

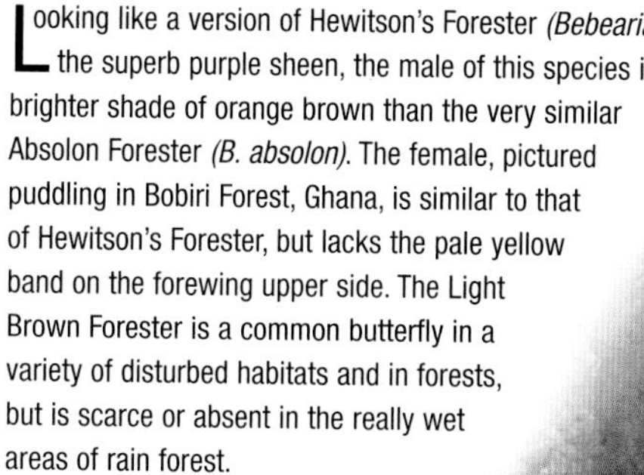

DATA

Scientific name: *Bebearia zonara*

Family: Nymphalidae

Wingspan: About 1.8 in (4.5 cm).

Flight period: All year.

Larval food plants: *Hypselodelphys* in the arrowroot family (Marantaceae).

Range: Africa (Sierra Leone to western Uganda).

Red Rim

DATA

Scientific name: *Biblis hyperia*

Family: Nymphalidae

Wingspan: About 2.6 in (6.5 cm).

Flight period: All year.

Larval food plants: *Tragia volubilis* in the spurge family (Euphorbiaceae).

Range: From southern Texas to Paraguay; in most of the West Indies.

Resident in southern Texas and sometimes common there, this species, which inhabits open forest, sometimes ranges into central Texas but does not manage to penetrate any farther into the United States. Farther south it can be common in a variety of forest types, always preferring open spots rather than the gloomier understory of primary forest. It is pictured here on the edge of rain forest in Trinidad. The red band along the rear margin of the hind wings is found in no other butterfly, making this species instantly recognizable in the field. Both sexes are similar, and the underside is nondescript.

Pearl-bordered Fritillary

Included for a long time in the genus *Clossiana*, this species is undergoing long-term decline in Europe, especially in the British Isles. This may be caused in part by its need for a particular kind of habitat in the cool British climate, namely warm, semiwooded, south-facing slopes. The butterfly illustrated was photographed in just this kind of habitat in southwest England. The upper side is that of a typical fritillary—basically brownish orange with numerous black spots—and very similar to that of the Silver Meadow Fritillary *(Boloria selene)*. The underside is a complex mosaic of various shades of brown with a few white patches, especially along the border of the hind wing.

DATA

Scientific name: *Boloria euphrosyne*

Family: Nymphalidae

Wingspan: About 1.6 in (4 cm).

Flight period: May.

Larval food plants: Violets *(Viola)* in the family Violaceae.

Range: From western Europe through much of temperate Asia.

Silver Meadow Fritillary

DATA

Scientific name: *Boloria selene*

Other common name: Small Pearl-bordered Fritillary (in UK).

Family: Nymphalidae

Wingspan: About 1.6 in (4 cm).

Flight period: In summer, in up to three flights.

Larval food plants: Violets *(Viola)* in the family Violaceae.

Range: Western Europe eastward to Korea; also North America.

Seen above in England, this is very much a northern species in North America. It is not found much south of a line drawn from southern Oregon across to Virginia, although it is present in the high mountains of Colorado and New Mexico. The Silver Meadow Fritillary is a butterfly of heaths, moors, grassy places, moist meadows, bogs, and even short-grass prairie, but it avoids dense woodland. In warm lowland areas it produces three broods during the summer but only two farther north and just a single brood in high mountains and in Alaska. The underside is broadly similar to that of the Pearl-bordered Fritillary *(Boloria euphrosyne).*

The Joker

Sun-drenched savanna is the habitat preferred by this widespread species, and it is found in forest only when it is both open and seasonally dry. This mating pair was photographed in Sokoke Forest on the coast of Kenya. The Joker is also found in semidesert habitats, such as around the borders of the Sahara in West Africa, where it is absent from the wet-forest zone. The upper side is orange, with a scattering of black marks on the forewing and a broad black band some way in from the outer margin of the hind wing.

DATA

Scientific name: *Byblia ilithya*

Family: Nymphalidae

Wingspan: About 1.8 in (4.5 cm).

Flight period: All year.

Larval food plants: *Dalechampia* and *Tragia* in the spurge family (Euphorbiaceae).

Range: Over most of the drier areas of sub-Saharan Africa, eastward through the Arabian Peninsula to Pakistan, India, and Sri Lanka.

Aurelian 89

One of numerous members of the genus *Callicore* in which a pair of numerals is clearly marked on the underside of the hind wing, this species displays the number 89 particularly clearly. Other species have different numbers, including 69, 66, 80, and 88, although they are not always perfectly portrayed. In this species, seen here puddling on a track through rain forest in Peru's Tingo Maria National Park, the upper side is superb, featuring bold splashes of red and purple against a black background. This gorgeous combination is seen only when the butterfly is in flight because it closes its wings as soon as it lands.

DATA

Scientific name: *Callicore aurelia*

Family: Nymphalidae

Wingspan: About 2 in (5 cm).

Flight period: All year.

Larval food plants: Members of the soapberry family (Sapindaceae).

Range: Over much of tropical South America.

Cyllene 88

DATA

Scientific name: *Callicore cyllene*

Family: Nymphalidae

Wingspan: About 2 in (5 cm).

Flight period: All year.

Larval food plants: Probably members of the soapberry family (Sapindaceae).

Range: Over much of tropical South America.

Like all members of the genus, this species is often found puddling on muddy ground. It is pictured here at rest on a tree trunk in the rain forest that surrounds the spectacular Iguaçu Falls in Argentina, which is about as far south as many widespread tropical butterflies are found in South America. The upper side of the forewing is red on the basal half and black on the rest, with a faint whitish mark near the wing tip. The hind wing is mainly blackish brown with three blue spots near the rear margin. As can be seen, the hind-wing underside bears a rather imprecise 88, with only one of the numerals being at all clear. Most of the forewing underside is red, with a yellow-banded black tip.

The Dainty 80

DATA

Scientific name: *Callicore hystaspes*

Family: Nymphalidae

Wingspan: About 1.6 in (4 cm).

Flight period: All year.

Larval food plants: Probably members of the soapberry family (Sapindaceae).

Range: Widespread in tropical South America.

As can be seen, the pattern on the underside of this species is broadly similar to that of Aurelain 89 *(Callicore aurelia)*, except that the hind wing displays the number 80 rather than 89. The forewing upper side has a brilliant blue base followed by a broad red band and finally a black upper half, in which there is a narrow white band near the wing tip. Two-thirds of the hind wing (from its base) is black, while the rest is blue. As with most members of this genus, this species is most often found puddling on damp ground and is pictured here in rain forest in Peru's Tingo Maria National Park.

Zigzag 80

Pictured here puddling on only slightly damp ground in rain forest at Rancho Grande in the Amazon region of Brazil, this species has a particularly beautiful underside. Fortunately, the forewing has been raised somewhat more than usual above the hind wing, revealing the striking pattern of black, white, and magenta on the forewing underside. The hind-wing underside also bears a particularly noteworthy combination of bluish black, cream, and white, with the number 80 clearly visible. Above, the forewing is similar to what is seen here, but the upper side of the hind wing is entirely different, being black with a broad red band.

DATA

Scientific name: *Callicore sorana*

Family: Nymphalidae

Wingspan: About 2 in (5 cm).

Flight period: All year.

Larval food plants: Probably in the soapberry family (Sapindaceae).

Range: Very widespread in the South American tropics.

Mimic Crescent

Of the 13 members of the genus *Castilia* some, such as this one, are narrow-winged mimics of other butterflies, such as heliconiids and ithomiids, while others have broader wings and are nonmimetic. The male (on the right in this mating pair) is smaller than the female, and his upper side is dark orange with broad black bars and borders. The female is more of a yellowish brown and has broad black wing tips speckled with yellow spots, giving a more or less tiger-striped pattern. This is a butterfly of rain-forest margins and weedy, disturbed areas in forest, as seen here at Finca La Selva in Costa Rica.

DATA

Scientific name: *Castilia eranites*

Family: Nymphalidae

Wingspan: About 1.6 in (4 cm).

Flight period: All year.

Larval food plants: *Odontonema* and *Justicia* (Acanthaceae).

Range: Mexico to Colombia and Venezuela.

White-dotted Crescent

DATA

Scientific name: *Castilia ofella*

Family: Nymphalidae

Wingspan: About 1.4 in (3.5 cm).

Flight period: All year.

Larval food plants: *Justicia* and *Aphelandra* (Acanthaceae).

Range: Guatemala to Colombia, Venezuela, and Trinidad.

Formerly placed in the genus *Eresia*, this little butterfly is found in all kinds of disturbed forest, only entering dense rain forest along roads, trails, or wide rivers. The butterfly illustrated here was photographed in a typical habitat on a weedy roadside near houses and vegetable patches on the edge of disturbed rain forest in Trinidad's Northern Range. Both sexes are similar, having blackish upper sides with a white band across all four wings. The underside pattern is broadly similar but considerably paler.

Common Pathfinder

Whereas most butterflies, including this one, are cryptic on the undersides and hold their wings shut when at rest, this species spends much of its time on the forest floor with its wings spread wide, exposing the upper sides. These are similar to the undersides and bear a very disruptive pattern that helps the butterfly blend in with the ground in the dappled shade of the rain forest, as seen here in Kenya's Kakamega Forest. When walking along a forest path, these butterflies frequently flutter along low in front of you for some distance, landing and taking flight again repeatedly, reluctant to abandon the path and veer off into the forest.

DATA

Scientific name: *Catuna crithea*

Family: Nymphalidae

Wingspan: About 2.1 in (5.2 cm).

Flight period: All year.

Larval food plants: Mainly members of the Sapotaceae.

Range: From West Africa to Kenya and southward to Zambia.

Malay Lacewing

When choosing which illustration to use for this species the author was spoilt for choice, since this butterfly is spectacular on both sides. In the end the underside won, with its jazzy red, white, black, and orange pattern, as seen on this individual photographed in Khao Sok National Park, Thailand. It avoids deep forest—wooded roadsides and even backyards are more typical habitats. The upper side of the forewing is largely black with a broad yellowish band, while the rear portion is orange. This continues over most of the hind wings, which have broad black, scalloped borders. In fresh males the orange is flushed strongly with rose pink, making a most striking shade.

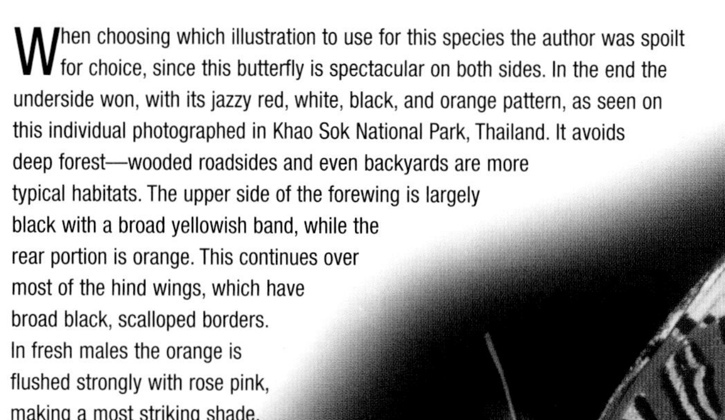

DATA

Scientific name: *Cethosia hypsea*

Family: Nymphalidae

Wingspan: About 3.3 in (8.5 cm).

Flight period: All year.

Larval food plants: *Adenia* climbers in the passionflower family (Passifloraceae).

Range: Myanmar (Burma), Thailand, Malay Peninsula.

Malagasy White-barred Gladiator

Members of this genus, especially the males, are often attracted to odors that are far from appealing to the human nose. In this case the smell that lured this butterfly, which is found in all forest types, was that of a rotting freshwater turtle that was squashed flat on a dirt road running through spectacular tropical dry forest near Morondava. As with many gladiators, the underside is a tapestry-like mix of colors impossible to describe, although the three sharply pointed tails on the hind wing are easily recognized. The upper side is brownish black with a white stripe down each wing, which is shortened and broken on the forewing.

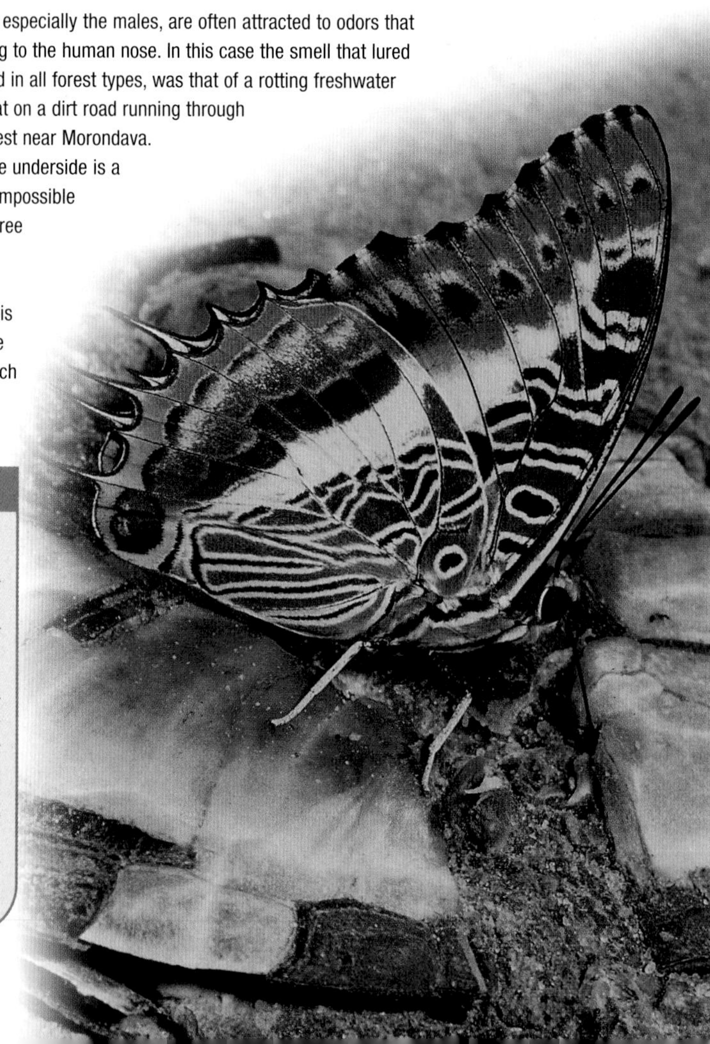

DATA

Scientific name: *Charaxes andara*

Family: Nymphalidae

Wingspan: About 3.2 in (8 cm).

Flight period: All year.

Larval food plants: Unknown.

Range: Madagascar.

Bamboo Gladiator

DATA

Scientific name: *Charaxes boueti*

Family: Nymphalidae

Wingspan: About 3 in (7.5 cm).

Flight period: All year.

Larval food plants: Bamboo (Poaceae).

Range: Africa (from Gambia to Uganda).

Caught on camera as he briefly spread his gorgeous wings while running toward some civet dung, this male was photographed in Ghana's Bobiri Forest. The upper side is red with broad black bands near the outer wing margins. The female is slightly larger and has a broad yellowish white band inward from the black marginal bands. In both sexes the underside is pinkish brown with a few darker markings, far less attractive than in many members of the genus. Formerly considered a scarce butterfly of the forest–savanna transition zone, this species is now often found near villages, where it breeds on planted Indian bamboo.

White-barred Gladiator

Gladiators tend most often to be attracted to fruit, dung, or sap rather than mud, but they occasionally come down to puddle on paths, especially after unusual dry season rainfall, as illustrated here in Ghana's Bobiri Forest. In this common and widespread (but seldom abundant) species the upper side is similar in both sexes—black with a white band down the center of each wing. The underside, as shown here, also carries a white band, but this time combined with a complex and beautiful pattern that is absent from the upper side. The White-barred Gladiator is found in dry and wet forests, including small groups of trees surrounded by farmland.

DATA

Scientific name: *Charaxes brutus*

Family: Nymphalidae

Wingspan: About 3.4 in (8.5 cm).

Flight period: All year.

Larval food plants: Varied, in several families, e.g., *Grewia* (Tiliaceae) and *Melia* (Meliaceae).

Range: Over much of sub-Saharan Africa.

Green-veined Gladiator

DATA

Scientific name: *Charaxes candiope*

Family: Nymphalidae

Wingspan: About 3.2 in (8 cm).

Flight period: All year.

Larval food plants: *Croton* in the spurge family (Euphorbiaceae).

Range: Most of sub-Saharan Africa; the islands of Socotra and São Tomé.

The white sap oozing from this fallen tree in Kenya's Shimba Hills had begun to ferment. Its powerful smell lured a variety of insects, including the Green-veined Gladiator pictured here with its pale green proboscis probing deeply into the sap. Found in city backyards as well as in forest and savanna, this is a common species, in which both sexes are similar. The upper side is tawny with yellowish brown wing bases and black and tawny spots toward the wing edges. The pale brownish underside is variable, and the costal and basal veins of the forewing are green.

Giant Gladiator

Civet dung is a great lure for members of this genus, and that is what had attracted this Giant Gladiator in Uganda's Kibale Forest National Park. The habitat here is rain forest, but this butterfly is found in a wide variety of forest types, both wet and dry, as well as in town and village backyards and even in open savanna as long as there are some trees. Both sexes are similar, the upper side being brownish black with a yellow band on the forewing, continued as two connected spots on the hind wing. Toward the rear of the hind wing, near the "tails," is a series of blue spots. The underside, as seen here, bears a complex pattern of a type seen in many gladiators.

DATA

Scientific name: *Charaxes castor*

Family: Nymphalidae

Wingspan: About 3.7 in (9.5 cm).

Flight period: All year.

Larval food plants: Very varied.

Range: Over most of sub-Saharan Africa.

Western Red Gladiator

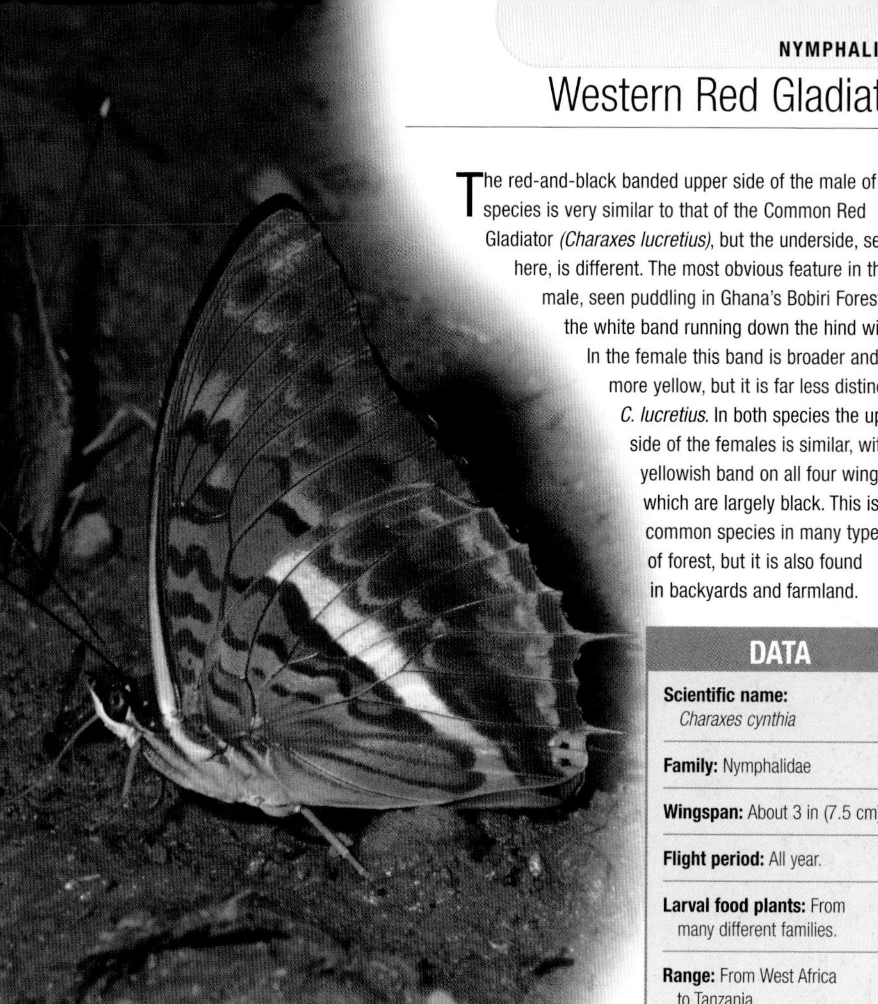

The red-and-black banded upper side of the male of this species is very similar to that of the Common Red Gladiator *(Charaxes lucretius)*, but the underside, seen here, is different. The most obvious feature in this male, seen puddling in Ghana's Bobiri Forest, is the white band running down the hind wing. In the female this band is broader and more yellow, but it is far less distinct in *C. lucretius*. In both species the upper side of the females is similar, with a yellowish band on all four wings, which are largely black. This is a common species in many types of forest, but it is also found in backyards and farmland.

DATA

Scientific name: *Charaxes cynthia*

Family: Nymphalidae

Wingspan: About 3 in (7.5 cm).

Flight period: All year.

Larval food plants: From many different families.

Range: From West Africa to Tanzania.

Blue-spotted Gladiator

In this genus it is rare for both sides of the adult to be equally beautiful. Usually one or other has the edge. In this species it is the striking white underside with its scattering of red spots that gets the author's vote. The upper side is far less satisfying. In the male it is largely black with a scattering of white spots on the forewing, which bears a row of three blue spots near its hind margin. The spots continue down the hind wing as a row of five. The female is also mainly black, but with a broad whitish band down all four wings. Found in forest, savanna, and even in the center of large cities, this species often comes to civet dung, as seen here in Ghana's Bobiri Forest.

DATA

Scientific name: *Charaxes etesipe*

Family: Nymphalidae

Wingspan: About 3 in (7.5 cm).

Flight period: All year.

Larval food plants: Many and varied.

Range: Over most of sub-Saharan Africa.

Demon Gladiator

DATA

Scientific name: *Charaxes etheocles*

Family: Nymphalidae

Wingspan: About 2.6 in (6.5 cm).

Flight period: All year.

Larval food plants: Mainly in the pea family (Fabaceae), e.g., *Albizia, Entada, Griffonia.*

Range: Africa (Senegal to Ethiopia, Kenya, and Zambia).

The 12 species of black *Charaxes* make a variable group. Identification is often difficult to achieve with any certainty and, in the case of the butterfly illustrated, the choice of name has been based mainly on the fact that this species is by far the most common, occurring in various types of forest. An important fact is that the male is deep black with little or no blue or green sheen. The male illustrated was one of several puddling in Bobiri Forest, Ghana, spending most of their time with their wings fully open, which is unusual in *Charaxes.* The female is dark brown, with or without a broken pale band down each wing. In both sexes the underside is brown with variable amounts of pale mottling.

Forest Pearl Gladiator

DATA

Scientific name: *Charaxes fulvescens*

Family: Nymphalidae

Wingspan: About 3.5 in (9 cm).

Flight period: All year.

Larval food plants: *Allophylus* in the soapberry family (Sapindaceae).

Range: From West Africa to Kenya, Tanzania, and Zambia.

This is a butterfly of shady rain forest, seen here feeding on fermenting sap on a tree in Kenya's Kakamega Forest. As will be obvious, the underside bears a convincing resemblance to a dead leaf, with lovely green veins. On the upper side the basal area of each wing is whitish yellow, the rest of each wing being a mixture of brownish orange and black. Both sexes are similar. A number of subspecies have been described, of which this is subspecies *monitor*, found mainly in East Africa from Sudan to Zambia.

Silver-striped Gladiator

This very local butterfly is restricted to forest and woodland along the Indian Ocean coasts of Kenya and Tanzania. It is pictured here in Makadara Forest in Kenya's Shimba Hills, feeding on the same sap run as the Green-veined Gladiator *(Charaxes candiope)* on page 209. Above, the male is a rich reddish orange with a black tip to the forewing and a row of black spots near the outer margin of the hind wing. The female is similar but has a pale yellowish band partway down the middle of each wing. In both sexes the underside is reddish brown, with a whitish line down the middle of the hind wing.

DATA

Scientific name: *Charaxes lasti*

Family: Nymphalidae

Wingspan: About 2.8 in (7 cm).

Flight period: All year.

Larval food plants: *Afzelia* in the pea family (Fabaceae).

Range: Africa (Kenya and Tanzania).

Common Red Gladiator

DATA

Scientific name: *Charaxes lucretius*

Family: Nymphalidae

Wingspan: About 2.8 in (7 cm).

Flight period: All year.

Larval food plants: *Hugonia* in the flax family (Linaceae) and *Annona* in the custard apple family (Annonaceae).

Range: From West Africa to Kenya, Tanzania, and Zambia.

Obtaining pictures of the upper side of a *Charaxes* is not easy. One way is to crouch beside some dung and wait for the butterflies to arrive. They have a habit of landing a short way from the dung and running toward it, opening and closing their wings. That is how this picture of a male Common Red Gladiator was obtained, after a long wait in the hot sun in Ghana's Bobiri Forest and some quick reactions by the photographer in pressing the camera's shutter button. In the female the red band along the wings is replaced by pale cream. The male's underside is brick red, but the female's is paler. This is a common butterfly in all types of forest.

Loadice Untailed Gladiator

One of the smaller members of the genus, this species is most common in relatively undisturbed forest, as seen here in Ghana's Bobiri Forest. However, it is also found in degraded forest and in farmland, such as cocoa farms. The male pictured here had just been forced off some civet dung by a throng of very pushy competitors and was trying to edge himself back in among the busily feeding melee, which consisted of seven species of charaxes. The upper side is mainly black, with a sprinkling of blue spots on the forewing and a double row near the hind-wing margin. In the female, which is brown, this is reduced to a single row. In both sexes the underside is brown.

DATA

Scientific name: *Charaxes lycurgus*

Family: Nymphalidae

Wingspan: About 2.6 in (6.5 cm).

Flight period: All year.

Larval food plants: Various, in several families.

Range: From West Africa to Uganda and Tanzania.

Square-winged Red Gladiator

DATA

Scientific name: *Charaxes pleione*

Family: Nymphalidae

Wingspan: About 2.2 in (5.5 cm).

Flight period: All year.

Larval food plants: *Acacia* in the pea family (Fabaceae).

Range: From West Africa to Kenya and Tanzania.

One of the smaller members of the genus, this forest butterfly is widespread but seldom occurs in any numbers. It is one of the few gladiators that is commonly seen basking with its wings spread wide, although it usually seems to be males that do this, displaying the orange upper side very clearly. The forewings have broad black tips. The female is much paler, while in both sexes the underside creates a very convincing imitation of a dead leaf, as will be obvious from this specimen feeding on civet dung in Bobiri Forest, Ghana.

Black-bordered Gladiator

A widespread species of forests, parks, and disturbed habitats, this butterfly does not seem to be very common. The individual pictured here, feeding on civet dung in Uganda's Kibale Forest National Park, was the only one seen by the author during a stay of several weeks in various East African forests. It is far from being a pristine specimen, but it illustrates the complex pattern on the underside. In this species the two long hind-wing tails are accompanied by several smaller "tails," which are extensions of the wing veins. The upper side is golden brown with broad black borders—the female being paler than the male.

DATA

Scientific name: *Charaxes pollux*

Family: Nymphalidae

Wingspan: About 3.2 in (8 cm).

Flight period: All year.

Larval food plants: Members of Meliaceae, Sapindaceae, Acanthaceae, and Euphorbiaceae.

Range: Over most of tropical Africa, south to Zimbabwe and Mozambique.

Flame-bordered Gladiator

Few gladiators spend much time with their wings open, and this picture is the result of a long patient wait in the coastal rain forest at Bimbia in Cameroon. This male flew up from a tiny speck of dung and was reluctant to return, constantly flying past but not landing. Finally, he dropped onto the muddy path and briefly opened his wings as he ran toward the dung, enabling this single picture to be hastily snatched. In the female of this forest butterfly the orange wing borders are narrower and paler, and she has a broad white band on each wing. In both sexes the underside is light brown with a purplish flush and a pale orange margin.

DATA

Scientific name: *Charaxes protoclea*

Family: Nymphalidae

Wingspan: About 3 in (7.5 cm).

Flight period: All year.

Larval food plants: In the pea, myrtle, and grass families (Fabaceae, Myrtaceae, and Poaceae).

Range: Over most of tropical Africa, south to Zambia and Mozambique.

Ornate Green Gladiator

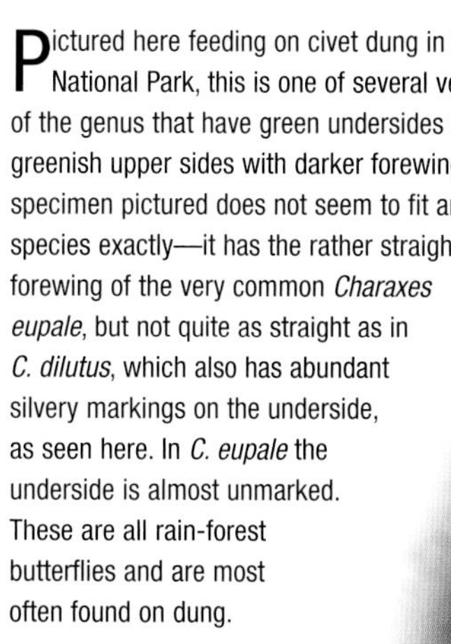

Pictured here feeding on civet dung in Uganda's Kibale Forest National Park, this is one of several very similar members of the genus that have green undersides and silvery greenish upper sides with darker forewing tips. The specimen pictured does not seem to fit any of the species exactly—it has the rather straight-edged forewing of the very common *Charaxes eupale*, but not quite as straight as in *C. dilutus*, which also has abundant silvery markings on the underside, as seen here. In *C. eupale* the underside is almost unmarked. These are all rain-forest butterflies and are most often found on dung.

DATA

Scientific name: *Charaxes subornatus*

Family: Nymphalidae

Wingspan: About 2.2 in (5.5 cm).

Flight period: All year.

Larval food plants: Uncertain.

Range: From West Africa to Uganda and western Kenya.

Common Blue Gladiator

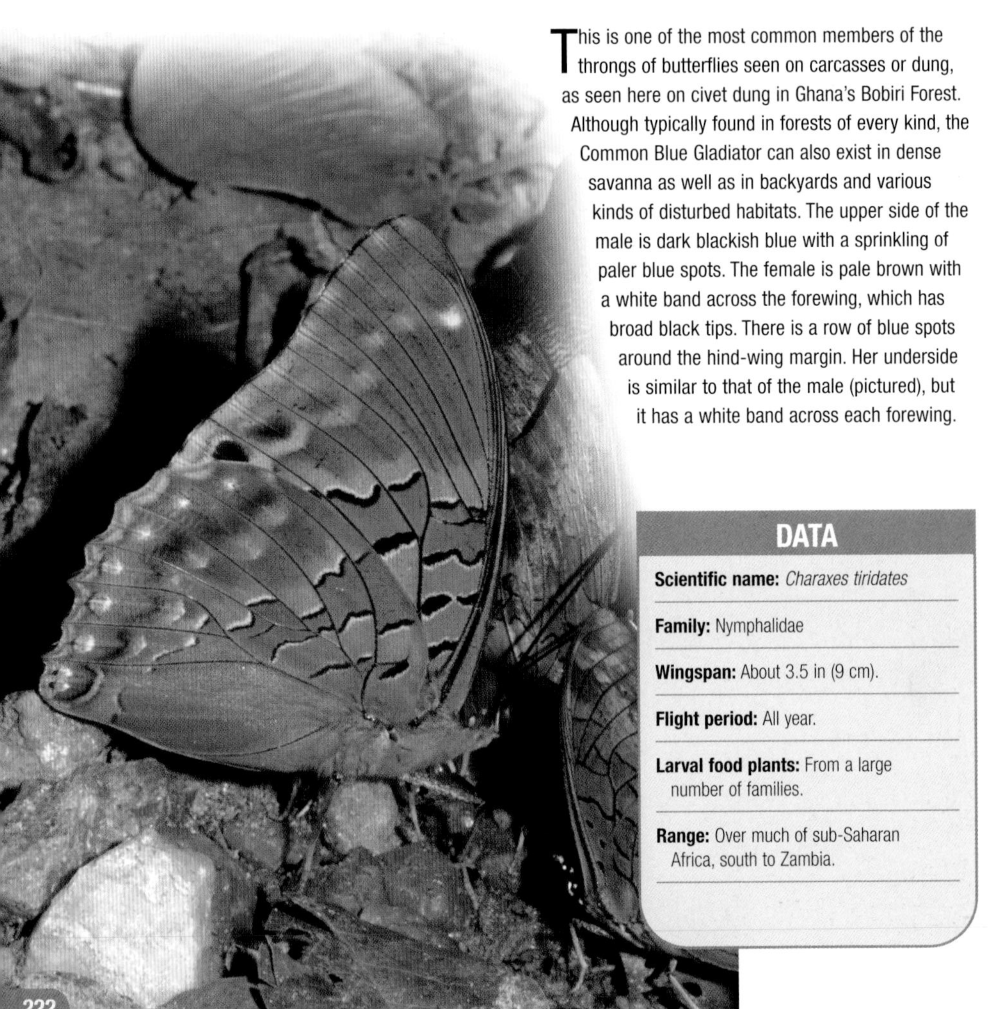

This is one of the most common members of the throngs of butterflies seen on carcasses or dung, as seen here on civet dung in Ghana's Bobiri Forest. Although typically found in forests of every kind, the Common Blue Gladiator can also exist in dense savanna as well as in backyards and various kinds of disturbed habitats. The upper side of the male is dark blackish blue with a sprinkling of paler blue spots. The female is pale brown with a white band across the forewing, which has broad black tips. There is a row of blue spots around the hind-wing margin. Her underside is similar to that of the male (pictured), but it has a white band across each forewing.

DATA

Scientific name: *Charaxes tiridates*

Family: Nymphalidae

Wingspan: About 3.5 in (9 cm).

Flight period: All year.

Larval food plants: From a large number of families.

Range: Over much of sub-Saharan Africa, south to Zambia.

Pearl Gladiator

This species is rarely seen on dung or carcasses, being mainly attracted to ripe fruit, so this picture of a male on civet dung in Uganda's Kibale Forest National Park is unusual. The Forest Pearl Gladiator *(Charaxes fulvescens)* is very similar, but in the Pearl Gladiator the tip of the forewing is far more strongly hooked, as can be seen clearly in the accompanying illustration. In both species the upper side has white wing bases grading outward to orange and then to black. The underside is a very passable imitation of a dead leaf. This very successful butterfly is found in almost every type of habitat except for desert and very wet rain forest. It is also at home in leafy parks and backyards in large cities.

DATA

Scientific name: *Charaxes varanes*

Family: Nymphalidae

Wingspan: About 3.2 in (8 cm).

Flight period: All year.

Larval food plants: Members of the cashew and soapberry families (Anacardiaceae and Sapindaceae).

Range: Over most of Africa south and east of the Sahara.

Club-tailed Gladiator

DATA

Scientific name: *Charaxes zoolina*

Family: Nymphalidae

Wingspan: About 2 in (5 cm).

Flight period: All year.

Larval food plants: Mainly thorn trees *(Acacia)* in the pea family Fabaceae.

Range: Africa (from Ethiopia and Sudan to Angola and South Africa); also Madagascar.

This is a species of dry forests, dense thornbush country, and savannas, and it avoids the wet tropical forests preferred by most other members of the genus. The upper side is usually white with either brown or black borders, but it is also often all-over orange, or a mix of the two. The underside makes a convincing representation of a dead leaf, as seen here in subspecies *betsimaraka* in the dry Kirindy Forest near Morondava in Madagascar. The presence of two hind-wing tails indicates that this is a female, since males have just a single tail.

Sagebrush Checkerspot

DATA

Scientific name: *Chlosyne acastus*

Family: Nymphalidae

Wingspan: About 1.5 in (3.8 cm).

Flight period: March–July.

Larval food plants: Rabbit brush *(Chrysothamnus viscidiflorus)* in the sunflower family (Asteraceae).

Range: From southern Canada (Alberta) to Arizona and California.

Once thought of as a subspecies of the Pearly Checkerspot *(Chlosyne gabbii)*, this butterfly is now regarded as a species in its own right. The change was based on breeding tests which demonstrated that caterpillars resulting from crossing the former "subspecies" of *C. gabbii* soon died, while caterpillars resulting from matings within each subspecies thrived. The Sagebrush Checkerspot is usually found in sagebrush scrub but also inhabits meadows and juniper or pinyon woodland to quite high altitudes, as seen here in the Rockies in Utah. The base of the hind wing is darker than the base of the forewing, a feature that is important in distinguishing this butterfly from other similar species. The underside is checkered with black, white, and orange.

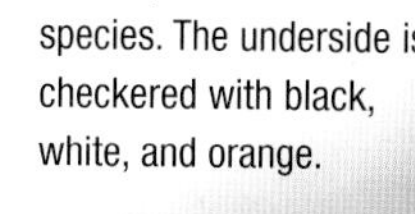

Desert Checkerspot

This is another former subspecies of the Pearly Checkerspot *(Chlosyne gabbii)*, but it is often regarded as a subspecies of the Sagebrush Checkerspot (*C. acastus*). This mating pair is in typical desert habitat, in California's Joshua Tree National Monument. A characteristic feature of this species is the especially bright orange tone of the upper side, which is far more vivid than in *C. acastus*. The zigzag black lines on the wings are also narrower than in any of the closely related species. The underside is a mix of black, white, and orange bands, a small section being just visible on the lowermost butterfly.

DATA

Scientific name: *Chlosyne neumoegeni*

Family: Nymphalidae

Wingspan: About 1.5 in (3.8 cm).

Flight period: March–June.

Larval food plants: Asters, especially Mojave aster *(Machaeranthera tortifolia)* in the sunflower family (Asteraceae).

Range: Nevada and Utah to Arizona, California, and Baja California.

Giant Patch

DATA

Scientific name: *Chlosyne janais*

Family: Nymphalidae

Wingspan: About 2 in (5 cm).

Larval food plants: Mainly *Odontonema* (Acanthaceae).

Flight period: All year.

Range: From Texas to Colombia.

This common butterfly of scrubby woodland, fields, and backyards is distinguished from other similar species by the scattered white spots on the forewing upper side, which do not join up to form a band. The hind wing's upper side is reddish orange with broad black borders. The underside of the forewing is similar to the upper side, but the hind wing's underside is most attractive, being a series of yellow, red, and black bands. When found in areas of rain forest this species tends to fly around the edges, such as on roadsides—as seen here near Jalapa in Veracruz State in Mexico—or in areas that have been disturbed by human activities.

Zebra

As with some of the lycaenids, such as the Aetolus Stripestreak *(Arawacus aetolus)*, the pattern on the underside of this butterfly has evolved to direct the observer's attention away from the butterfly's real head (seen here on the left) and toward a headlike pattern at the tip of the hind wings. The upper side is blackish brown with a broad yellow band across each forewing. The adults are fond of overripe fruit but will also feed on sap, dung, and mud, as seen here in Trinidad. Zebras are found in all forest types but especially in secondary growth, where their host trees, which are pioneer species, often abound.

DATA

Scientific name: *Colobura dirce*

Family: Nymphalidae

Wingspan: About 2.8 in (7 cm).

Flight period: All year.

Larval food plants: *Cecropia* in the fig family (Moraceae).

Range: Throughout the tropical zones of the Americas and the West Indies.

Dusky Peacock

DATA

Scientific name: *Cybdelis mnasylus*

Family: Nymphalidae

Wingspan: About 1.8 in (4.5 cm).

Flight period: All year.

Larval food plants: Unknown.

Range: Colombia and Venezuela.

The range stated here is that quoted in books and on the Internet, and yet the butterfly pictured above was photographed puddling in subtropical rain forest in Finca El Rey National Park in northern Argentina, several thousand miles outside the given range. The coloration is correct for this species, especially the blue and white eyespot on each brownish red hind wing and the four white patches on each black forewing. *Cybdelis phaesyla*, subspecies *boliviana*, also has hind-wing eyespots, but they are plain blue. Other forms of *C. phaesyla* lack eyespots, so its seems that the amount of variability in this genus is considerable, and the current situation with regard to number of species may need some revision.

Becker's Creamy Yellow Glider

There are few butterflies in which the sexes are so attractively dissimilar as in this beautiful rain-forest species. In the male, seen here feeding on a fallen fig in Bimbia Forest, Cameroon, the upper side is a rich creamy yellow with a broad black border to the hind wing. His underside is brown, spotted with white. In the female the forewing upper side is black with a scattering of white spots, while the hind wing is mostly white with a white-spotted black margin and a yellow patch near the apex. This coloration has a defensive purpose because the female is a mimic of various unpalatable, day-flying moths in the genus *Otroeda* (Geometridae).

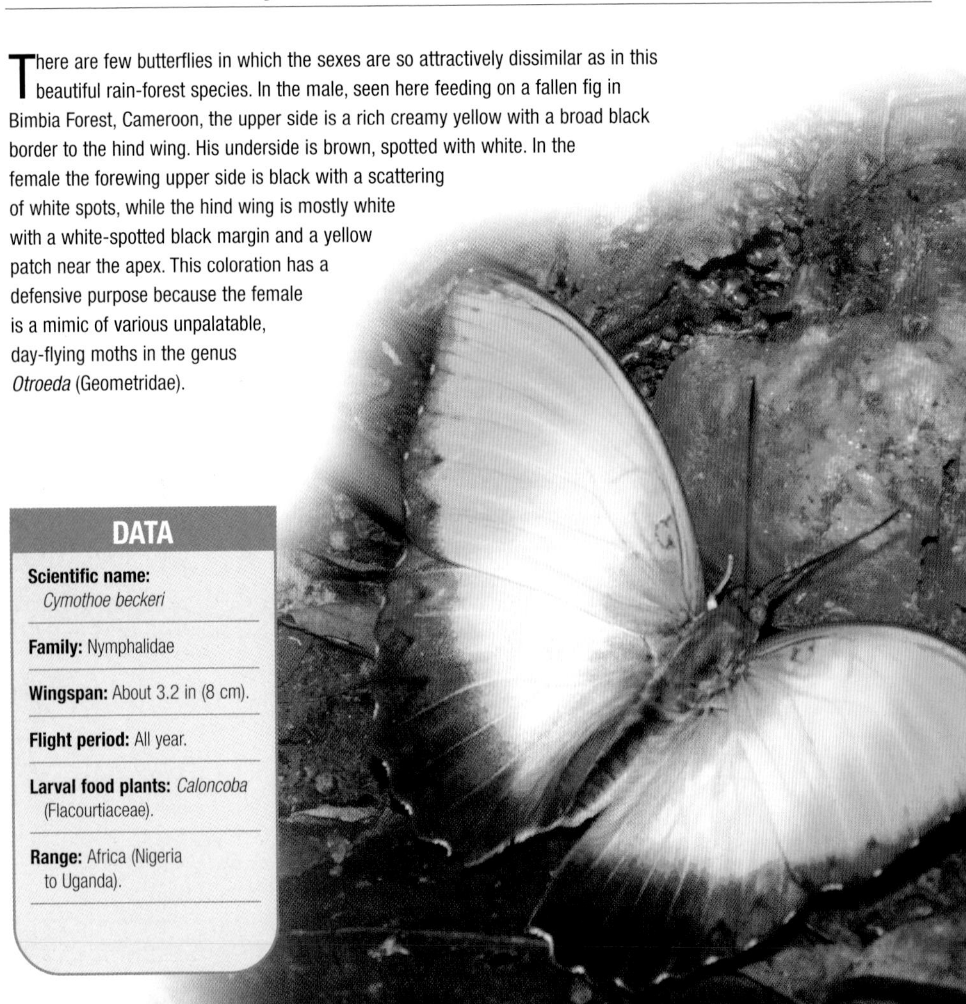

DATA

Scientific name: *Cymothoe beckeri*

Family: Nymphalidae

Wingspan: About 3.2 in (8 cm).

Flight period: All year.

Larval food plants: *Caloncoba* (Flacourtiaceae).

Range: Africa (Nigeria to Uganda).

Common Glider

DATA

Scientific name: *Cymothoe caenis*

Family: Nymphalidae

Wingspan: About 2.4 in (6 cm).

Flight period: All year.

Larval food plants: Mainly Flacourtiaceae.

Range: From West Africa to Uganda, Angola, and Zambia.

More common in secondary habitats than in primary rain forest, this species occasionally occurs in astronomical numbers during mass migrations stimulated by a local population explosion. In the male (pictured here in Bobiri Forest, Ghana) the upper side is whitish with a few small black patches on the forewings and a zigzag row of black around the hind wing margin. Beneath, he is greenish white with a narrow dark band down each wing. The female's upperside is brown with a broad white band down each wing. Below, she is similar but paler.

Common Yellow Glider

DATA

Scientific name: *Cymothoe egesta*

Family: Nymphalidae

Wingspan: About 3.2 in (8 cm).

Flight period: All year.

Larval food plants: *Rinorea* in the violet family (Violaceae).

Range: From West Africa to Uganda and Tanzania.

It is a characteristic of this genus that the two sexes look very different. In this species the ground color of the male's upper side is yellow, overlaid on the hind wing with large areas of brown, especially toward the base. In the female, pictured here puddling in Ghana's Bobiri Forest, the upper side is dark brown with a narrow white band down all four wings. In both sexes the underside is vaguely like a dead leaf. This is a butterfly of primary rain forest and reasonably mature second-growth areas, and it is apparently unable to adapt to severe disturbance of its habitat.

Scalloped Yellow Glider

DATA

Scientific name: *Cymothoe fumana*

Family: Nymphalidae

Wingspan: About 3.2 in (8 cm).

Flight period: All year.

Larval food plants: *Rinorea* in the violet family (Violaceae).

Range: Africa (Sierra Leone to the Congo region).

The Scalloped Yellow Glider tends to keep a little higher than some of the other gliders, and the males can be elusive. The author was fortunate, therefore, to find this fine male puddling on damp ground in Ghana's Bobiri Forest. This was the only specimen noted during a period of six weeks, and it was present only for a few minutes, indicating the large part that luck plays in seeing and photographing butterflies. As can be seen, the male's upper side is yellow with a large area of brown. The female is mainly brown with yellowish wing borders. In both sexes of this forest butterfly the underside is rather like a dead leaf.

Lurid Glider

DATA

Scientific name: *Cymothoe lurida*

Family: Nymphalidae

Wingspan: About 2.4 in (6 cm).

Flight period: All year.

Larval food plants: *Rinorea* in the violet family (Violaceae).

Range: Africa (Côte d'Ivoire to Kenya, Tanzania, and Angola).

Occurring mainly in primary rain forest, this species is also found in second-growth habitats as long as plenty of large trees are present. It spends much of its time high up in the forest canopy but comes down to feed on fallen fruit, such as figs, and—like this male pictured in Kakamega Forest in western Kenya—on muddy ground. The form from this area and in neighboring Uganda is subspecies *butleri.* The female is basically dark brown with a faint white band across the forewing (a large pure white band in subspecies *hesione*).

Western Red Glider

DATA

Scientific name: *Cymothoe mabillei*

Family: Nymphalidae

Wingspan: About 2 in (5 cm).

Flight period: All year.

Larval food plants: *Rinorea* in the violet family (Violaceae).

Range: Africa (Sierra Leone to Ghana).

One of several similar-looking butterflies, the males of this species are slightly more orange than in the Common Red Glider *(Cymothoe coccinata)*, with which it sometimes flies and with which it was at one time included. This striking butterfly is mainly an inhabitant of rain forest, where it can be seasonally common, as in Ghana's Bobiri Forest, where the accompanying picture was taken. The males spend much of their time feeding on mud or fallen fruit on the shady rain-forest floor, but they occasionally come into more open spots to feed on flowers. The female is whitish on both sides, patterned with dark brown, while the male (pictured) has a brown leaflike underside.

Striped Glider

DATA

Scientific name: *Cymothoe oemilius*

Family: Nymphalidae

Wingspan: About 3.5 in (9 cm).

Flight period: All year.

Larval food plants: *Caloncoba* (Flacourtiaceae).

Range: Africa (Nigeria to Congo).

Anyone who has been lucky enough to see this superb butterfly floating around low over the rain-forest floor on its large, elegantly striped wings is not likely to forget the experience in a hurry. The white band across each black wing is edged with what to the human eye is a very subtle shade of blue, although this tends to be rendered as rather more of a gray in photographs. The underside is dark silvery gray with a narrowish white band down each wing and twin rows of silvery spots, similar to those on the upper side. The butterfly pictured here dropped in all too briefly to feed on fallen figs in Cameroon's Bimbia Forest.

Acilia Mapwing

The seven species of butterflies in this genus are most often found puddling on the ground, as seen here in rain forest at the Wau research facility in New Guinea. With its brown, white-banded wings and orange hind-wing bases this species bears a superficial resemblance to some species of *Adelpha* and *Doxocopa* from the American tropics—see the Erotia Sister *(A. erotia)* on page 166 and Linda's Emperor *(D. linda)* on page 244. However, only *Cyrestis acilia* has a row of small eyespots down the margin of each hind wing. The underside consists mainly of a complex pattern of brown and white stripes.

DATA

Scientific name: *Cyrestis acilia*

Family: Nymphalidae

Wingspan: About 2 in (5 cm).

Flight period: All year.

Larval food plants: Figs *(Ficus)* in the family Moraceae.

Range: Moluccas, New Guinea, and several Pacific islands.

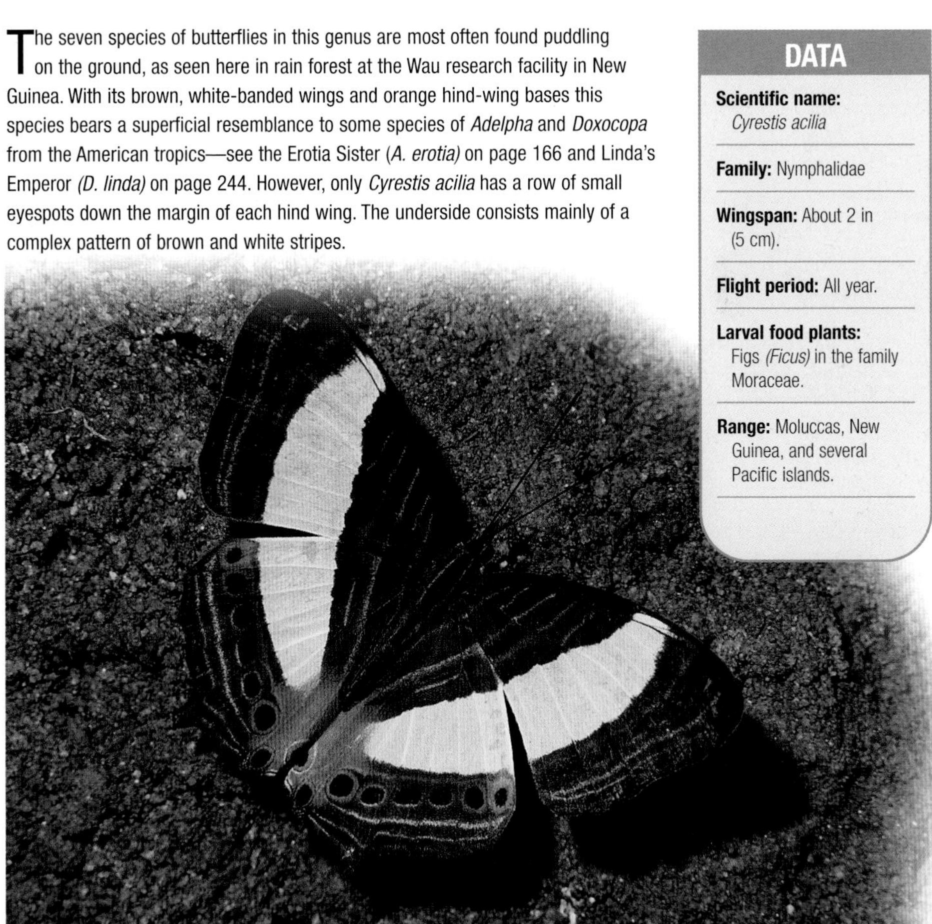

African Map Butterfly

DATA

Scientific name: *Cyrestis camillus*

Family: Nymphalidae

Wingspan: About 2.8 in (7 cm).

Flight period: All year.

Larval food plants: Mainly members of the fig family (Moraceae).

Range: Over most of sub-Saharan Africa south to Zimbabwe; also on Madagascar.

As with the previous species, the African Map Butterfly is usually found puddling on some muddy track, as seen here in Kakamega Forest in western Kenya. Although it is found in primary rain forest, this is more a butterfly of secondary growth and disturbed areas. It has the unusual habit of always sitting with its wings held out flat, even when at rest beneath a leaf. With its pattern of black and pale orange bands against a white background, coupled with tailed hind wings, it is like no other African butterfly. The underside is broadly similar but paler. Note the definite suggestion of a "false head" pattern at the tips of the hind wings.

Agathina Emperor

Many of the 30 or so species in this genus are noted for the exquisite metallic blue coloration of the males, and this species is one of the most intensely colored of all. In most of the species the forelegs are green and the undersides of the wings a rather drab pale brown. The females do not usually resemble the males in any respect and often look more like species of *Adelpha*. These are among the most fast-flying butterflies in the American tropics and can be very difficult to approach. Males busy feeding on urine-soaked ground are regularly the exception, this individual seen here in Peru's Tingo Maria National Park being an example.

DATA

Scientific name: *Doxocopa agathina*

Family: Nymphalidae

Wingspan: About 1.8 in (4.5 cm).

Flight period: All year.

Larval food plants: Members of the elm family (Ulmaceae), probably *Celtis* (hackberries).

Range: Over most of tropical South America.

Turquoise Emperor

DATA

Scientific name: *Doxocopa cherubina*

Family: Nymphalidae

Wingspan: About 2.8 in (7 cm).

Flight period: All year.

Larval food plants: Members of the elm family (Ulmaceae).

Range: Mexico to Paraguay.

This is exactly how you would wish to find emperor butterflies—with their wings spread flat along the ground, fully exposing the wonderful upper side. In this species the basic color of the upper side of the male (pictured here in rain forest in Peru's Tingo Maria National Park) is dark brown, with a turquoise blue band on each wing that does not extend to the margin. In the female the shade of brown is much paler, and each wing bears a narrower band that is white with a blue flush. This species was formerly regarded as a subspecies of *Doxocopa laurentia*.

Cyan Emperor

The basic color of the upper side in the male of this striking species (depicted here puddling on damp ground in rain forest near Satipo in Peru) is rich brownish black. There is a large bright metallic blue patch on each hind wing and a smaller darker blue patch near the base of each forewing. The female upper side is similar to that seen in both sexes of the Silver Emperor *(Doxocopa laure)*. In both sexes the underside is basically pale brown. This is one of the most regularly seen members of the genus, especially the males, who visit mammal dung and sewage-enriched riversides. The females are seldom seen.

DATA

Scientific name: *Doxocopa cyane*

Family: Nymphalidae

Wingspan: About 2.4 in (6 cm).

Flight period: All year.

Larval food plants: Hackberries *(Celtis)* in the elm family (Ulmaceae).

Range: Mexico to Peru.

Orange-spotted Emperor

DATA

Scientific name: *Doxocopa elis*

Family: Nymphalidae

Wingspan: About 2 in (5 cm).

Flight period: All year.

Larval food plants: Members of the elm family (Ulmaceae).

Range: Colombia to Peru.

The pale green proboscis typical of most members of this genus is just about visible here on this male, seen puddling on a dirt road between Tingo Maria and Pucallpa in Peru. When the bus the author was on stopped for its passengers to enjoy a meal break in a small rain-forest settlement, he took the chance to snatch a few pictures of several butterflies feeding on the roadside. They were attracted to the spot where the bus passengers relieved themselves during long journeys, public rest rooms being scarce in Peru. The striking blue sheen visible on the wings is not obvious from some angles, while the pinkish orange spots that form a band on the forewing can be much more intense than seen here.

Silver Emperor

This is one of the few *Doxocopa* species in which male and female are similar, both of them resembling an *Adelpha*. In the male the upper side is brown with an orange band down each forewing, grading into white near the rear margin and lining up with a white band on the hind wing. The white bands are overlaid with a beautiful purple sheen, clearly visible in this photograph of a male on the edge of a coffee plantation near Jalapa in Veracruz State, Mexico. In the female there are plain white bands on all four wings and an orange spot near the tip of each forewing. The underside is pale brownish in both sexes. This lovely butterfly is more common in secondary forest and disturbed areas than in primary rain forest.

DATA

Scientific name: *Doxocopa laure*

Family: Nymphalidae

Wingspan: About 3 in (7.5 cm).

Flight period: All year.

Larval food plants: Hackberries *(Celtis)* in the elm family (Ulmaceae).

Range: Mexico to Brazil.

Linda's Emperor

So close is the resemblance of this species to an *Adelpha* that it was under that genus that the author first looked when attempting an identification. As can be seen, the upper side is very similar to that of *A. erotia*. However, the shape of the forewing is a giveaway, since it has a squared-off tip not seen in *Adelpha*. The orange forewing patch and white wing bands are very much as seen in several species of *Adelpha*, but the "false head" pattern at the tips of the hind wings is better developed in the butterfly depicted here. This is subspecies *selina*, formerly treated as a species in its own right. It was puddling on a forested roadside in the Chapada de Guimarães, Brazil.

DATA

Scientific name: *Doxocopa linda*

Family: Nymphalidae

Wingspan: About 2.2 in (5.5 cm).

Flight period: All year.

Larval food plants: Members of the elm family (Ulmaceae).

Range: Over much of tropical South America.

Pavon Emperor

DATA

Scientific name: *Doxocopa pavon*

Family: Nymphalidae

Wingspan: 2.2 in (5.5 cm).

Flight period: All year.

Larval food plants: Hackberries *(Celtis)* in the elm family (Ulmaceae).

Range: Mexico to Bolivia and Peru.

Some substance on the surface of a log in rain forest was keeping the butterfly illustrated above very busy when the author happened to pass by in Peru's Tingo Maria National Park. Flicking its wings open and closed, this male exposed his gorgeous blue upper side only briefly, and even then not with the wings held flat. This is still the only specimen of this species seen by the author after long periods spent in the wilds of Central and South America, even though the Pavon Emperor occurs in all types of forest. The female looks very like a pale version of Linda's Emperor *(Doxocopa linda)*.

Mylitta Butterfly

DATA

Scientific name: *Dynamina mylitta*

Family: Nymphalidae

Wingspan: About 1.6 in (4 cm).

Flight period: All year.

Larval food plants: *Dalechampia* (Euphorbiaceae).

Range: Throughout the tropics of Central and South America.

It is on wet sand that you are most likely to find the male of this very widespread little butterfly, seen here in rain forest in Peru's Tingo Maria National Park. As will be obvious, the male's upper side is a bright metallic shade of bluish green. The female is very different, being black and white with two slightly indistinct eyespots near the hind-wing margin. In both sexes the underside is a bold combination of brown and silvery white, in stripes and circular blobs, with two eyespots on each hind wing. This is a butterfly of rain-forest edges and roadsides and disturbed forest of many different types.

Thecla Banner

In its habit of sitting with its head pointing downward on tree trunks, this widespread butterfly is like a small version of the crackers *(Hamadryas)* illustrated on pages 282 to 287. Unlike the crackers, however, the Thecla Banner is silent. In the female (the upper of the two butterflies seen here mating in Peru's Tingo Maria National Park) the upper side is gray and the tips of the forewings are rounded. In the male the upper side is more of a brownish gray, and the tips of his forewings are more pointed and contain a small dark eyespot. In both sexes there is a broad white band across each forewing, and the underside is tan colored.

DATA

Scientific name: *Ectima thecla*

Family: Nymphalidae

Wingspan: About 2 in (5 cm).

Flight period: All year.

Larval food plants: *Dalechampia* (Euphorbiaceae).

Range: Most of the South American tropics.

Azure-winged Triangle

DATA

Scientific name: *Epiphele orea*

Family: Nymphalidae

Wingspan: About 2.2 in (5.5 cm).

Flight period: All year.

Larval food plants: *Serjania* and *Paullinia* in the soapberry family (Sapindaceae).

Range: Costa Rica to Brazil.

In the butterflies of this genus, which contains some 12 species, the males and females are so different that they often appear to belong to two different species. Photographed in rain forest in Peru's Tingo Maria National Park, the male illustrated above was behaving in typical fashion, perching open winged on a leaf in a light gap and rushing out to intercept passing butterflies. The forewings are basically brownish black, shot through with a lovely blue shimmer that is clearly visible here, and with two pinkish orange bands. The hind wings are bright iridescent blue. By contrast, the female is plain brown with a single orange band across each forewing.

Three-barred Tiger Crescent

DATA

Scientific name: *Eresia alsina*

Family: Nymphalidae

Wingspan: About 2.2 in (5.5 cm).

Flight period: All year.

Larval food plants: *Pilea pittieri* in the nettle family (Urticaceae).

Range: Nicaragua and Costa Rica.

Wet rain forest above about 1,000 feet (300 m) is the favored habitat for this species, photographed here in Braulio Carrillo National Park, Costa Rica. This is certainly a wet piece of forest—the author well remembers the three days of solid rain that accompanied his first visit there. Butterflies of this species are usually found as solitary individuals fluttering around near the ground in deep shade, as seen here. Its color combination of black, orange, and yellow places it firmly in the tiger-striped mimicry grouping. The underside is similar to the upper side shown here, but paler. Both sexes are alike.

Two-banded Tiger Crescent

DATA

Scientific name: *Eresia eunice*

Family: Nymphalidae

Wingspan: About 2.2 in (5.5 cm).

Larval food plants: Probably Acanthaceae.

Range: Throughout most of the American tropics from Panama southward.

Most of the butterflies in this genus have long narrow wings and are mimics of other species. The models for the Two-banded Tiger Crescent are various unpalatable members of the tiger-striped mimicry grouping, such as the Disturbed Tigerwing *(Mechanitis polymnia)* and the Isabella Longwing *(Eueides isabella)*. This species, seen here in rain forest in Peru's Tingo Maria National Park, even behaves like its models, sitting on a leaf and repeatedly opening and closing its wings. The underside is similar to the upper side but paler.

Square-tipped Crescent

DATA

Scientific name: *Eresia philyra*

Family: Nymphalidae

Wingspan: About 2.4 in (6 cm).

Flight period: All year.

Larval food plants: Unknown.

Range: Mexico.

Another member of the so-called tiger-striped mimicry group, the pattern on the upper side of this species is very similar to that of the Two-banded Tiger Crescent *(Eresia eunice)*—a combination of yellow, black, and orange. As can be seen in the accompanying illustration, the female (on the right) is considerably bigger than the male, and has wings that are relatively broad compared with their length. This is a butterfly of disturbed forest and rain-forest edges, seen here on a roadside through a small area of residual rain forest in Veracruz State, Mexico.

Bechina Purplewing

DATA

Scientific name: *Eunica bechina*

Family: Nymphalidae

Wingspan: About 2.4 in (6 cm).

Flight period: All year.

Larval food plants: Members of the Caryocaraceae.

Range: Colombia to Brazil.

The genus *Eunica* contains some 50 species of forest butterflies found in the tropical regions of Central and South America, although several species just manage to stray into the southern United States. In a number of species, including the beautiful species illustrated here (at Rancho Grande in the Amazon region of Brazil), the males exhibit a stunning purplish blue sheen, which is more obvious from some angles than others, so the butterfly seems to flicker as it moves. The females are generally brown with a white bar on each forewing. In both sexes of this species the underside is pale mottled brownish with some small eyespots.

Ceres Forester

DATA

Scientific name: *Euphaedra ceres*

Family: Nymphalidae

Wingspan: About 2.8 in (7 cm).

Flight period: All year.

Larval food plants: Known to breed on *Deinbollia pinnata* in the soapberry family (Sapindaceae).

Range: Africa (Sierra Leone to the Congo region).

Containing some 200 species, *Euphaedra* is the largest butterfly genus in Africa, with the exception of *Acraea*. The Ceres Forester is one of the commonest species in the rain forests of West Africa, and one of the most adaptable. It is one of the species most likely to be found away from forests, being quite at home in such places as suburban backyards and around villages. It was one of thousands of butterflies puddling in Bobiri Forest, Ghana, as seen here. The upper side is metallic bluish, with a broad black margin to the hind wings. The outer three-quarters of the forewing is black, crossed by a whitish band, this being broader in the otherwise similar female. The underside is greenish with black spotting.

Edwards's Forester

With an appearance that gives an uncanny impression of its wings being made of plastic, this highly distinctive butterfly is not like any other. The forewing upper side is blackish brown with a greenish sheen and a touch of orange toward the base. The hind wing is orange with a broad dark border and three large black spots toward the base. The underside is roughly similar. Often found on fallen fruit or puddling on the ground, this species is ecologically tolerant and is found from forest into almost open country. It is seen here basking in the early morning in Ghana's Bobiri Forest.

DATA

Scientific name: *Euphaedra edwardsi*

Family: Nymphalidae

Wingspan: About 2.8 in (7 cm).

Flight period: All year.

Larval food plants: *Lecaniodiscus cupanioides* in the soapberry family (Sapindaceae).

Range: Africa (Sierra Leone to Uganda).

Common Blue-banded Forester

DATA

Scientific name: *Euphaedra harpalyce*

Family: Nymphalidae

Wingspan: About 3.2 in (8 cm).

Flight period: All year.

Larval food plants: *Blighia sapida*, *Lecaniodiscus cupanoides*, and other Sapindaceae.

Range: Africa (Guinea-Bissau to Rwanda and Uganda).

This large brown butterfly with its blue-banded hind wings is usually seen flying fast and low along some forest track before suddenly dropping down to feed on a fallen fig or patch of muddy ground. From its upper side it is impossible to distinguish this species from the Western Blue-banded Forester *(Euphaedra eupalus)*. However, in that species there is a series of white spots down the greenish hind-wing underside, which are absent in *E. harpalyce*. Seen here basking in Bobiri Forest, Ghana, this highly adaptable species is found in forests of all types as well as in backyards in large cities, such as Ghana's capital, Accra.

Janetta Themis Forester

Several species of *Euphaedra* have strikingly marked undersides, but this is one of the most beautiful of all. The basic color is a lovely deep yellow, with a large red patch near the base of each hind wing and a small red patch at the base of each forewing. There is a row of black spots down the outer margins and a few more scattered around, especially on the forewing. The upper side is greenish blue, heavily flushed with gold, with a broad black tip to the forewing, in which there is a more or less circular golden patch. There is always a small red spot near the base of the hind wing. This is mainly a rain-forest species, seen here feeding on fallen fruit in Cameroon's Bimbia Forest, but it can also survive in degraded habitats.

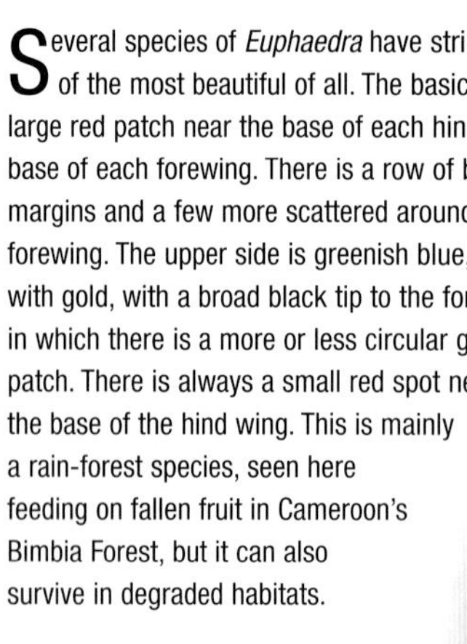

DATA

Scientific name: *Euphaedra janetta*

Family: Nymphalidae

Wingspan: About 2.8 in (7 cm).

Flight period: All year.

Larval food plants: Members of the soapberry family (Sapindaceae).

Range: Africa (Sierra Leone to the Congo region).

Dark Brown Forester

DATA

Scientific name: *Euphaedra losinga*

Family: Nymphalidae

Wingspan: About 3.2 in (8 cm).

Flight period: All year.

Larval food plants: Members of the soapberry family (Sapindaceae).

Range: Africa (Nigeria to Congo region).

Brown might not seem to be a very exciting color for a butterfly, but the Dark Brown Forester is an impressive species. This is especially true when a specimen of this large butterfly is seen flapping low down near the rain-forest floor or pausing to feed on a fallen fig, as here in Cameroon's Bimbia Forest. The yellow band across the forewing is very distinctive, but the white tips to the forewings are common to several other brown species. The underside is green, overlaid with silvery scales. This is mainly a species of good-quality rain forest, colonizing second-growth areas only if they retain a good canopy.

Widespread Forester

DATA

Scientific name: *Euphaedra medon*

Family: Nymphalidae

Wingspan: Male about 2.4 in (6 cm); female about 3 in (7.5 cm).

Flight period: All year.

Larval food plants: Members of the soapberry family (Sapindaceae).

Range: Over most of tropical Africa.

This is the most common and widespread member of the genus, found in almost every kind of habitat from degraded forests to gardens and gallery forest. Rain forest is certainly its preferred habitat, however. It is the only member of its genus in which the two sexes are completely dissimilar. The female, pictured here in Bobiri Forest in Ghana, is dark olive brown, with a violet area on the hind wing and along the inner margins of the forewings. The male, which is generally much smaller, is mostly bottle green with blackish margins and a dark apex to the forewing, on which there is a yellowish orange band. In both sexes the underside is mainly a pale brownish green color.

Gold-banded Forester

Found in coastal forests, woodlands, and plantations along the Indian Ocean coast of Africa, from Kenya to KwaZulu-Natal in South Africa, this species is usually seen fluttering around near the forest floor. More than most members of the genus it also frequently lands on the ground with wings spread flat, as seen in this male resting on the sandy soil of Kenya's Sokoke Forest. It will also feed on fallen fruits, even those that are relatively hard, for example, some palms. The sexes are similar, but the female is larger. The basic upper-side color is a lovely violet blue with black wing tips crossed by a yellow bar. The underside is a pale fawn color.

DATA

Scientific name: *Euphaedra neophron*

Family: Nymphalidae

Wingspan: About 2.8 in (7 cm).

Flight period: All year.

Larval food plants: *Deinbollia* in the soapberry family (Sapindaceae).

Range: Africa (Kenya to South Africa).

Bronze Forester

DATA

Scientific name: *Euphaedra paradoxa*

Family: Nymphalidae

Wingspan: About 2.4 in (6 cm).

Flight period: All year.

Larval food plants: Members of the soapberry family (Sapindaceae).

Range: Africa (Kenya, Uganda, Tanzania, and Zambia).

With its black wings overlaid with bronzy brown on the basal areas, this is a very unusual member of the genus. It is also a little smaller than most. There are four white spots forming a slightly broken bar across the black tip of the forewing. The velvety black body is ornamented with a number of white spots. Like most foresters, this species is often found on the ground beneath trees that are dropping ripe fruits, as here on a path in Kakamega Forest, Kenya.

Perseis Mimic Forester

With its rich red, black, and cream coloration this splendid butterfly is a mimic of unpalatable day-flying moths in the genus *Xanthospilopteryx*. This is a relatively scarce butterfly of good-quality rain forest. It is seldom seen in numbers, although one or two individuals were present over several weeks while the author was in Ghana's Bobiri Forest, where the accompanying photograph was taken. The underside is broadly similar but paler. Three other species—*Euphaedra eusemoides*, *E. imitans*, and *E. zaddachii*—have similar coloration to the upper side but lack the white spots in the black borders of the hind wings.

DATA

Scientific name: *Euphaedra perseis*

Family: Nymphalidae

Wingspan: About 2.8 in (7 cm).

Flight period: All year.

Larval food plants: Members of the soapberry family (Sapindaceae).

Range: Africa (Guinea to Ghana).

Common Ceres Forester

Although it has rather limited distribution, this species can be abundant where found and is one of the commonest members of the genus in Ghana, where this photograph was taken, in Bobiri Forest. One of the reasons for its abundance is the range of forest types that seem to be suitable, including disturbed areas. The upper side is bluish green, the forewing being mostly black crossed by a yellowish or pale cream band that is narrower than in the very similar Ceres Forester *(Euphaedra ceres)*. The hind wing has a broad dark border. The greenish underside has a pale yellowish band across the forewing and a row of black spots on the hind-wing margin.

DATA

Scientific name: *Euphaedra phaetusa*

Family: Nymphalidae

Wingspan: About 2.8 in (7 cm).

Flight period: All year.

Larval food plants: Members of the soapberry family (Sapindaceae).

Range: Africa (Guinea to Togo).

Ravola Ceres Forester

DATA

Scientific name: *Euphaedra ravola*

Family: Nymphalidae

Wingspan: About 2.8 in (7 cm).

Flight period: All year.

Larval food plants: Members of the soapberry family (Sapindaceae).

Range: Africa (Côte d'Ivoire to Congo region).

Even in its preferred habitat of relatively good-quality rain forest this species tends to be found in the shadier spots, rather than in light gaps or on the edges of clearings. Not often seen, it is best sought out beneath a fig tree that is dropping the ripe fruits to which this butterfly is most attracted, as depicted here in Cameroon's Bimbia Forest. The sexes are similar, both having a metallic bluish green upper side with a dark apex to the forewing, on which there is a whitish or yellowish bar. Below, the hind wing is mainly yellow with dark borders, while the forewing is pale greenish with two yellow patches.

Common Orange Forester

DATA

Scientific name: *Euphaedra ruspina*

Family: Nymphalidae

Wingspan: About 3 in (7.5 cm).

Flight period: All year.

Larval food plants: Members of the soapberry family (Sapindaceae).

Range: Africa (Ghana to Congo, Tanzania, Angola, and Zambia).

Depicted here in Cameroon's Bimbia Forest, this is a butterfly of shady rain forest, although it is also found in somewhat degraded habitats. The ground color is bright reddish orange, and on the black apex to the forewing there are three white spots forming an incomplete band. The hind wing has a broad black border in which there is a row of white spots. The underside is mainly pale greenish orange. The distinctive pattern on the upper side seems to mimic that of certain unpalatable day-flying moths, such as *Aletis helcita* (Geometridae) and *Phaegorista similis* (Hypsidae).

Common Themis Forester

This was one of the most abundant members of the genus when the author made a six-week stay in Ghana's Bobiri Forest, where this puddling male was photographed. Apart from size (the female being larger), the sexes are similar, although the female has a more pointed forewing. On the upper side the ground color is a shining bluish green, and most of the forewing is black with a yellowish band across the apical half. The hind wing has a broad black border, and there is usually a red dot at the base of the forewing. The underside is mainly gold with red wing bases and black-spotted borders. This species is more common in drier forests and disturbed areas than in virgin rain forest.

DATA

Scientific name: *Euphaedra themis*

Family: Nymphalidae

Wingspan: About 2.8 in (7 cm).

Flight period: All year.

Larval food plants: Members of the soapberry family (Sapindaceae).

Range: Africa (Sierra Leone to Cameroon).

Uganda Forester

DATA

Scientific name: *Euphaedra uganda*

Family: Nymphalidae

Wingspan: About 3.2 in (8 cm).

Larval food plants: Members of the soapberry family (Sapindaceae).

Range: Africa (Uganda, Kenya, and Tanzania).

Although most abundant in the rain forests of Uganda, this species can also be very common locally in the remaining forests of extreme western Kenya, as in Kakamega Forest, where this picture was taken. During the author's single visit to this threatened forest, this was one of only two members of the genus seen. It was abundant on the tracks through the forest wherever figs or other attractive fruits had fallen from the trees above. The sexes are similar, the ground color being a rather iridescent blue in the female (pictured) and slightly more purple in the male. There is a black apex to the forewing, on which there is a row of four white spots. The hind-wing borders are dark, and the underside is plain greenish.

Common Pink Forester

There are few butterflies anywhere in the world that can rival the sheer elegance of the colors seen beneath the wings of this species, revealed here in all their glory as a male feeds on fallen fruit in Ghana's Bobiri Forest. It is the hind wing that is most striking, being mainly a beautiful shade of pinkish red. The forewing underside is bluish green, crossed by a white band. The upper side is similar to that found in several other species—basically bluish green with a mostly black forewing crossed by a white band below the apex. Fortunately, this is a common butterfly in most types of forest, including those that have been badly degraded.

DATA

Scientific name: *Euphaedra xypete*

Family: Nymphalidae

Wingspan: About 2.6 in (6.5 cm).

Flight period: All year.

Larval food plants: Members of the soapberry family (Sapindaceae).

Range: Africa (Guinea-Bissau to Cameroon).

Marsh Fritillary

DATA

Scientific name: *Euphydryas aurinia*

Family: Nymphalidae

Wingspan: About 1.4 in (3.5 cm).

Flight period: May–June.

Larval food plants: Mainly plantains *(Plantago)* in the Plantaginaceae and scabious *(Succisa)* in the Dipsacaceae.

Range: From western Europe across temperate Asia to Korea.

A damp, tussocky, rough pasture with plenty of devil's-bit scabious *(Succisa pratensis)* is a typical habitat for this species, although it is also found on dry grassy banks, in open areas within woodland, and on the marshy edges of lakes. The upper side is pretty typical for a fritillary, being basically brownish orange with a variable degree of black marking. There is a row of whitish spots within the dark hind-wing border. The underside is the usual fritillary mosaic of black, white, and pale orange. This seems to be a declining species, and urgent conservation measures are currently underway in countries such as England.

Chalcedon Checkerspot

DATA

Scientific name: *Euphydryas chalcedona*

Family: Nymphalidae

Wingspan: About 1.8 in (4.5 cm).

Flight period: March–July, depending on location and altitude.

Larval food plants: Members of the Scrophulariaceae, e.g., paintbrushes *(Castilleja)* and monkey flower *(Mimulus)*.

Range: United States (Oregon to Arizona) and in Mexico (Baja California).

This is a very variable butterfly that exists in a series of subspecies, some of which are often now regarded as separate species. Unfortunately, the situation is complicated by the way that one form often seems to grade into another. Many of the forms are of very local occurrence. The one pictured above is the lowland desert form, photographed in Arizona. The upper side is typically black with bands of small yellowish spots. It is a common species, found in a wide range of habitats, from coasts to open mountainsides.

Common Harlequin

DATA

Scientific name: *Euptera elabontas*

Family: Nymphalidae

Wingspan: About 1.6 in (4 cm).

Flight period: All year.

Larval food plants: Members of the Sapotaceae.

Range: Africa (Côte d'Ivoire to Congo region, Kenya, Tanzania, and Zambia).

One of several very similar-looking species, all of which are found in rain forest, the specimen pictured here was puddling on a path through Kenya's Kakamega Forest. It is the only one that the author has ever seen. The sexes are very similar, except that in the female the markings on the upper side are white, while in the male they are pale cream. The underside is basically similar, but the ground color is much paler, being light brown rather than black.

Variegated Fritillary

DATA

Scientific name: *Euptoieta claudia*

Family: Nymphalidae

Wingspan: About 2 in (5 cm).

Flight period: All year in south; summer in north.

Larval food plants: Very varied, e.g., May apple *(Podophyllum)* in the Berberidaceae and beggarticks *(Desmodium)* in the Fabaceae.

Range: United States to Argentina.

In the south of its range and in the southernmost parts of the United States, such as in south Texas, this species is on the wing all year. In Florida it flies from March to December, while farther north it may be common in late summer only after a northward migration, sometimes as far as southern Canada. It is found in a wide range of open habitats, including waste lots, fields, roadsides, and open woodland. It also often comes into backyards, as seen here in South Carolina. The upper side is tawny with a complicated black pattern—the one on the hind wing being unique and easily identifying this species. The underside bears a complex mix of browns.

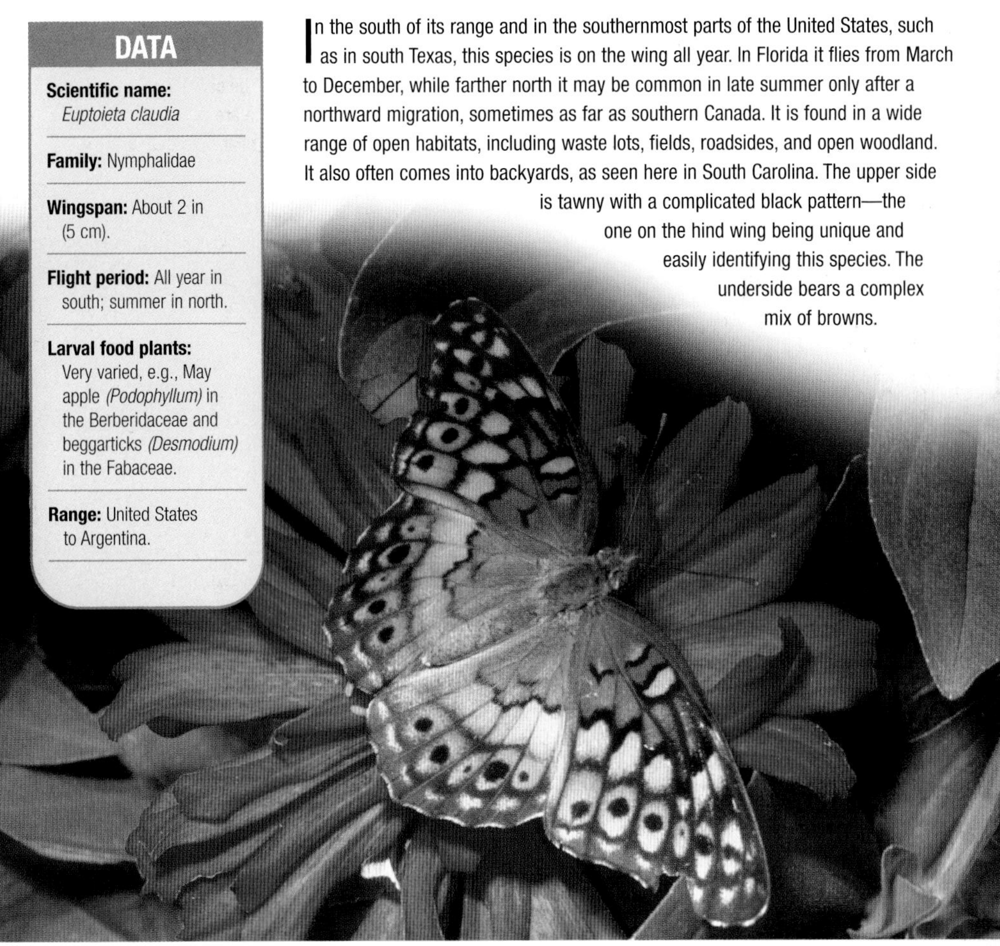

Mexican Fritillary

DATA

Scientific name: *Euptoieta hegesia*

Family: Nymphalidae

Wingspan: About 2 in (5 cm).

Larval food plants: Varied. *Passiflora foetida* (family Passifloraceae) in Texas.

Range: United States to Argentina.

The only place where this basically tropical butterfly has a permanent home in the United States is southern Texas, where it is on the wing from July through December. In summer it often migrates a little farther north, sometimes straying into southern California. It occurs in a wide variety of mostly open habitats, such as scrublands, open woodland, backyards, and roadsides, as seen here in Oaxaca State, Mexico. The upper side is a richer shade of orange than in the Variegated Fritillary *(Euptoieta claudia)*, and the black markings are less complex, especially on the hind wing, where they are much reduced. The underside is a complex mix of browns.

Lazy Nymph

The 70 or so species of the large genus *Euriphene* are restricted to the tropical regions of Africa. All except one, *E. iris*, are butterflies of dense forest, poorly adapted to survive in degraded or disturbed areas. In most species, including this one, the males are brown with a bluish purple sheen that varies in intensity from species to species. The females always look different, in this case being brown with a pattern of wavy-edged yellow bars. Nymphs spend a lot of their time just sitting around on leaves, often along the sides of forest tracks and paths, which is where this female was found in Kenya's Kakamega Forest.

DATA

Scientific name: *Euriphene ribensis*

Family: Nymphalidae

Wingspan: About 2 in (5 cm).

Flight period: All year.

Larval food plants: Unknown.

Range: Africa (Gabon to Uganda and Kenya).

Common Nymph

Scientific name: *Euriphene barombina*

Family: Nymphalidae

Wingspan: About 2 in (5 cm).

Flight period: All year.

Larval food plants: *Combretum* (Combretaceae).

Range: Africa (Côte d'Ivoire to Uganda and Angola).

Usually the commonest member of the genus in most localities, this species is able to survive in very poor-quality habitats, such as small groves of trees. In large areas of relatively good forest it can be very abundant, as it was during the author's visit to Bobiri Forest in Ghana, where the accompanying photograph of a basking male was taken. The overall topside coloration is a violet shade of blue with a dark underlying pattern and some small white spots near the apex of the forewing. The female is very different, being brownish orange, with the black outer three-quarters of the forewing crossed by a broken white band.

Common Commander

DATA

Scientific name: *Euryphura chalcis*

Family: Nymphalidae

Wingspan: About 2 in (5 cm).

Flight period: All year.

Larval food plants: In several families, e.g., *Hugonia platysepala* in the flax family (Linaceae).

Range: From West Africa to Kenya and Zambia.

When the author returned from West Africa in 2005, the number of butterfly species thought to have been photographed in Bobiri Forest in Ghana had to be somewhat reduced. This was because, on checking the identification books, at least five supposed species were found to be females of the Common Commander. They can be pale green, pale blue, brown and yellow, black and white, or brown and green, the latter being the author's favorite form, illustrated here. The smaller males are less variable—dark reddish brown being the most common color. The underside is fairly plain brown in both sexes. Mainly a forest butterfly, this species is also found in very disturbed habitats and even in backyards.

Suffert's Commander

DATA

Scientific name: *Euryphura togoensis*

Family: Nymphalidae

Wingspan: About 2.4 in (6 cm).

Flight period: All year.

Larval food plants: Unknown.

Range: Africa (Sierra Leone to Cameroon).

With its brilliant golden hind wings this is a particularly striking species. It is restricted to rain forest of good quality, such as Ghana's Bobiri Forest, where the accompanying photograph of a puddling specimen was taken. The forewing is mainly dark brownish black with a few silvery spots. The sexes are similar, except that the male has a more falcate hind wing, the tip being drawn out to something of a point (while it is rounded in the female). In both sexes the underside is like a very drab, muted version of the upper side.

Golden Piper

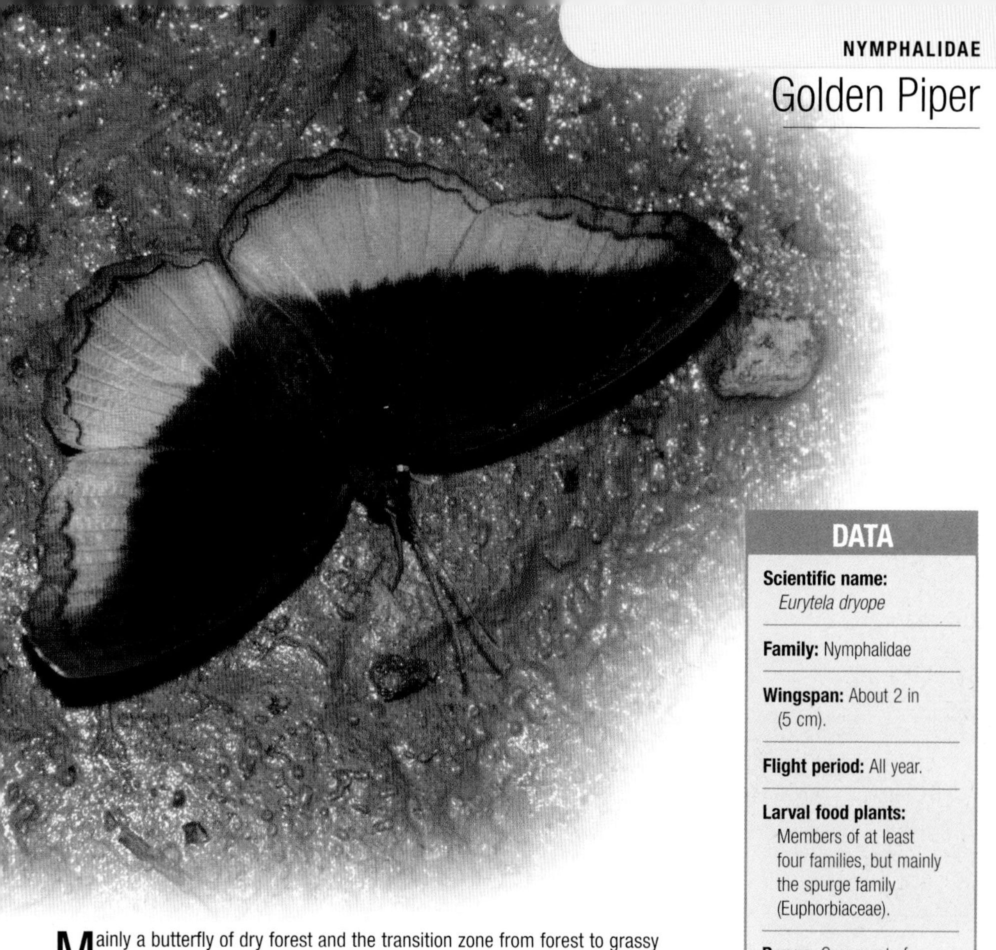

Mainly a butterfly of dry forest and the transition zone from forest to grassy savanna with scattered trees, this species is not common in dense rain forest. The specimen shown here was photographed puddling beside a small stream in a mosaic of patches of forest and farmland near Kpalimé in Togo. In both sexes the upper side is brown with a broad orange band down each wing margin. The underside is similar but very pale.

DATA

Scientific name: *Eurytela dryope*

Family: Nymphalidae

Wingspan: About 2 in (5 cm).

Flight period: All year.

Larval food plants: Members of at least four families, but mainly the spurge family (Euphorbiaceae).

Range: Over most of sub-Saharan Africa and on Madagascar.

Pied Piper

DATA

Scientific name: *Eurytela hiarbas*

Family: Nymphalidae

Wingspan: About 2 in (5 cm).

Flight period: All year.

Larval food plants: Castor-oil *(Ricinus communis)* and other Euphorbiaceae.

Distribution: Over most of sub-Saharan Africa.

This is a butterfly of dry forest, disturbed scrubby areas, forest edges, and secondary forest. It is seldom common and usually occurs as the odd individual—the one depicted here was puddling beside a stream near Kpalimé in Togo. The upper side is darker than in the Golden Piper *(Eurytela dryope)*, being a very dark chocolate brown with a fairly broad white band down each wing and set well in from the margins. The underside is similar but rather paler.

Common Forest Queen

DATA

Scientific name: *Euxanthe eurinome*

Family: Nymphalidae

Wingspan: About 3.2 in (8 cm).

Flight period: All year.

Larval food plants: *Afzelia* (Fabaceae); *Phialodiscus*, *Deinbollia*, and *Blighia* (Sapindaceae).

Range: Africa (Senegal to Kenya, Ethiopia, and Angola).

Although it is a widespread species, the Common Forest Queen is seldom found in significant numbers. With its black wings covered in pale blue spots, this species looks very similar to the African Blue Tiger *(Tirumala petiverana)*, of which it could possibly be a mimic. However, the fact that *Euxanthe eurinome* has a bright orange-yellow abdomen indicates that it is probably distasteful, so any mimicry involved would be of the Muellerian variety. While it is predominantly a forest butterfly (seen here in Bobiri Forest in Ghana), this species occurs in a variety of habitats, including backyards in large cities such as Accra, Ibadan, and Abidjan.

Dark Forest Queen

DATA

Scientific name: *Euxanthe tiberius*

Family: Nymphalidae

Wingspan: About 3.7 in (9.5 cm).

Flight period: All year.

Larval food plants: *Deinbollia* (Sapindaceae).

Range: Africa (Kenya and Tanzania).

Forests along the coasts of Kenya and Tanzania and inland as far as Mount Kenya and the Meru Forest are home to this splendid butterfly. The males spend much of their time sitting head downward on tree trunks, dashing out to intercept intruders, including the author, as happened in the Shimba Hills in Kenya where this picture was taken. The upper side of the forewing is black with rows of greenish white spots and a reddish brown patch near the base. The hind wing is black with three white spots and a row of white marginal dots. The female is similar, but the forewing spots are white and she has a large white patch on the hind wing.

Wakefield's Forest Queen

Although mainly a butterfly of coastal forests this species is also found far inland. It is readily attracted to fermenting fruit, but it will also come to fermenting sap, as seen here oozing from a fallen tree in Makadara Forest in Kenya's Shimba Hills. The wings on both sides are velvety black with numerous semitranslucent greenish blue markings. In the male (pictured) the forewing is more rounded than in the female, whose markings are also paler, often almost white.

DATA

Scientific name: *Euxanthe wakefieldi*

Family: Nymphalidae

Wingspan: About 3.2 in (8 cm).

Flight period: All year.

Larval food plants: *Deinbollia* (Sapindaceae).

Range: Kenya, Tanzania, Mozambique, Zimbabwe, and South Africa.

Red Cracker

DATA

Scientific name: *Hamadryas amphinome*

Family: Nymphalidae

Wingspan: About 3 in (7.5 cm).

Flight period: All year.

Larval food plants: *Dalechampia* in the spurge family (Euphorbiaceae).

Range: Mexico to the Amazon Basin. Vagrant in southern United States.

This attractive species gets its common name from the large red patch on the underside of the hind wings. This is clearly visible in this photograph of a female hanging beneath a *Dalechampia* vine as she lays her eggs in a series of neat rows, a little piece of domestic drama that took place on a forested roadside in Trinidad. The upper side is blackish with a mottled pattern of bluish gray spots and a jagged white forewing band. The Red Cracker is found mainly in second-growth forests, and is only a relatively scarce member of the canopy community in primary rain forest.

Azure Cracker

DATA

Scientific name: *Hamadryas arinome*

Family: Nymphalidae

Wingspan: About 2.8 in (7 cm).

Flight period: All year.

Larval food plants: *Dalechampia* in the spurge family (Euphorbiaceae).

Range: Mexico to the Amazon Basin.

With its pattern of bright azure spots this is probably the most striking member of the genus, and arguably the most beautiful. In the female, pictured here on a tree trunk in tropical dry forest in Santa Rosa National Park, Costa Rica, the jagged white forewing band is very distinct. By contrast, it is rather indistinct in the male. The forewing underside is blackish with a broad white band, while the hind wing is black with a row of red marginal spots. This species is found in all forest types, but in dense rain forest it is mainly a canopy insect.

Gray Cracker

This was the first cracker seen (or heard) by the author, and the amazingly loud cracking sound made by several butterflies as they dashed out from a small group of trees came as a great surprise. This happened during a brief stop on a long drive in Veracruz State, Mexico, and this is one of the photographs that resulted. As will be obvious, with its cryptic mottled brownish upper side this species is very well camouflaged when at rest with open wings on a tree trunk, which is where it spends much of the day. This tropical species occurs in various types of forest as well as in cultivated areas and is an occasional visitor to southern Texas.

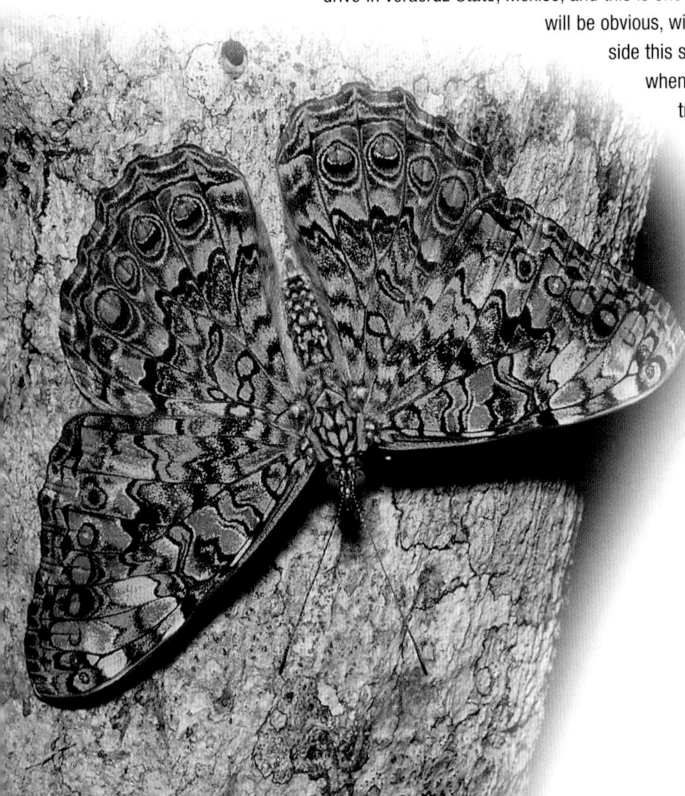

DATA

Scientific name: *Hamadryas februa*

Family: Nymphalidae

Wingspan: About 2.8 in (7 cm).

Flight period: All year.

Larval food plants: *Dalechampia* in the spurge family (Euphorbiaceae).

Range: Southern United States to Argentina.

Yellow Cracker

DATA

Scientific name: *Hamadryas fornax*

Family: Nymphalidae

Wingspan: About 3 in (7.5 cm).

Larval food plants: *Dalechampia* in the spurge family (Euphorbiaceae).

Range: Mexico to Brazil and Bolivia.

The common name of this butterfly is derived from the large yellowish orange patch that covers almost the entire area of the hind-wing underside. There is a smaller patch on the rear of the forewing, the rest of which is pale brown with silvery spots. The upper side, as seen here, is the usual mottled cracker pattern, consisting of grayish blue spots against a dark background and with several silvery gray patches forming two indistinct bands on the forewing. Mainly a butterfly of rain forest, the Yellow Cracker is not a common butterfly in Costa Rica, and the author was very fortunate to get this photograph of a specimen seen on a roadside tree on the coast near Manuel Antonio National Park.

Pale Cracker

DATA

Scientific name: *Hamadryas glauconome*

Family: Nymphalidae

Wingspan: About 3 in (7.5 cm).

Flight period: All year.

Larval food plant: *Dalechampia* in the spurge family (Euphorbiaceae).

Range: Mexico to Costa Rica.

Occurring only in forests that have marked wet and dry seasons, this species becomes vary scarce during the many months without rain. However, a few individuals can usually be seen even at the height of the drought. In Costa Rica this species is generally found in the dry forests on the Pacific slope, especially in Guanacaste Province, where this Pale Cracker was photographed in Santa Rosa National Park. It is unmistakable, being the only member of the genus with a large white area at the wing tips; the rest are gray.

Starry Cracker

Crackers are most often found on tree trunks, but they will also spend a fair amount of time on the ground, feeding on fallen fruit or on salty ground, like the male photographed here in rain forest in Tingo Maria National Park, Peru. The Starry Cracker is the darkest member of the genus and is also noted for its very rounded wing shape. Above, the wings are velvety black with a pattern of bright turquoise spots. The female has a white band across the forewing. The underside is an iridescent bluish black with red spots around the hind margin. The coloration seems to be of a "warning" nature because this species is apparently unpalatable to birds.

DATA

Scientific name: *Hamadryas laodamia*

Family: Nymphalidae

Wingspan: About 2.8 in (7 cm).

Flight period: All year.

Larval food plants: *Dalechampia* in the spurge family (Euphorbiaceae).

Range: Mexico to the Amazon Basin.

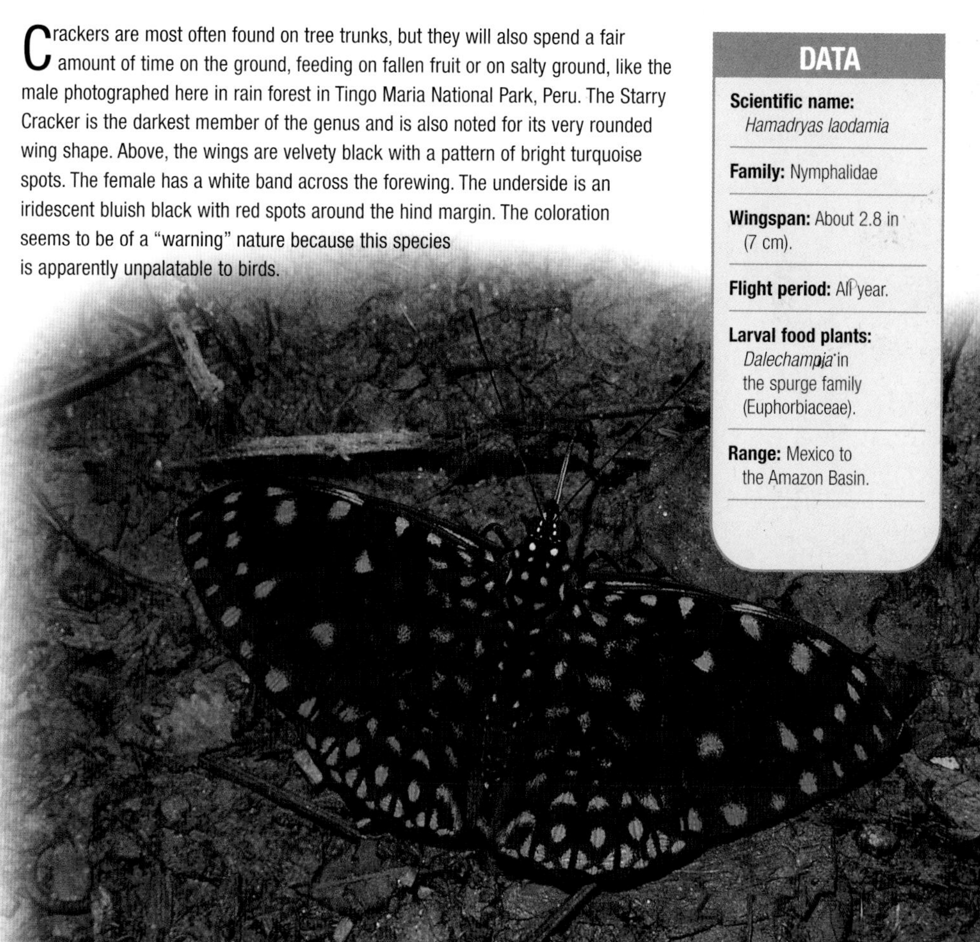

Guineafowl Butterfly

Over a vast swath of Africa south of the Sahara, wherever there is open grassy savanna or bush, this species is almost sure to crop up. The destruction of extensive areas of forest by humans over the last 100 years, especially in West Africa, has opened up large areas of new habitat for this butterfly, which has become quite common on agricultural land in the main forest zone. It spends much of its time with its gray, silver-spotted wings spread wide on open bare ground, as seen here on a campsite in the Masai Mara, one of Kenya's prime "big game" reserves. The underside is brownish orange.

DATA

Scientific name: *Hamanumida daedalus*

Family: Nymphalidae

Wingspan: About 2.2 in (5.5 cm).

Flight period: All year.

Larval food plants: *Combretum* (Combretaceae).

Range: Over most of sub-Saharan Africa.

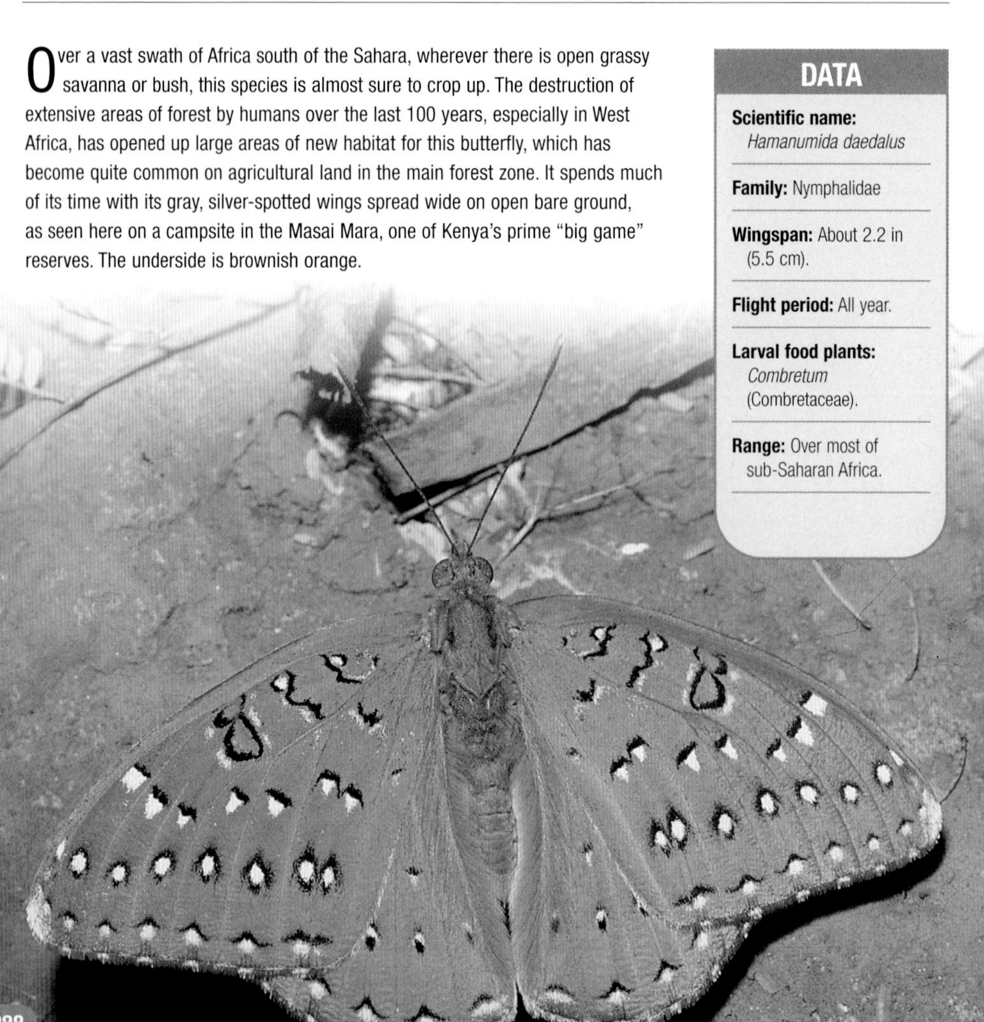

Angular Glider

DATA

Scientific name: *Harma theobene*

Family: Nymphalidae

Wingspan: About 2.6 in (6.5 cm).

Larval food plants: Members of the family Flacourtiaceae.

Range: Africa (Sierra Leone to Kenya and Zambia).

Containing just this single species, the genus *Harma* is under attack at present from those who wish to include it in *Cymothoe*, with which it is very closely related. Both the DNA and larval stages are certainly very similar. However, the strongly angled wing shape is very distinctive and serves to distinguish this species instantly from all other similar butterflies. The male, seen here puddling at Bobiri in Ghana, is pale brown with a yellow stripe down each wing. The female is pale brown without yellow bands and with or without a gray suffusion across the outer two-thirds of the wings. Found in small patches of trees as well as in various forest types, this is a very adaptable species.

Orange Mapwing

Most often found feeding on rotting fruits on the forest floor, both sexes of this butterfly will also sometimes visit flowers, especially those of the sunflower family (Asteraceae), as seen here on a roadside near Jalapa in Veracruz State, Mexico. The upper side is brownish orange, with a black forewing apex on which there are several brownish orange spots. There is a narrow black bar across the forewing, not far from its base. The toothlike tail on the hind wing is typical of all members of the genus. This is a species of disturbed forest and second growth, rather than dense primary forest.

DATA

Scientific name: *Hypanartia lethe*

Family: Nymphalidae

Wingspan: About 2.2 in (5.5 cm).

Flight period: All year.

Larval food plants: Members of the elm family (Ulmaceae) and nettle family (Urticaceae).

Range: Mexico to Brazil.

Variable Diadem

Unlike the Diadem *(Hypolimnas misippus),* in this species both sexes are highly variable and mimic species of unpalatable black-and-white butterflies, such as the Small Monk *(Amauris damocles)* and *A. niavius*. The various forms differ mainly in the size and number of white patches on the forewings and the extent of pale creamy yellow on the hind wings. Illustrated below is subspecies *wahlbergi*, photographed in Kakamega Forest in western Kenya. Both sexes may visit fallen fruit or flowers. Although mainly a forest butterfly, the Variable Diadem is found in more open habitats, including city backyards.

DATA

Scientific name: *Hypolimnas anthedon*

Family: Nymphalidae

Wingspan: About 3 in (7.5 cm).

Flight period: All year in tropics; October–April in South Africa.

Larval food plants: Mainly in the nettle family (Urticaceae), e.g., *Urera*, *Fleurya*, and *Urtica*.

Range: Over most of sub-Saharan Africa and on Madagascar.

Common Eggfly

Over its vast range this butterfly is somewhat variable, the largest and finest race being subspecies *nerina*, photographed here on Townsville Common in Queensland, Australia. The male is velvety black with a blue-edged white spot in the center of each wing. The female is very variable, from almost plain bluish black to heavily marked specimens with white patches on all four wings and an orange patch on each forewing. The underside is as seen here in this mating pair. The Common Eggfly is found in most types of habitat, from open woodland to town backyards.

DATA

Scientific name: *Hypolimnas bolina*

Family: Nymphalidae

Wingspan: About 3.2 in (8 cm).

Flight period: All year in north; late summer (January–March) in south.

Larval food plants: In many families.

Range: India to New Guinea, Australia, and Samoa.

Dark Eggfly

DATA

Scientific name: *Hypolimnas deois*

Family: Nymphalidae

Wingspan: About 3.4 in (8.5 cm).

Flight period: All year.

Larval food plants: Various.

Range: Moluccas and New Guinea.

Originally described from the Moluccas, *Hypolimnas deois* is variable. The butterfly illustrated is subspecies *divina* from New Guinea, seen puddling in rain forest at Wau. The very dark brown, unmarked forewings make it obvious that this is a male. In the female the ground color is slightly lighter, and the forewings bear a large whitish patch. In both sexes there is an orange and white patch on each hind wing, plus a few small ocelli. The underside is basically similar, but in the male there is a large whitish patch on the hind wing, bearing five eyespots surrounded by orange.

Malagasy Diadem

DATA

Scientific name: *Hypolimnas dexithea*

Family: Nymphalidae

Wingspan: About 3.5 in (9 cm).

Flight period: All year.

Larval food plants: Unknown.

Range: Madagascar.

This is one of the most beautiful members of the genus. The heavily scalloped hind margins to the wings are picked out with blue lines, while the orange band on the hind wing contrasts beautifully with the white basal area. The underside is reddish brown with a white band across the forewing and a large white patch occupying most of the hind wing. The scalloped margins are picked out in white rather than blue. This species flies mainly near forested rivers, especially in open spots, as shown here in Montagne d'Ambre National Park in the north of Madagascar.

Diadem

In recent years the Diadem has been expanding its worldwide range and has now reached Brazil. It is a butterfly of open grassland and bush, found only in disturbed areas in forest, and can be common in city backyards and on agricultural land around villages. The male is deep velvety black. Each forewing has two oval white patches, with a single patch on each hind wing. Each white patch is surrounded by a narrow diffuse band of iridescent violet. The female, illustrated here puddling in Ghana's Bobiri Forest, is a convincing mimic of the Common Tiger *(Danaus chrysippus)*, although it seldom mimics the *alcippus* morph seen on page 58.

DATA

Scientific name: *Hypolimnas misippus*

Family: Nymphalidae

Wingspan: About 2.8 in (7 cm).

Flight period: All year in tropics; summer in temperate areas.

Larval food plants: Numerous, in several families.

Range: Over much of the world except North America and much of South America.

Blue Diadem

Males of this large species tend to spend much of their time perched high up along a forest track, well out of photographic reach, and dash out to engage in skirmishes with other large butterflies. Fortunately, the male seen here was perched low down, basking on a morning of cool Harmattan winds in Ghana's Bobiri Forest. The blue bands on the male are replaced by white in the female. The three white spots in the black wing apex are missing in the otherwise similar Scarce Blue Diadem *(Hypolimnas monteironis)*. The Blue Diadem is mainly a butterfly of open disturbed forest. Both sexes often puddle on muddy ground.

DATA

Scientific name: *Hypolimnas salmacis*

Family: Nymphalidae

Wingspan: About 3.5 in (9 cm).

Flight period: All year.

Larval food plants: *Fleurya* and *Urera* in the nettle family (Urticaceae).

Range: Africa (Sierra Leone to Tanzania) and on the islands of Bioko and São Tomé.

Peacock

Despite seeing well over 1,000 species of tropical butterflies, the author still considers this to be one of the most strikingly colored butterflies in the world. When at rest, the wings are usually kept closed, exposing the blackish and very leaflike undersides. When danger threatens, the wings are instantly snapped open, suddenly revealing the four large eyespots, a defensive display designed to make a possible enemy back off in surprise. The ground color is a kind of reddish chocolate brown, although this becomes faded in specimens that have overwintered, this being undertaken in the adult stage. The Peacock spends most of its time on flowers, as seen here in England.

DATA

Scientific name: *Inachis io*

Family: Nymphalidae

Wingspan: About 2.2 in (5.5 cm).

Flight period: April–May and July–September.

Larval food plants: Nettles *(Urtica)* in the family Urticaceae.

Range: From western Europe through temperate Asia to Japan.

Queen of Spain Fritillary

DATA

Scientific name: *Issoria lathonia*

Family: Nymphalidae

Wingspan: About 1.6 in (4 cm).

Flight period: Most of the summer, in 2–3 broods.

Larval food plants: Violets *(Viola)* in the family Violaceae.

Range: From Western Europe, North Africa, and the Canary Islands to western China.

A noted migrant, this species is unusual in being able to hibernate as an egg, a caterpillar, or an adult, depending on the local conditions prevailing in the fall. The upper-side coloration and pattern are typical of a fritillary, being a warm brownish orange with a fairly evenly spaced scattering of black dots. The underside of the hind wing is marked with a number of large silvery white spots. This is a butterfly of open places such as rough meadows, flowery roadsides (as seen here in France), and mountainsides.

Handkerchief

DATA

Scientific name: *Janatella leucodesma*

Family: Nymphalidae

Wingspan: About 1.4 in (3.5 cm).

Flight period: All year.

Larval food plants: Unknown.

Range: Nicaragua to Venezuela and Trinidad.

The three species of *Janatella* were formerly included in *Phyciodes*, along with a number of other genera such as *Castilia* and *Tegosa*. The Handkerchief has rather rounded wings that are dark on top. A broad white band crosses each wing, and there is a white patch near the tip of the forewing. Below, the hind wing is mainly white with a brown border containing some blackish eyespots. The forewing is a mixture of black, white, and pale brown. Although sometimes found in the rain-forest interior, this is mainly a butterfly of forest edge, such as roadsides, as seen in the photograph above of a mating pair in Trinidad.

Peacock Pansy

DATA

Scientific name: *Junonia almana*

Family: Nymphalidae

Wingspan: About 1.8 in (4.5 cm).

Flight period: All year.

Larval food plants: Members of the Acanthaceae.

Range: From India and Sri Lanka to China, Japan, and Australia.

Like most members of the genus, this is a butterfly of disturbed areas rather than dense forest. The one illustrated above was in the garden surrounding the headquarters buildings at Thale Ban National Park in southern Thailand. This is subspecies *javana*, which is slightly smaller than subspecies *almana*. The latter is found in areas with marked variations in rainfall, where it develops a distinct dry-season form with more angled wings and undersides that are much more leaflike. This form is only weakly developed in *javana*, which inhabits areas with less seasonal patterns of rainfall.

White-banded Pansy

Restricted to the remaining areas of rain forest found along the eastern side of Madagascar, this butterfly does not seem to be particularly common. In fact, the one shown below photographed in the Ranomafana National Park, was the only specimen seen by the author after six months spent on this fascinating island of biodiversity. As can be seen, on the adult upper side the white band down each wing grades into a subtle shade of blue along its outer edge, and there is a long slender tail from the tip of each hind wing.

DATA

Scientific name: *Junonia andremiaja*

Family: Nymphalidae

Wingspan: About 1.8 in (4.5 cm).

Flight period: All year.

Larval food plants: Members of the Acanthaceae.

Range: Madagascar.

Garden Inspector

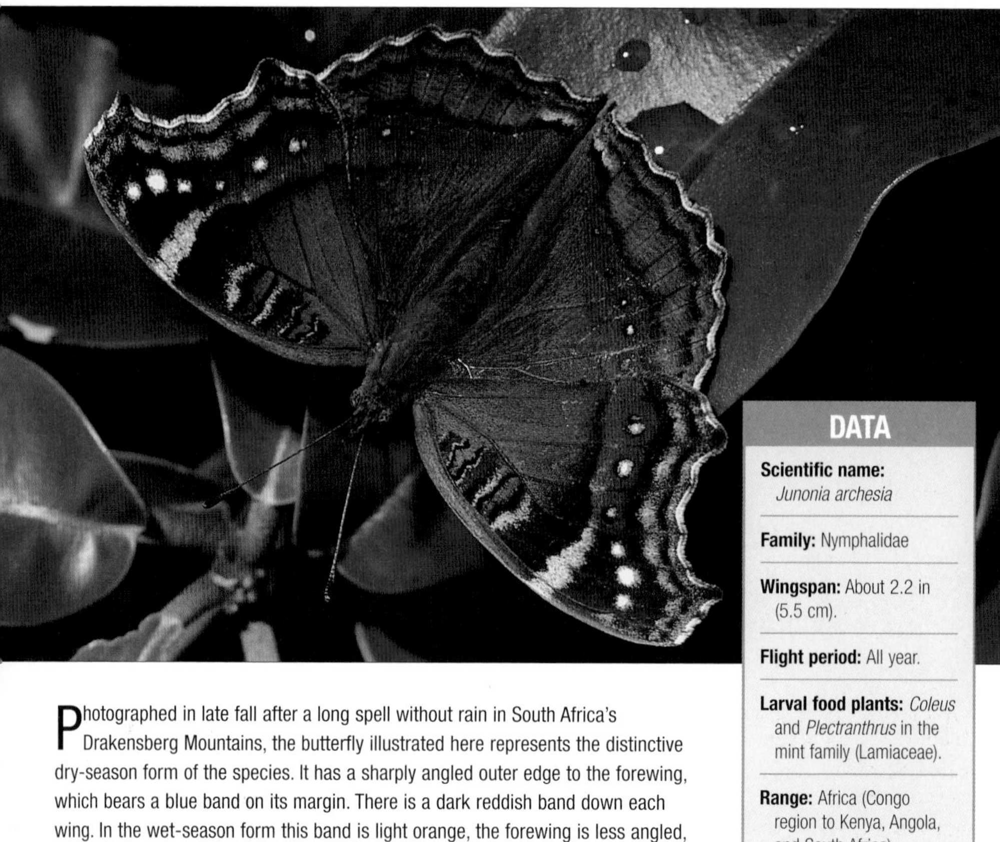

DATA

Scientific name: *Junonia archesia*

Family: Nymphalidae

Wingspan: About 2.2 in (5.5 cm).

Flight period: All year.

Larval food plants: *Coleus* and *Plectranthrus* in the mint family (Lamiaceae).

Range: Africa (Congo region to Kenya, Angola, and South Africa).

Photographed in late fall after a long spell without rain in South Africa's Drakensberg Mountains, the butterfly illustrated here represents the distinctive dry-season form of the species. It has a sharply angled outer edge to the forewing, which bears a blue band on its margin. There is a dark reddish band down each wing. In the wet-season form this band is light orange, the forewing is less angled, and there is no blue band. In both forms the underside resembles a dead leaf. The sexes are similar, but the female is usually larger. This is a common species in open areas such as parks, backyards, and savanna.

Gray Pansy

DATA

Scientific name: *Junonia atlites*

Family: Nymphalidae

Wingspan: About 2.4 in (6 cm).

Flight period: All year.

Larval food plants: *Hygrophila* (Acanthaceae).

Range: Over most of tropical Asia.

With its silvery gray ground color this butterfly is really like no other in the region. The black-and-red eyespots around the hind margins of all four wings are also distinctive and very attractive. As with most members of the genus, the underside of the Gray Pansy looks like a dead leaf. Parks, backyards, roadsides, and open secondary forest is where you will most often find it. The specimen illustrated here was photographed in Malaysia's Taman Negara National Park. As would be expected, it was basking on the edge of the rain forest in one of the backyards near the visitor center rather than in the forest itself, where few butterflies were on show.

Marsh Commodore

DATA

Scientific name: *Junonia ceryne*

Family: Nymphalidae

Wingspan: About 2 in (5 cm).

Flight period: All year.

Larval food plants: Acanthaceae and Dipsacaceae.

Range: Over most of sub-Saharan Africa.

As its name suggests, the Marsh Commodore is associated with swamps and streams, usually in fairly open situations such as savanna and often in hill country, as seen here in the Drakensberg Mountains in South Africa. The wet-season form (illustrated) has a slightly less angular margin to the forewing than the dry-season form. In the latter the underside resembles a dead leaf, while in the wet-season form it is a paler version of the upper side, with its brown ground color and lovely pale orange band on each wing.

Buckeye

DATA

Scientific name: *Junonia coenia*

Family: Nymphalidae

Wingspan: About 2.2 in (5.5 cm).

Flight period: All year in south; in summer farther north.

Larval food plants: Numerous, in many families.

Range: Canada to Mexico, Bermuda, Cuba, and the Bahamas.

Pictured here feeding on flowers on the edge of a desert wash near Saltillo in Coahuila State, Mexico, the Buckeye is found in a wide variety of generally open situations. Flying all year around in Texas, Florida, and southern California, migratory flights take egg-laying females northward in summer, and they sometimes reach as far as Canada. Adults can be distinguished from the Smoky Buckeye *(Junonia evarete)* by the generally much brighter coloration, especially the orange band along the margin of the hind wing, and the generally larger and more iridescent eyespots. The underside is mainly pale brown with a single large eyespot on the forewing.

Smoky Buckeye

DATA

Scientific name: *Junonia evarete*

Family: Nymphalidae

Wingspan: About 2.2 in (5.5 cm).

Flight period: All year.

Larval food plants: Members of Scrophulariaceae and Verbenaceae.

Range: Southern United States to Argentina.

The buckeyes belong to a difficult group, and it is possible that the butterfly currently known as the Smoky Buckeye could, in fact, be a mix of several species. Hybridization with the Buckeye *(Junonia coenia)* also causes complications. In its "classic" dark form, subspecies *nigrosuffusa* (depicted below), the upper side is very dark, especially compared with the Buckeye, and the eyespots are smaller and less brightly colored. The underside is darkish brown with a single largish eyespot (but often smaller than that of the Buckeye) on the forewing. As with most members of the genus, this is an insect of open habitats, pictured here in semidesert near Monte Alban in Oaxaca State, Mexico.

Gregori's Brown Pansy

DATA

Scientific name: *Junonia gregorii*

Family: Nymphalidae

Wingspan: About 2 in (5 cm).

Flight period: All year.

Larval food plants: Various members of the family Acanthaceae.

Range: Africa (Nigeria to Uganda and Kenya).

This rather drab species was formerly regarded as a subspecies of the Brown Pansy *(Junonia stygia)*, but it is generally rather darker than that species and has a more distinct and regular pattern of black markings. In particular, the row of small eyespots on the hind wing is usually far more distinct in *J. gregorii*. The underside is quite leaflike, and the number of eyespots is reduced, but each one is far more distinct than on the upper side. This is a butterfly of forest edges and clearings, photographed here in Kenya's Kakamega Forest.

Brown Soldier

The Brown Soldier is typically found in damp habitats and is pictured here in a swampy clearing in rain forest near Wau in New Guinea. The general coloration is a rather somber shade of brown, with black along the hind margins of the wings and on the tip of the forewing. There is a row of small eyespots along the margins of the wings, most noticeable on the hind wings. The underside is dark brown and very like a dead leaf. This is a variable butterfly, and several races occur, some of which lack any black on the upper side.

DATA

Scientific name: *Junonia hedonia*

Family: Nymphalidae

Wingspan: About 2.4 in (6 cm).

Flight period: All year.

Larval food plants: Various.

Range: Moluccas, New Guinea, Australia, Solomons, and various other Pacific islands

Yellow Pansy

DATA

Scientific name: *Junonia hierta*

Family: Nymphalidae

Wingspan: About 2 in (5 cm).

Flight period: All year.

Larval food plants: *Justicia*, *Asystasia*, etc. (Acanthaceae).

Range: Over most of Africa and the Arabian Peninsula eastward to India and Myanmar (Burma); also on Madagascar.

Although members of this genus are most often found on flowers and in the tropics are often almost the only butterflies commonly seen in such situations, they occasionally feed on damp ground, as seen here in the Kirindy Forest in Madagascar. This is subspecies *paris*, which is restricted to Madagascar. The ground color varies from yellow to a fairly rich orange (as seen here), with blackish borders and margins to the wings and a bright blue iridescent spot on each hind wing. This is an abundant species in bush country, savanna, open forests, and backyards.

Gaudy Commodore

There is no butterfly in the world that occurs in such spectacularly different seasonal forms as the Gaudy Commodore. In fact, the two forms were originally described as separate species. The dry-season form (illustrated) is iridescent blue with a row of red spots down each wing. The underside is very like a brown dead leaf. The wet-season form is orange on both sides with a pinkish flush and is also much smaller. The dry-season form spends much of its time hidden away in caves or holes in termite mounds but also visits flowers. Seen here is subspecies *sesamus*, photographed in typical open grassy habitat in South Africa's Drakensberg Mountains.

DATA

Scientific name: *Junonia octavia*

Family: Nymphalidae

Wingspan: 1.8–2.8 in (4.5–7 cm).

Flight period: All year.

Larval food plants: *Coleus*, *Rabdosia*, etc., in the mint family (Lamiaceae).

Range: Over most of sub-Saharan Africa.

Blue Pansy

In just about any open weedy spot over much of Africa, whether it be a backyard, roadside verge, city waste lot or forest clearing, this will often be the first butterfly to be seen. The basic upper side coloration is black, with a few white spots on the forewings and in a row down the hind-wing margins. The most conspicuous feature of the male (as seen here in Madagascar) is the large iridescent blue spot on each hind wing. This may be present in a reduced and rather paler form on the female, but may also be absent. The underside is mainly yellowish brown.

DATA

Scientific name: *Junonia oenone*

Family: Nymphalidae

Wingspan: About 2.2 in (5 cm).

Flight period: All year.

Larval food plants: *Barleria, Justicia, Ruellia,* etc. (Acanthaceae).

Range: Most of sub-Saharan Africa; also on the Arabian Peninsula and Madagascar.

Eyed Pansy

Originally described in 1758 from China, this widespread butterfly is split into several subspecies, of which this is *madagascariensis* from Africa and Madagascar. This is a butterfly of open places and it can be common in backyards, even in large cities. In the male, photographed here while basking on a pile of buffalo dung in savanna in the Masai Mara in Kenya, the upper side is a rich dark blue, with white-spotted black wing tips and several small orange-ringed eyespots. The female is blackish blue near the wing bases, paler blue beyond, with much larger eyespots than in the male. The underside is fairly leaflike.

DATA

Scientific name: *Junonia orithya*

Family: Nymphalidae

Wingspan: About 1.8 in (4.5 cm).

Flight period: All year.

Larval food plants: In many families.

Range: From Africa and Madagascar through the Middle East to China, New Guinea, and Australia.

Common Commodore

DATA

Scientific name: *Junonia pelarga*

Family: Nymphalidae

Wingspan: About 2 in (5 cm).

Flight period: All year.

Larval food plants: *Solenostemon rotundifolius* and *Coleus* in the mint family (Lamiaceae); sometimes also cocoa *(Theobroma cacao)* in the Sterculiaceae.

Range: West and Central Africa.

As with a number of other species, the Common Commodore exhibits two distinct seasonal forms. The butterfly pictured here in Bobiri Forest, Ghana, is the female dry-season form. Note how the margin of the forewing is so heavily scalloped that it produces a hooked tip. The broad bands across each wing are a beautiful light pinkish blue, edged with red. In the wet-season form these bands are pale orange, and the forewing is not hooked at the tip. The underside is pale orange with darker margins, while in the dry-season form the underside resembles a dead leaf. The Common Commodore is found in all types of forest, in well-wooded savanna and in backyards, even coming into large cities.

Royal-blue Pansy

DATA

Scientific name: *Junonia rhadama*

Family: Nymphalidae

Flight period: All year.

Larval food plants: Members of the Acanthaceae.

Range: Madagascar.

Despite supposedly being a common and widespread species on Madagascar, during six months on the island the author found the beautiful Royal-blue Pansy only in one place—in the Parc Tsimbazaza in the capital city, Antananarivo. This park is home to the zoological gardens, and dozens of Royal-blue Pansies were fluttering around in the semiwild areas between the exhibits. In some ways this species is like the Eyed Pansy *(Junonia orithya),* but it has more blue and lacks the black on the forewings. In the male there is only a single red-ringed eyespot on each hind wing, as opposed to the two found in the female illustrated above.

Little Commodore

One of the most common African butterflies, the Little Commodore is found in all kinds of habitats from open forest to savanna, riversides, city parks, and backyards. In large tracts of rain forest it occurs only in cleared areas or along broad logging roads. It is seen here basking on the weeds that spring up in abundance in the camping area in Kakamega Forest, Kenya. The ground color is blackish brown, the basal area of the forewing being a rich chestnut. There are pale orange or yellowish bands down each wing. The underside is lighter and bears a complex pattern.

DATA

Scientific name: *Junonia sophia*

Family: Nymphalidae

Wingspan: About 1.6 in (4 cm).

Flight period: All year.

Larval food plants: Various Acanthaceae.

Range: West Africa to Zambia and Malawi.

Soldier Commodore

DATA

Scientific name: *Junonia terea*

Family: Nymphalidae

Flight period: All year.

Larval food plants: Various Acanthaceae.

Range: Over most of sub-Saharan Africa.

The ground color of this rather round-winged butterfly is blackish brown. Each wing bears a broad pale orange band, while the base is a pale brown color. There are a few blue-centered red eyespots near the wing margins, especially near the rear margin of the hind wing. The underside is basically straw colored. No other butterfly resembles this species to any great extent, making it instantly recognizable in the field. The Soldier Commodore is most likely to be seen along logging roads in forest or in cleared areas around buildings, its presence being a sure indicator of habitat disturbance.

Andean Buckeye

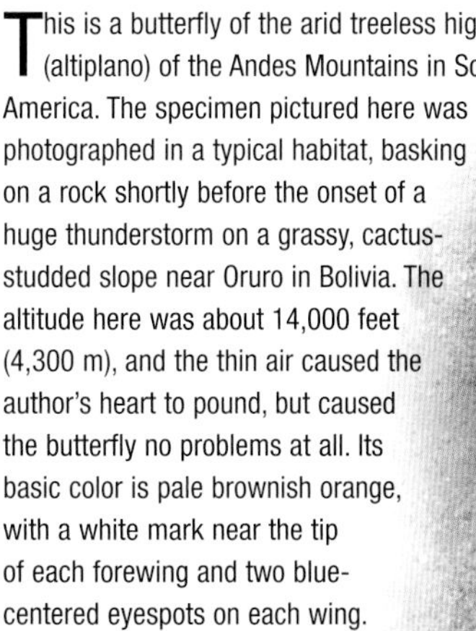

This is a butterfly of the arid treeless high plains (altiplano) of the Andes Mountains in South America. The specimen pictured here was photographed in a typical habitat, basking on a rock shortly before the onset of a huge thunderstorm on a grassy, cactus-studded slope near Oruro in Bolivia. The altitude here was about 14,000 feet (4,300 m), and the thin air caused the author's heart to pound, but caused the butterfly no problems at all. Its basic color is pale brownish orange, with a white mark near the tip of each forewing and two blue-centered eyespots on each wing.

DATA

Scientific name: *Junonia vestina*

Family: Nymphalidae

Wingspan: About 1.8 in (4.5 cm).

Flight period: Mainly November–April.

Larval food plants: Various.

Range: Bolivia and Peru.

Blue-spot Pansy

This species in unusual in the genus in having males and females that look like different species. In the male—seen here on a campsite in savanna in Kenya's Masai Mara national reserve—the ground color is a deep velvety black. There is a large orange patch on each wing and a blue patch near the front edge of the hind wing. The female is much drabber, being a dull brownish red with deeper brown veins. In both sexes the underside is reasonably leaflike. Although mainly a forest butterfly, the Blue-spot Pansy is also found in savanna if sufficient trees are present.

DATA

Scientific name: *Junonia westermannii*

Family: Nymphalidae

Wingspan: About 2.2 in (5.5 cm).

Flight period: All year.

Larval food plants: Members of the Acanthaceae and Amaranthaceae.

Range: Africa (Côte d'Ivoire to Ethiopia, Kenya, and Tanzania).

African Leaf Butterfly

Although the underside of this forest butterfly provides a good imitation of a dead leaf, the adults never seem to roost among dead leaves; instead, they always hang beneath green plants. The males often perch on leaves, ready to intercept intruding butterflies, as seen here in the forest below Wli Falls in Ghana. Note how the tip of the hind wing is drawn out to suggest a leaf stalk. Above, the male is dark brown with a broad violet band across the forewing. The apical third of the forewing is almost black and is crossed by a small orange band. The female is also brown, with a broad whitish band on the forewing and usually also on the hind wing.

DATA

Scientific name: *Kallimoides rumia*

Family: Nymphalidae

Wingspan: About 2.8 in (7 cm).

Flight period: All year.

Larval food plants: *Brillantaisia* (Acanthaceae).

Range: West Africa to Tanzania.

The Archduke

DATA

Scientific name: *Lexias dirtea*

Family: Nymphalidae

Wingspan: About 3.2 in (8 cm).

Flight period: All year.

Larval food plants: *Calophyllum* (Clusiaceae).

Range: India to the Philippines.

For many years this species was included in the genus *Euthalia*. The only way to distinguish it from the almost identical *Lexias pardalis* is by looking at the tip of the antenna. This is black above (but orange below) in *dirtea* and orange all over in *pardalis*. In the male (illustrated) the wings are deep blackish brown with a broad blue band along the rear margin of the hind wing and a narrower greenish blue band on the forewing margin. The female is totally different, being brown with a dense scatter of golden spots. Both sexes feed on muddy patches in forest, as seen here in Bako National Park in Borneo.

Southern White Admiral

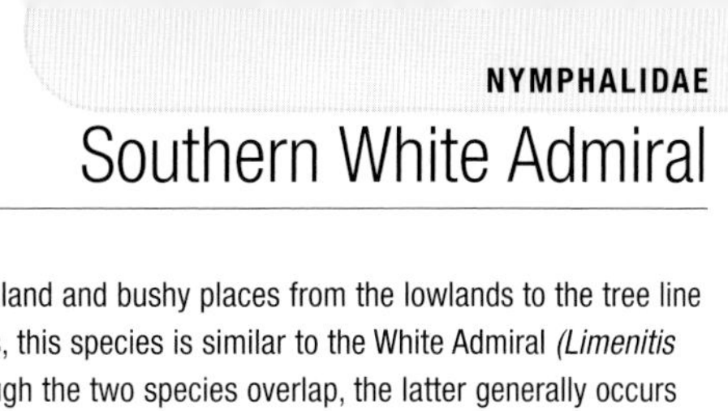

Found in woodland and bushy places from the lowlands to the tree line on mountains, this species is similar to the White Admiral *(Limenitis camilla)*. Although the two species overlap, the latter generally occurs farther north. The obvious difference lies in the row of spots near the hind-wing margin. As can be seen in the photograph, there is a single row in this species, but in *L. camilla* there is a double row. In both species the upper side is bluish black with a series of white patches forming partial bars on each wing, which are almost complete on the hind wing. The adult seen here in dark woodland in France had recently emerged from its chrysalis.

DATA

Scientific name: *Limenitis reducta*

Family: Nymphalidae

Wingspan: About 2 in (5 cm).

Flight period: May onward in 2–3 broods in south; in Switzerland single brood in July.

Larval food plants: Honeysuckle *(Lonicera)* in the Loranthaceae.

Range: Southern and central Europe to Syria and Iran.

Classic West Indian

DATA

Scientific name: *Lucinia sida*

Family: Nymphalidae

Wingspan: About 1.8 in (3.5 cm).

Flight period: All year.

Larval food plants: *Serjania diversifolia* (Sapindaceae).

Range: Cuba, Hispaniola, and the Bahamas.

This is a relatively local species, found on just three West Indian islands, although it can be common where it occurs. The specimen pictured here was photographed in a hotel garden on Cuba, although open forest or coastal mangrove swamps would be a more typical habitat. The upper side is rather drab, and it is the underside that bears the most striking pattern, as seen here. The underside of the forewings is mainly pale brownish orange, with dark tips bearing a white spot. The edges of the hind wings are heavily scalloped.

Orange Daggerwing

As its name suggests, the Orange Daggerwing is distinguished from other similar butterflies by the pale orange ground color of the upper side. The pattern of black bars is not unlike that found in *Marpesia alcibiades*, but that species is brown. The underside of *M. berania* is a dull yellow. This is a butterfly of many different habitats, although it is most common in rain forest, as shown by this specimen seen puddling in Peru's Tingo Maria National Park. This species is known to form large nocturnal roosts of 50 or more individuals that may remain faithful to the roost for a period of several months.

DATA

Scientific name: *Marpesia berania*

Family: Nymphalidae

Wingspan: About 2.4 in (6 cm).

Flight period: All year.

Larval food plants: Members of the fig family (Moraceae).

Range: From Mexico southward throughout the American tropics.

Crethon Daggerwing

DATA

Scientific name: *Marpesia crethon*

Family: Nymphalidae

Wingspan: About 2.4 in (6 cm).

Flight period: All year.

Larval food plants: Members of the fig family (Moraceae).

Range: Venezuela and Colombia to Peru.

As with all other members of the genus, this species bears a long tail near the tip of each hind wing, hence the generic common name of daggerwings. Daggerwings are sometimes found on flowers but are more often seen puddling on damp ground, as here in Peru's Tingo Maria National Park. This species is very similar to *Marpesia orsilochus*, which also has a single white bar down each brown wing. However, in *M. crethon* there is a scattering of unconnected white spots on the outer half of the forewing, whereas in *M. orsilochus* there is rather a faint white bar. Note the red eyespots forming a "false head" on the hind wings.

Red Daggerwing

It is the distinctly hooked tip of the forewing that makes this species instantly recognizable. The wings are, in fact, a dull shade of orange rather than red. The males often puddle on mud, but both sexes visit flowers, as seen here in tropical dry forest in Santa Rosa National Park, Costa Rica. The Red Daggerwing also occurs in rain forest, disturbed habitats, and even in city backyards. In the United States it is resident only in Florida, but migrants from Mexico often reach Texas and sometimes fly as far north as Nebraska. When at rest, adults often hang beneath a leaf with their wings closed, bearing a strong resemblance to brown dead leaves.

DATA

Scientific name: *Marpesia petreus*

Family: Nymphalidae

Wingspan: About 3 in (7.5 cm).

Flight period: All year.

Larval food plants: Figs *(Ficus)* in the family Moraceae.

Range: Southern United States to Argentina.

Purple-washed Daggerwing

DATA

Scientific name: *Marpesia themistocles*

Family: Nymphalidae

Wingspan: About 2.4 in (6 cm).

Flight period: All year.

Larval food plants: Members of the fig family (Moraceae).

Range: Over much of tropical South America.

This is one of the drabber members of the genus. Its upper side is generally dark brown with a broad band of paler brown along the outer margin of the forewing. The underside is leaflike, with a falcate forewing and a relatively long tail on the hind wing. The shade of brown is much paler than on the upper side and is suffused with a beautiful purplish pink sheen that is just visible here on the lower half of the hind wing. This individual was photographed as it puddled on the ground in rain forest in Tingo Maria National Park, Peru.

Spotted Fritillary

The Spotted Fritillary occurs in three subspecies, of which this is *meridionalis*, photographed in the Pyrenees Mountains in France. This subspecies lives on mountain slopes and has just a single brood, usually in June and July. As can be seen in this mating pair, the underside is mainly white with orange bands and numerous black spots. The upper side is the usual fritillary combination of brownish orange with black markings, but these are generally scarcer and less distinct than in most other species. In the females the ground color is often partly obscured by a distinctive silvery suffusion.

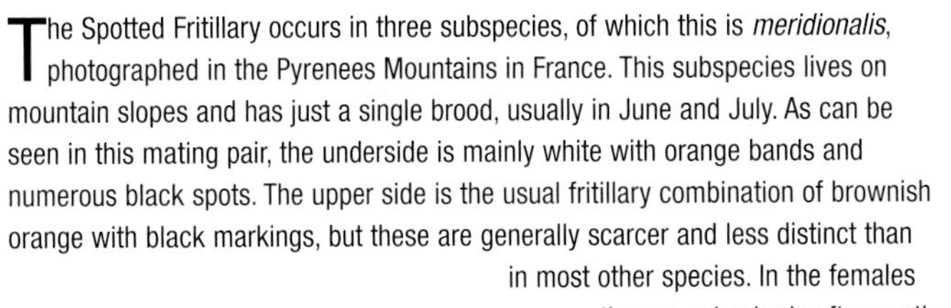

DATA

Scientific name: *Melitaea didyma*

Family: Nymphalidae

Wingspan: About 1.6 in (4 cm).

Flight period: May onward, in several broods.

Larval food plants: Mainly plantain *(Plantago)* in the Plantaginaceae and toadflax *(Linaria)* in the Scrophulariaceae.

Distribution: From southern and Western Europe and North Africa to central Asia.

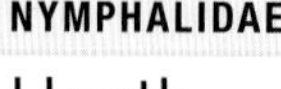

Heath Fritillary

DATA

Scientific name: *Mellicta athalia*

Family: Nymphalidae

Wingspan: About 1.4 in (3.5 cm).

Flight period: Mainly June–July.

Larval food plants: Mainly plantain *(Plantago)* in the Plantaginaceae and cow wheat *(Melampyrum)* in the Scrophulariaceae.

Range: From Western Europe through temperate Asia to Japan.

Over most of Europe this is the commonest and most widespread member of the genus. It is also very variable, which has led to the description of several subspecies. This is subspecies *athalia*, found north of the Alps and photographed here in southern England, where it is extremely rare. In fact, the colony to which this specimen belonged went extinct two years after this picture was taken. Outside England the habitat varies from moorland and mountainsides to flowery meadows and roadsides. The underside is unusual—it is patterned with brown, as is typical in many fritillaries, but without any white spots.

The Elf

Although it occasionally strays north into Arizona and Texas, this single member of the genus *Microtia* is a tropical butterfly. It is seen here in dry forest in Santa Rosa National Park, Costa Rica. Much of the forest in this area has been converted to pasture, where this butterfly is generally more common than in the nearby undisturbed forest. In rain forest it is restricted to associated pasture and open areas. The dark brown wings with their orange patches are like those of no other species, allowing instant recognition in the field. The underside is much drabber.

DATA

Scientific name: *Microtia elva*

Family: Nymphalidae

Wingspan: About 1.2 in (3 cm).

Flight period: All year.

Larval food plants: Unknown.

Range: Southern United States to Costa Rica.

Orsis Bluewing

The 10 members of the genus *Myscelia* can be recognized by the blue banding on the upper side, the hooked apex to the forewing, and the cryptic underside. In this species the wing margins are black and there are some faint white "chalk marks" here and there, as well as an inconspicuous dark red spot on the black tip of the forewing. The underside is mainly dark and drab, like a dead leaf. This is a rain-forest butterfly, photographed here as it basked briefly on a leaf in the private reserve at Rancho Grande in Brazilian Amazonia. Both sexes feed on rotting fruits.

DATA

Scientific name: *Myscelia orsis*

Family: Nymphalidae

Wingspan: About 1.8 in (4.5 cm).

Flight period: All year.

Larval food plants: Members of the spurge family (Euphorbiaceae).

Range: Honduras, Colombia, and Peru to Brazil and Argentina.

Eastern Scalloped Sailor

DATA

Scientific name: *Neptidopsis fulgurata*

Family: Nymphalidae

Wingspan: About 1.8 in (4.5 cm).

Flight period: All year.

Larval food plants: *Dalechampia* and *Tragia* (Euphorbiaceae).

Range: Kenya, Tanzania, South Africa, and Madagascar.

This is one of just two species in *Neptidopsis*. On both the upper side and the underside the wings are a patchwork of black and white, paler on the underside, as seen here. This specimen—photographed in Kirindy Forest in Madagascar—is roosting in the early evening. By hanging head downward from a twig and spreading its forewings away from its hind wings (in a manner never usually seen in living butterflies), it managed to create a very convincing imitation of a silvery dead leaf. This is a species of dry forest, found mainly on the coast in its east African range.

Scalloped Sailor

The Scalloped Sailor looks very much like a species of *Neptis* and is often wrongly included as such in collections. However, despite the visual similarity, there is no close biological relationship. In particular, the forewing veins have swollen bases, which is never true of *Neptis*. The Scalloped Sailor is a butterfly of forest edges and secondary growth. The mating pair shown here was photographed in Kenya's Kakamega Forest. The wings are mainly black with broad white bands, but paler on the underside.

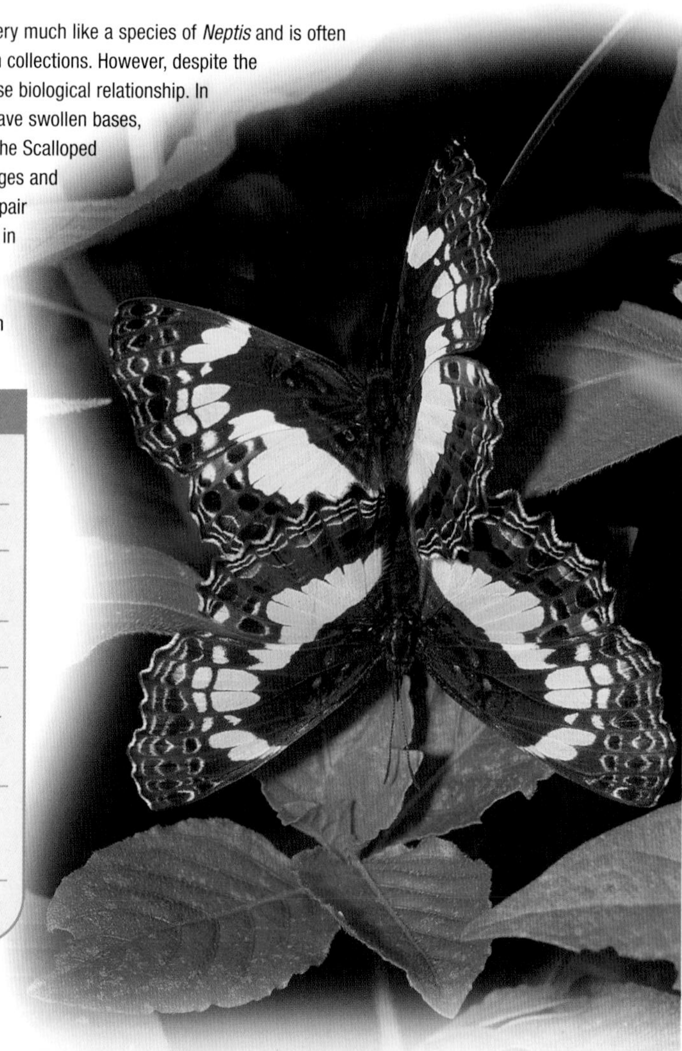

DATA

Scientific name: *Neptidopsis ophione*

Family: Nymphalidae

Wingspan: About 1.8 in (4.5 cm).

Flight period: All year.

Larval food plants: *Tragia benthamii* and probably castor-oil plant *(Ricinus communis)* in the family Euphorbiaceae.

Range: Over most of sub-Saharan Africa, south to Zimbabwe and Mozambique.

Common Club-dot Sailor

The genus *Neptis* contains some 150 described species, of which just less than a half occur in Africa. This is a difficult group, and numerous additional species undoubtedly remain to be described. With just one or two exceptions, all the African species are black and white, as with the species pictured here in Kenya's Kakamega Forest. It is the commonest member of the genus and also one of the most common of all African forest butterflies. Unlike some *Neptis*, it is able to thrive in severely disturbed forests. As with all members of the genus, the underside is similar to the upper side but paler.

DATA

Scientific name: *Neptis agouale*

Family: Nymphalidae

Wingspan: About 1.6 in (4 cm).

Flight period: All year.

Larval food plant: *Abrus canescens*, *Acacia ataxacantha*, *Dalbergia hostilis* in the pea family (Fabaceae).

Range: West Africa to Tanzania and Zambia.

Common Sailor

DATA

Scientific name: *Neptis hylas*

Family: Nymphalidae

Wingspan: About 1.6 in (4 cm).

Flight period: All year.

Larval food plants: In many different families.

Range: India and Sri Lanka to China, Japan, and Indonesia.

Found in a wide variety of wooded habitats, over its huge range this common species has been split into a plethora of subspecies. However, since many of them probably grade into one another, they are likely to be of little real significance. This is subspecies *kamarupa*, photographed in Thale Ban National Park in southern Thailand. This subspecies merges gradually into subspecies *papaja* of northern Thailand. There are numerous black-and-white species similar to this one; all are difficult to tell apart without looking at the detail of the white bars and spots.

Variable Sailor

Sailors seldom visit flowers or fermenting fruits but are often seen puddling on muddy ground, as here in Ghana's Bobiri Forest. This species may not be as variable as its common name implies because it probably constitutes a number of different species (up to a dozen or more) that have yet to be suitably separated from one another and described. At present it is easier to distinguish the larvae rather than the adults, most of which are superficially similar to the one illustrated here. This is a butterfly of seasonally dry forests, occurring mainly in disturbed areas within wetter forest types.

DATA

Scientific name: *Neptis nysiades*

Family: Nymphalidae

Wingspan: About 1.8 in (4.5 cm).

Flight period: All year.

Larval food plants: Unknown.

Range: West Africa to the Congo region and Angola.

Velvet Olive

Just five species from Central and South America make up the genus *Nessaea*. They are easily distinguished by their green undersides, although it is possible that *Nessaea* will eventually prove to be part of *Catonephele*. All the species feed on rotting fallen fruit, as seen here in a swampy area of rain forest in the Tambopata National Reserve in Peru, a typical habitat. This shows a very newly emerged adult in which the black of the wings is extremely intense and velvety, contrasting with the blue bar on each forewing and the orange hind-wing bars. The underside is mainly green. For a long time this species was known as *N. ancaeus*.

DATA

Scientific name: *Nessaea obrinus*

Family: Nymphalidae

Wingspan: About 2.6 in (6.5 cm).

Flight period: All year.

Larval food plants: *Alchornea* (Euphorbiaceae).

Range: Over most of the South American tropics.

Large Tortoiseshell

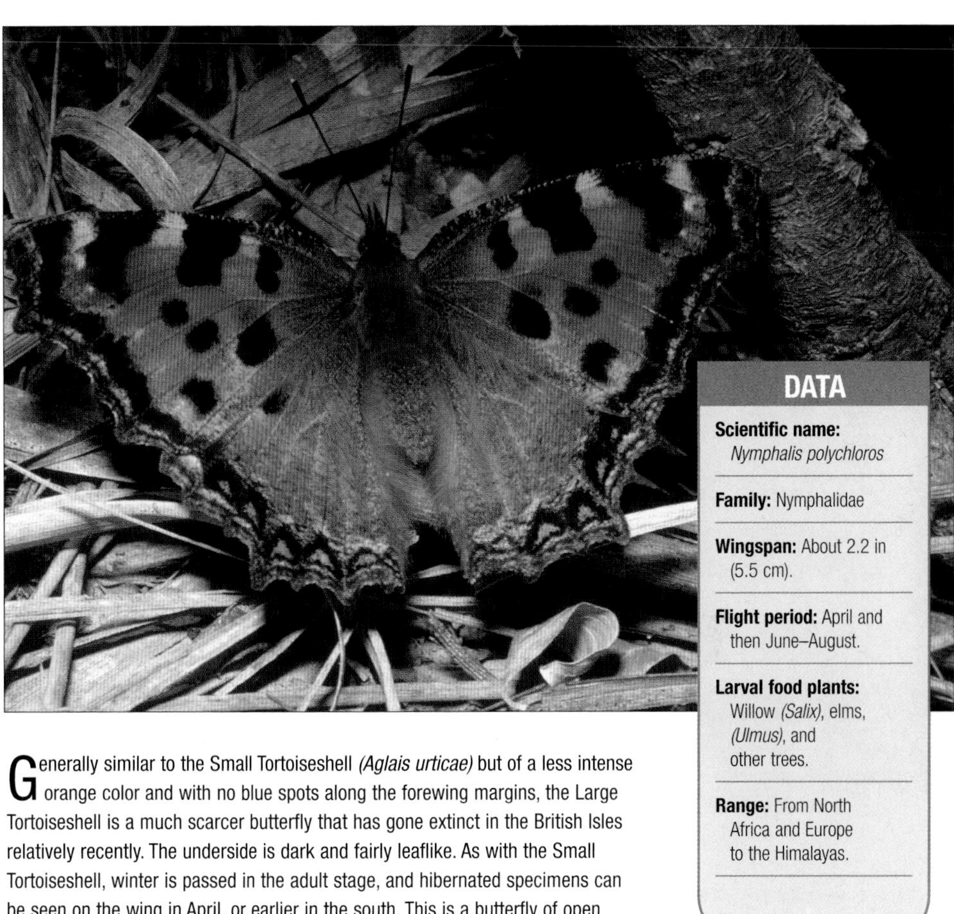

DATA

Scientific name: *Nymphalis polychloros*

Family: Nymphalidae

Wingspan: About 2.2 in (5.5 cm).

Flight period: April and then June–August.

Larval food plants: Willow *(Salix)*, elms, *(Ulmus)*, and other trees.

Range: From North Africa and Europe to the Himalayas.

Generally similar to the Small Tortoiseshell *(Aglais urticae)* but of a less intense orange color and with no blue spots along the forewing margins, the Large Tortoiseshell is a much scarcer butterfly that has gone extinct in the British Isles relatively recently. The underside is dark and fairly leaflike. As with the Small Tortoiseshell, winter is passed in the adult stage, and hibernated specimens can be seen on the wing in April, or earlier in the south. This is a butterfly of open woodland, pictured here in France.

Ussher's Palla

DATA

Scientific name: *Palla ussheri*

Family: Nymphalidae

Wingspan: About 3 in (7.5 cm).

Flight period: All year.

Larval food plants: *Dichapetalum* (family Dichapetalaceae), *Prevostea breviflora* and *Bonomia* (family Convolvulaceae), and *Toddalia* (family Rutaceae).

Range: West Africa to Tanzania and Zambia.

There are just four species in the genus *Palla*, all of which are restricted to the tropical regions of Africa. The males perch on low vegetation, especially along forest roads (as seen here in Ghana's Bobiri Forest) and rush out to intercept passing butterflies. In this species the male can be distinguished by the fact that most of the hind-wing band is reddish brown, while the white forewing band is narrow and barely tinged with blue. The female is broadly similar but much paler. The underside is somewhat like a dead leaf. This is the commonest member of the genus and is found in most forest types.

Common Leopard Fritillary

This widespread butterfly has been split into three subspecies. This is *aethiopica*, found over much of Africa and southwestern Arabian Peninsula, including most of the offshore islands (except on Socotra, where subspecies *granti* is present). The upper side is yellowish orange with a few black spots and a row of black V-shaped spots around the wing margins. The underside is similar but much paler. Mainly found in open dry woodland and savanna, this species also occurs in cleared areas in rain forest, as here in Kenya's Kakamega Forest.

DATA

Scientific name: *Phalanta phalantha*

Family: Nymphalidae

Wingspan: About 2 in (5 cm).

Flight period: All year.

Larval food plants: Very varied.

Range: Much of Asia, Arabian Peninsula, Africa.

Field Crescent

The Field Crescent could easily be mistaken for some of the checkerspots or fritillaries, but it is a considerably smaller butterfly. The upper-side ground color is blackish with a pattern of brownish orange spots and pale fringes. The underside is yellowish brown with rusty markings and two to three small black patches on the inner margin of the forewing. The Field Crescent is found in a variety of open habitats, such as streamsides, fields, meadows, woodland clearings, and roadsides, as seen here in Wyoming.

DATA

Scientific name: *Phyciodes campestris*

Wingspan: About 1.2 in (3 cm).

Flight period: April–October, depending on location and altitude.

Larval food plants: Various members of the sunflower family (Asteraceae).

Range: Alaska to Mexico, but only west of the Great Plains.

Pearl Crescent

DATA

Scientific name: *Phyciodes tharos*

Family: Nymphalidae

Wingspan: About 1.2 in (3 cm).

Flight period: All year in south; May–August in north.

Larval food plants: Members of the sunflower family (Asteraceae).

Range: Alberta to Mexico, omitting a large area west of the Great Plains.

Because of the large amount of orange on the upper side, this is one of the more attractive of the crescents. It is similar to the noticeably larger Orange Crescent *(Phyclodes morpheus)*, in which the orange markings are not divided by such prominent dark lines. In both species the underside is much paler with a few dark markings. In some localities these two very similar butterflies can be difficult to tell apart. The Pearl Crescent tends to be found in moist habitats, such as damp meadows, moist prairie, and streamsides, as seen here in South Carolina.

Arachne Checkerspot

DATA

Scientific name: *Poladryas arachne*

Family: Nymphalidae

Wingspan: About 1.6 in (4 cm).

Flight period: April–September.

Larval food plants: Beardtongue *(Penstemon)*, family Scrophulariaceae.

Range: United States (over most of the Southwest).

This small checkerspot is found mainly in flowery mountain fields and meadows, but also occurs in hot lowland deserts, as seen here in Arizona. The upper side is dark brownish orange with a pattern of distinct dark lines. The underside, as seen here in a mating pair, is an attractive mosaic of white, orange, and black. The white spots of the hind-wing margins are edged with black. Courtship and mating in this species often take place on and around flowers, mostly belonging to the sunflower family (Asteraceae), as is the case here.

Comma

DATA

Scientific name: *Polygonia c-album*

Family: Nymphalidae

Wingspan: About 1.8 in (4.5 cm).

Flight period: March–April; June and August.

Larval food plants: Various, especially nettle *(Urtica)*, elm *(Ulmus)*, and hop *(Humulus)*.

Range: Europe and North Africa to Japan.

As can be seen in this specimen photographed on the edge of an English woodland, this butterfly's resemblance to a shriveled, ragged-edged oak leaf is very close. The white commalike marking on the underside gives rise to its name. The upper side is brownish orange, with a somewhat irregular pattern of black marks. The Comma hibernates as an adult during winter, emerging in March or April. It is found in many kinds of habitats, such as parks, backyards, roadsides, and woodland edges. In North America there are five species of *Polygonia*, of which the most similar species to this is the Green Comma *(P. faunus)*.

Question Mark

DATA

Scientific name: *Polygonia interrogationis*

Family: Nymphalidae

Wingspan: About 2.8 in (7 cm).

Flight period: June to early August, then again in late August.

Larval food plants: Elms *(Ulmus)*, nettles *(Urtica)*, and hops *(Humulus)*.

Range: Southern Canada to Mexico, but absent from much of the west.

This is the largest member of the genus in North America. Unlike the others, the wing margins in the Question Mark are not ragged, although the forewing is noticeably hooked and there is a prominent tail on each hind wing. The orange and black pattern on the upper side is not dissimilar from that of the other species in the genus, including the Comma *(Polygonia c-album)*, although the pale wing borders of the Question Mark are unique. The underside is pale brown, with a conspicuous white "question mark." Wooded areas are its favored habitat, but this species can be common in suburban parks and backyards, as seen here in New Jersey.

Western Blue Beauty

DATA

Scientific name: *Protogoniomorpha cytora*

Family: Nymphalidae

Flight period: All year.

Wingspan: About 3.2 in (8 cm).

Larval food plants: Acanthaceae.

Range: West Africa (Guinea to Togo).

It seems to be quite rare to find this beautiful butterfly feeding; it is most often seen perched on low vegetation along a logging road or track through rain forest, as here in Ghana's Bobiri Forest. This is a female, distinguishable by the whitish patches on her blackish brown wings. In the males, which spend much of their time dive-bombing passing butterflies, the wing patches are blue. As with several other members of this genus, the underside is a passable imitation of a brown dead leaf.

Forest Mother-of-pearl

DATA

Scientific name: *Protogoniomorpha parhassus*

Family: Nymphalidae

Wingspan: About 3.5 in (9 cm).

Flight period: All year.

Larval food plants: *Brillantaisia*, *Isoglossa*, *Justicia*, and other Acanthaceae.

Range: Over most of the forested parts of Africa except for the far south.

When walking along a forest track just about anywhere in Africa, it is common for one of these large butterflies to fly up from beneath a leaf as you approach. That is where it will have spent the night, or most of the day if it is dull, invariably hanging with its head downward and exposing its silvery underside like a pale dead leaf. Each wing bears two red, white, and blue eyespots, as seen below in this male, which was puddling on a muddy track in Kenya's Kakamega Forest. The upper side is silver with a lovely lilac sheen and some black spots.

Eastern Blue Beauty

The underside of this large and spectacular butterfly could easily be dismissed as being merely "dull brown" but, as the accompanying illustration shows, there is a subtle blue sheen across large parts of each wing, and some attractive eyespots. In males the upper side is a brilliant metallic blue, grading into brown toward the rear of the hind wing, which bears a single large eyespot and three very tiny ones. The female is similar but less intensely blue. Although mainly a forest butterfly, seen here in Kenya's Kakamega Forest, this species is also found in open agricultural areas.

DATA

Scientific name: *Protogoniomorpha temora*

Family: Nymphalidae

Wingspan: About 3.2 in (8 cm).

Flight period: All year.

Larval food plants: Acanthaceae.

Range: Africa (Nigeria to Sudan, Ethiopia, the Congo region, Kenya, and Tanzania).

Common False Legionnaire

DATA

Scientific name: *Pseudacraea eurytus*

Family: Nymphalidae

Wingspan: About 2.8 in (7 cm).

Flight period: All year.

Larval food plants: Sapotaceae such as *Chrysophyllum*, *Malacantha*, and *Aningeria*.

Range: West Africa to Uganda and Tanzania.

This species occurs in a number of different forms, which are superb mimics of some of the larger legionnaires formerly in *Bematistes*, such as the Jodutta Legionnaire *(Acraea jodutta)*. Unlike the Mocker Swallowtail *(Papilio dardanus)* and the Diadem *(Hypolimnas misippus)*, both sexes of *Pseudacraea eurytus* are mimetic. The great variation observed in the species means it is impossible to give a description except to say that two basic patterns are involved: brownish orange with black or white with black. Several forms usually fly together and have been thought of as separate species, but recent molecular evidence suggests otherwise. Forest is the main habitat, as here at Bobiri in Ghana.

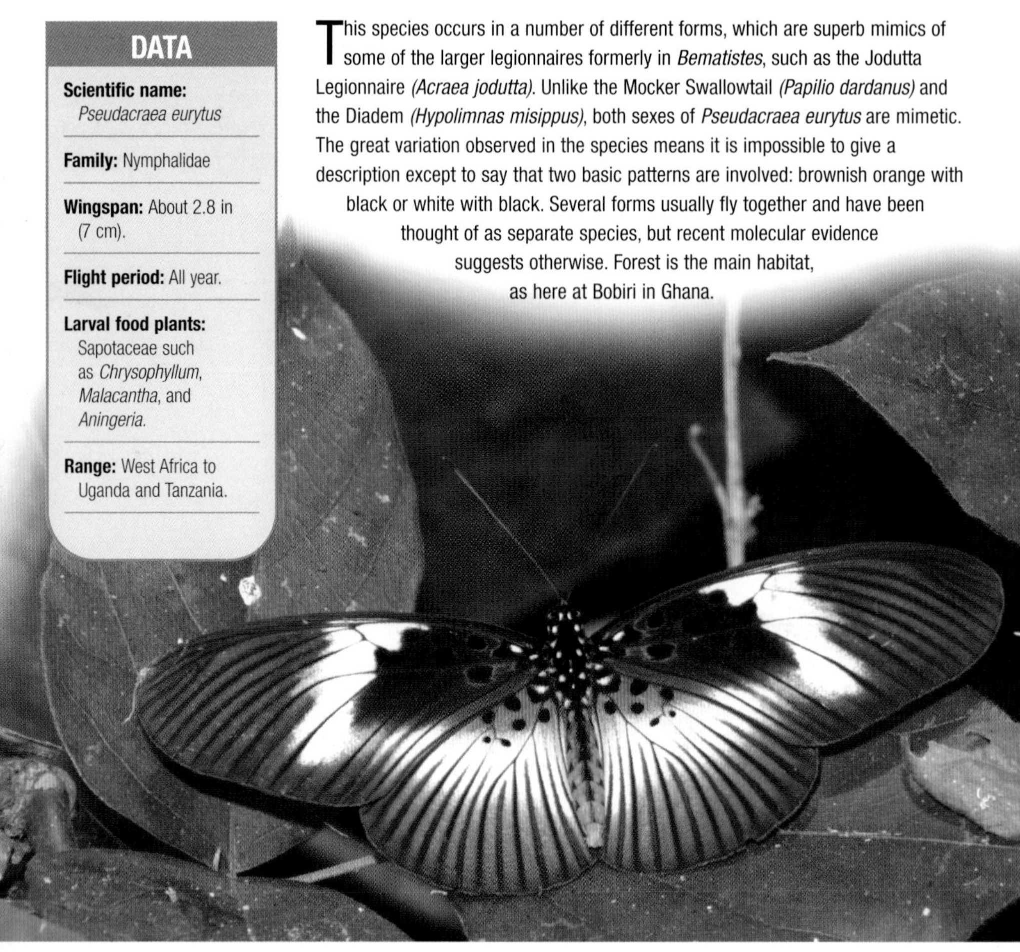

False Diadem

DATA

Scientific name: *Pseudacraea lucretia*

Family: Nymphalidae

Wingspan: About 2.8 in (7 cm).

Flight period: All year.

Larval food plants: Members of the Sapotaceae.

Range: Over most of sub-Saharan Africa.

Throughout much of Africa there are few patches of forest or woodland where you will not come upon this species sooner or later. The adult butterflies often feed on fermenting fruit or sap and also visit the dung of mammals such as civets, as seen here in Kakamega Forest in Kenya. The black-and-white banding on the upper side is vaguely similar to that of a number of *Acraea* and *Danaus* species, but is not sufficiently faithful to any to be considered a specific mimic. The False Diadem could be a generalized mimic, avoided by enemies that have learned to shun all black-and-white butterflies of this size and general pattern. The underside is similar but paler.

Incipient False Legionnaire

Scientific name: *Pseudacraea warburgi*

Family: Nymphalidae

Wingspan: About 2 in (5 cm).

Flight period: All year.

Larval food plants: *Manilkara* (Sapotaceae), *Strephonema*, *Combretum* (Combretaceae).

Range: Africa (Sierra Leone to Uganda).

Although the pattern on this species is vaguely reminiscent of some legionnaires, it is not generally regarded as in any way mimetic. The outer part of the forewing is blackish and has some pale markings, while its base is reddish brown with many black spots, as is the base of the hind wing. The rest of the hind wing is orange with a black margin containing some small, rounded orange spots. The underside is similar but paler. Never apparently found on flowers or fruit, this species will puddle on muddy ground. The specimen illustrated below was photographed basking in Ghana's Bobiri Forest.

Sibylline False Sergeant

DATA

Scientific name: *Pseudathyma sibyllina*

Family: Nymphalidae

Wingspan: About 1.8 in (4.5 cm).

Flight period: All year.

Larval food plants: Members of the Sapotaceae.

Range: Africa (Sierra Leone to Nigeria).

The small genus *Pseudathyma*, which is closely related to *Euptera*, contains just 14 forest species. These butterflies have a fast flight and seldom seem to settle for long, although they can be attracted to traps baited with fermenting fruit. Males also come down to the ground to puddle, as seen here in Ghana's Bobiri Forest. In the male the edge of the forewing is strongly falcate, bending inward about halfway along—a feature shared only by *Pseudathyma falcata*. The black-and-white pattern on the upper side is found in various permutations in all the other species. The underside is similar but paler.

Green-spotted Banner

The fast-flying males of this rain-forest butterfly perch along forest tracks in the early morning but then break off to spend the rest of the day puddling on the ground. They are often found on riverbanks, as here in Peru's Tingo Maria National Park. The females are rarely seen and are also fast fliers. The upper side is dark brown with a broad greenish band down each wing, broken into three pieces on the forewing. The underside is white bordered with red, a general pattern seen in all members of the genus, although in this species there is no small tail on the hind wing.

DATA

Scientific name: *Pyrrhogyra edocla*

Family: Nymphalidae

Wingspan: About 2.4 in (6 cm).

Flight period: All year.

Larval food plants: *Paullinia*, *Serjania* (Sapindaceae).

Range: Mexico to the Amazon Basin.

Orange Leafwing

The Orange Leafwing is found only on the island of Madagascar, in rain forest. This individual was photographed in Montagne d'Ambre National Park in the north of the island. Although it may look as though it is sitting with its wings open, this rarely happens. In fact, the specimen seen here was flitting across the ground in a jerky fashion, opening and closing its wings—meaning that the photographer needed very fast reactions to get this shot. The upper side is brownish orange with a purple sheen, just visible on the upper hind wing. The tips of the forewings are black with a white patch. The underside is a wonderful copy of a dead leaf, seen at its best when the butterfly perches (always head downward) on a twig.

DATA

Scientific name: *Salamis anteva*

Family: Nymphalidae

Wingspan: About 2.1 in (5.4 cm).

Flight period: All year.

Larval food plants: Acanthaceae.

Range: Madagascar.

Rusty-tipped Page

DATA

Scientific name: *Siproeta epaphus*

Family: Nymphalidae

Wingspan: About 3 in (7.5 cm).

Flight period: All year.

Larval food plants: *Ruellia*, *Blechum* (Acanthaceae).

Range: Mexico to Peru.

The butterflies in this genus of just five species have in the past all been placed in various genera (often misapplied); this species was formerly included in *Metamorpha*. It is a butterfly of disturbed areas, secondary forest, and wooded roadsides and is seen here on the edge of a coffee plantation near Jalapa in Veracruz State, Mexico. The rusty-tipped forewings are separated from the dark brown wing bases by a narrow white band. The hind-wing margin bears a number of small tail-like projections. The underside is similar to the upper side but much paler.

Malachite

Although one of the most common butterflies throughout the American tropics, in the United States the Malachite is a very rare species, resident only in the south of Florida and Texas, where at times it can be common. It is found mainly in disturbed forests and areas of second growth, but it can be seen frequently in leafy backyards even in large cities. As can be seen, the green on the underside is paler than on the upper side, a small portion of which is just visible in the accompanying illustration, taken in Peru's Tingo Maria National Park. Some people consider the Malachite to be a mimic of *Philaethria dido*.

DATA

Scientific name: *Siproeta stelenes*

Family: Nymphalidae

Wingspan: About 3 in (7.5 cm).

Flight period: All year.

Larval food plants: *Ruellia*, *Justicia*, and *Blechum* (Acanthaceae).

Range: United States to the Amazon Basin.

Blomfild's Beauty

DATA

Scientific name: *Smyrna blomfildia*

Family: Nymphalidae

Wingspan: About 3 in (7.5 cm).

Flight period: All year.

Larval food plants: *Urrera* in the nettle family (Urticaceae).

Range: Mexico to Peru.

The two species currently included in the genus *Smyrna* are recognized by their rounded wing shape and striking zebra-patterned undersides. In both species the food plant is *Urrera* and the caterpillar is very spiny. In this species the male upper side is golden brown, the outer third of each forewing being black with three white spots. The female is similar but rather a dull brown and with a cream band across each forewing. Found in both wet and dry forests, the adults of this species feed on rotting fruit and dung as well as puddling on the ground. This individual was seen in Peru's Tingo Maria National Park.

Crown Fritillary

Found in chaparral, sagebrush flats, and open conifer woodland, this species is most often seen on flowers, as depicted here in Utah, photographed in mid-August. The upper side is the typical fritillary combination of black spots on a brownish orange background, although the background is a more reddish orange in subspecies *semiramis* from southern California. The underside is always beautifully decorated with metallic silver spots, which are not ringed with black as in the very similar Zerene Fritillary *(Speyeria zerene)*.

DATA

Scientific name: *Speyeria coronis*

Family: Nymphalidae

Wingspan: About 2.8 in (7 cm).

Flight period: June–August.

Larval food plants: Violets *(Viola)* in the family Violaceae.

Range: Northwestern United States, south to California, Utah, Nevada, and Colorado.

The Senator

DATA

Scientific name: *Stibochiona coresia*

Family: Nymphalidae

Wingspan: About 2 in (5 cm).

Flight period: All year.

Larval food plants: Unknown.

Range: Java, Sumatra, Nias, and Borneo.

As with a number of other tropical butterflies, when at rest this rain-forest species always flips upside down beneath a leaf and flattens its wings against the underside, as seen here. As well as making the butterfly less conspicuous, this position provides shelter from heavy rain. In the male (illustrated) the wings are a deep chocolate brown, and there is a broad blue band along the margin of each hind wing. The female is much paler, and the hind-wing band is white on the outer part and bluish violet on the inner side. The specimen illustrated here was photographed in rain forest at Bukit Lawang in Sumatra.

Common Color Sergeant

DATA

Scientific name: *Symbrenthia hypatia*

Family: Nymphalidae

Wingspan: About 1.8 in (4.5 cm).

Flight period: All year.

Larval food plants: Members of the nettle family (Urticaceae).

Range: Southeast Asia.

Although looking superficially similar to a number of banded brown and orange Asian species in the genera *Athyma* and *Neptis*, the members of this genus are easily distinguished by having a short tail on each hind wing. However, these are a little worn in the specimen illustrated here, photographed in a rubber plantation near Bukit Lawang in Sumatra. The pattern of orange bands on a brown background is confusingly similar in a number of different species, each of which also shows some variation. In this species the underside bears an intricate pattern of dark brown lines on a pale brown background, rather like a dead leaf.

Etia Crescent

The genus *Tegosa* contains 15 species of rather small butterflies formerly included in the genus *Phyciodes*. Most of them have rather nondescript buff-colored undersides, as is the case with the species illustrated here, seen puddling on a track in rain forest in Peru's Tingo Maria National Park. On the upper side the ground color is dark brown with two orange bands on the forewing and two slightly indistinct wavy golden lines near the rear margin of the hind wing.

DATA

Scientific name: *Tegosa etia*

Family: Nymphalidae

Wingspan: About 3 cm (1.2 in).

Flight period: All year.

Larval food plants: Unknown.

Range: Colombia, Ecuador, and Peru.

Coppery Crescent

This widespread species is so variable that a number of subspecies have been described, some of which have recently been raised to the level of species. In its orange coloration with dark wing borders it resembles some of the small species of legionnaires *(Acraea)* from Africa, but they are not closely related. However, the resemblance may not be simply a coincidence, since the butterflies pictured here (at Tingo Maria in Peru) were constantly opening and closing their wings as they puddled. This habit is also seen in the chemically defended legionnaires, indicating that the Coppery Crescent is probably warningly colored.

DATA

Scientific name: *Tegosa liriope*

Family: Nymphalidae

Wingspan: About 1 in (2.5 cm).

Flight period: All year.

Larval food plants: Unknown.

Range: Over most of the South American tropics.

Orange-patched Crescent

DATA

Scientific name: *Telenassa teletusa*

Family: Nymphalidae

Wingspan: About 1.2 in (3 cm).

Flight period: All year.

Larval food plants: Unknown.

Range: Over most of the South American tropics.

The genus *Telenassa* is another genus that has been segregated from *Phyciodes*. In common with *Tegosa*, its members are relatively small butterflies with drab undersides. Little is known about their biology or early stages. As with *Tegosa*, the adults often come down to the rain-forest floor to puddle, as seen here in Peru's Tingo Maria National Park. The forewings are brown, speckled with gold near their bases and bearing three yellowish orange patches. The hind wing is crossed by a broad band of a similar orange color.

Orange Banner

Using the name "Orange Banner" for a butterfly shown here as being pink and blue might seem inappropriate, but this is very variable species and over much of its range the ground color is indeed orange. Its very falcate forewing with its squared-off apex easily distinguishes it from the only other member of the genus *(Temenis pulchra)*, which does not look as though it is closely related. The orange banner is found in dry forest but is more common in the wetter types, and is seen here in rain forest in the Rancho Grande reserve in Brazilian Amazonia.

DATA

Scientific name: *Temenis laothoe*

Family: Nymphalidae

Wingspan: About 2.2 in (5.5 cm).

Flight period: All year.

Larval food plants: *Serjania*, *Paullinia*, *Cardiospermum*, and *Urvillea* (Sapindaceae).

Range: Mexico to the Amazon Basin.

Clarissa Eastern Beauty

There is a fair amount of variation in this spectacular blue species, involving not only color but also wing shape. For example, in subspecies *malayanus* from peninsular Thailand and the Malay Peninsula the tip of the forewing is extended outward, forming a very falcate wing. Much of the hind wing is brown, grading into a straw-colored marginal zone, and it has a pronounced tail. In the form illustrated below, seen puddling on riverside pebbles in the Gunung Leuser National Park in Sumatra, there is no brown on the tailless hind wing, and the forewing is not at all falcate.

DATA

Scientific name: *Terinos clarissa*

Family: Nymphalidae

Wingspan: About 3 in (7.5 cm).

Flight period: All year.

Larval food plants: Members of the Violaceae and Euphorbiaceae.

Range: Thailand, Malaysia, Indonesia, and the Philippines (Mindanao).

Tiger Beauty

A close relative of *Colobura*, the genus *Tigridia* contains just a single species. The upper side is orange with black tips to the forewings, which are also crossed by a black bar. The underside is zebra patterned, especially on the hind wing. This is a rain-forest butterfly in which the males spend much of the day perched head downward on tree trunks in deep shade, as seen here in Peru's Tingo Maria National Park. The females are most often observed when they are searching for saplings on which to lay their eggs. Both sexes feed on fermenting fruit.

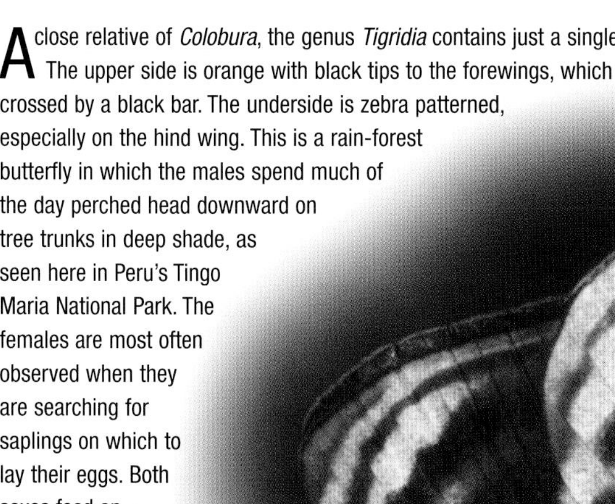

DATA

Scientific name: *Tigridia acesta*

Family: Nymphalidae

Flight period: All year.

Larval food plants: *Cecropia* and *Paruma* in the fig family (Moraceae).

Range: Costa Rica to the Amazon Basin.

West Coast Painted Lady

DATA

Scientific name: *Vanessa annabella*

Family: Nymphalidae

Wingspan: About 2 in (5 cm).

Flight period: Much of the year in south; summer in north

Larval food plants: Many plants in the mallow family (Malvaceae), e.g., globe mallow *(Sphaeralcea)* and alkali mallow *(Sida).*

Range: From British Columbia and Alberta through the western United States to Guatemala.

In earlier works this species was confused with the very similar *Vanessa carye* from South America. It is found in a wide variety of habitats, including roadsides, forest clearings, cultivated fields, vacant lots in cities, backyards, and chaparral—in fact, just about anywhere that is suitable for its food plants, many of which are very common. As in all other painted ladies, the upper side is black and orange, with a few white spots near the tip of the forewing. However, uniquely in the North American species, the four spots near the hind-wing margin are all of about equal size and have blue in the center.

Red Admiral

DATA

Scientific name: *Vanessa atalanta*

Family: Nymphalidae

Wingspan: About 2.2 in (5.5 cm).

Flight period: From spring to fall.

Larval food plants: Nettle *(Urtica)*, false nettle *(Boehmeria)*, and pellitory *(Parietaria)* in the family Urticaceae.

Range: Europe to Asia Minor and North Africa and in the Azores and Canary Islands. North America, southward to Guatemala; also in the West Indies. New Zealand and Hawaii (both introduced).

With its dark velvety black wings, strikingly marked with red bars and white spots, this is always an instantly recognizable butterfly in Europe and North America, where no other species are remotely similar. The underside is a complex mix of rather dark colors. Inhabiting every kind of habitat from city backyards and waste lots to roadsides, streamsides, canyons, and chaparral, the Red Admiral is a great wanderer. It often migrates in large numbers, as happens most years from southern Europe and North Africa to the British Isles, where the accompanying photograph was taken.

Painted Lady

DATA

Scientific name: *Vanessa cardui*

Family: Nymphalidae

Wingspan: About 2.2 in (5.5 cm).

Flight period: Over much of the summer.

Larval food plants: Numerous, including thistles (Asteraceae), mallows (Malvaceae), and fiddlenecks (Boraginaceae).

Range: Over most of the world except for South America and the ice caps.

The Painted Lady is the world's most widely distributed butterfly. Of the three species of painted ladies found in North America, this is the only one that does not have an angled forewing, making it easily recognizable. It is also the only one in which the spots along the hind-wing margin do not normally have blue centers and are very small. The Painted Lady is a noted migrant; every year millions head north from their warm year-round southern breeding grounds. They are often found on flowers, as seen here in England. Unfortunately, progeny of late breeders in the north are unable to survive the cold northern winters, and they all perish.

South American Painted Lady

DATA

Scientific name: *Vanessa carye*

Family: Nymphalidae

Wingspan: About 2 in (5 cm).

Larval food plants: Various.

Flight period: Mainly October–April.

Range: Colombia to Chile, Argentina, Uruguay, and Paraguay.

Over the tropical parts of its range, such as in Peru and Ecuador, this species is found only at high elevations in the Andean mountain range. Farther south, for example in Chile, it occurs down to sea level. The specimen pictured above was found basking on bare ground among clumps of southern beeches *(Nothofagus)* at the base of the Andes at Chillãn in southern Chile. The black-and-orange coloration is much as in other painted ladies, but in the South American Painted Lady the forewing is noticeably falcate with a squared-off tip.

Australian Painted Lady

Found in every kind of habitat, the Australian Painted Lady has a slightly more rounded apex to the forewing than the Painted Lady *(Vanessa cardui)*, of which it was once regarded as a subspecies. In addition, rather than being completely black, the four spots along the hind-wing margin have blue centers. The cryptic underside of the hind wing is typical of most painted ladies, and is seen here covering a large pinkish patch on the forewing. This species is hard to spot when at rest on dead vegetation, as here in woodland in the Grampian Mountains near Melbourne, Australia.

DATA

Scientific name: *Vanessa kershawi*

Family: Nymphalidae

Wingspan: About 2 in (5 cm).

Flight period: All year in north; August–May in three broods in south.

Larval food plants: Everlasting flowers *(Helichrysum, Ammobium*, and *Acrolinium)* in the sunflower family (Asteraceae).

Range: Australia and New Zealand.

American Painted Lady

DATA

Scientific name: *Vanessa virginiensis*

Family: Nymphalidae

Wingspan: About 2 in (5 cm).

Flight period: All year in south; two flights in summer in north.

Larval food plants: In several families, but prefers *Gnaphalium*, *Antennaria*, and *Anaphalis* (family Asteraceae).

Range: Southern Canada to Venezuela and the West Indies. An occasional stray to Europe, but resident in the Canary Islands.

The American Painted Lady is one of the most familiar North American butterflies, found in just about every kind of habitat, including woodlands, streamsides, fence rows, coastal chaparral, waste lots, roadsides, and backyards, as seen here in South Carolina. The most obvious difference from other painted ladies is the presence of a small white spot on the forewing (in one of the orange-colored cells about two-thirds of the way down from the tip). The hind-wing eyespots are large and have blue centers. The underside is the usual complex pattern seen in painted ladies—a large pink patch on the forewing and two large eyespots on the hind wing.

The Lady's Maid

Although very patchily distributed and absent from large areas within its range, and even from whole countries, such as Togo, this colorful little butterfly can be abundant where it occurs. In Kenya's Kakamega Forest, where this photograph was taken, the author found dozens puddling on the ground along the tracks through the rain forest. A few were also feeding on civet dung alongside larger butterflies such as various species of *Charaxes*. The broad orange bands on the upper side possibly have a defensive function, because the wings are constantly opened and closed—a common habit in toxic, warningly colored species. The underside is drab and vaguely leaflike.

DATA

Scientific name: *Vanessula milca*

Family: Nymphalidae

Wingspan: About 1.4 in (3.5 cm).

Flight period: All year.

Larval food plants: Unknown.

Range: West Africa to Kenya and Zambia.

Lesser Cruiser

DATA

Scientific name: *Vindula dejone*

Family: Nymphalidae

Wingspan: About 2.8 in (7 cm).

Flight period: All year.

Larval food plants: Passionflowers *(Passiflora)* in the family Passifloraceae.

Range: Thailand to the Philippines and New Guinea.

This fairly large robust butterfly is found mainly along paths and tracks in rain forest, often puddling on the ground, as this individual was in Thale Ban National Park in southern Thailand. In its overall coloration it is very similar to the even larger and more widespread Cruiser *(Vindula erota)*. The chief difference lies in the presence of a small third eyespot near the tip of the hind wing in *V. dejone*. Only the males, as seen here, are orange. In the females the wings are brownish, often flushed greenish, and there is a broad whitish stripe down each wing, although this is restricted to the forewings in some subspecies.

Chilean Fritillary

DATA

Scientific name: *Yramea modesta*

Family: Nymphalidae

Wingspan: About 1.2 in (3 cm).

Flight period: November–April.

Larval food plants: Violets *(Viola)* in the family Violaceae.

Range: Chile.

Seven fritillaries formerly included in the genus *Issoria* are now separated into the genus *Yramea*. In tropical countries such as Colombia and Bolivia they occur only in the Andes Mountains, but farther south they are found down to sea level. The specimen pictured here was photographed as it basked on the ground in an open forest of southern beech trees *(Nothofagus)* at Chillãn in southern Chile. The pattern of black spots and streaks on a brownish orange background is pretty much as seen in numerous species of fritillaries around the world.

Yellow Clubtail

DATA

Scientific name: *Atrophaneura neptunus*

Family: Papilionidae

Wingspan: About 3.2 in (8 cm).

Flight period: All year.

Larval food plants: Pipevines *(Aristolochia)* in the family Aristolochiaceae.

Range: Myanmar (Burma) to Indonesia.

Members of this genus are now often placed in *Parides*, with *Atrophaneura* retained as a subgenus. They are all warningly colored, highly toxic butterflies and are strictly avoided by predators. Their defensive compounds are absorbed from the food plant by the caterpillars. In the adults the hind wings always bear tails, these being particularly long and club-ended in the species illustrated here, seen in rain forest at Bukit Lawang in Sumatra. The upper side is similar to the underside, except that the patch of red on the hind wing is much larger.

Pipevine Swallowtail

DATA

Scientific name: *Battus philenor*

Family: Papilionidae

Wingspan: About 3.2 in (8 cm).

Flight period: Mostly three flights, May–September.

Larval food plants: Pipevines *(Aristolochia)* in the family Aristolochiaceae.

Range: United States to Costa Rica.

Summertime migrations take this robust butterfly to most parts of the continental United States except the Northwest. Its distinctive pattern of black wings with a bluish iridescence, especially on the hind wings, is mimicked by a number of perfectly palatable, innocuous species such as the Black Swallowtail *(Papilio polyxenes)*, the Spicebush Swallowtail *(P. troilus)*, and the dark female Eastern Tiger Swallowtail *(P. glaucus)*. These butterflies also mimic the Pipevine Swallowtail's underside, which is mainly black with a row of red spots around the margin of the hind wing. The Pipevine Swallowtail is found in most habitats and can be common in backyards, as seen here in Georgia.

Short-lined Kite Swallowtail

One of the most common members of the family in the American tropics, adults of this species are often seen in large numbers puddling on sandy riverbanks in rain forest, as here in Guatopo National Park in Venezuela. It is distinguished from several similar species by the fact that the black lines running inward from the front of the wing (this part of the wing being known as the costa) are all of about the same length. The upper side is similar to the underside seen here.

DATA

Scientific name: *Eurytides agesilaus*

Family: Papilionidae

Wingspan: About 3 in (7.5 cm).

Flight period: All year.

Larval food plants: Unknown.

Range: Mexico to Argentina.

Green-spotted Jay

Given its vast range, it is not surprising that this lovely butterfly occurs in a number of subspecies, differing mainly in size, wing shape, and length of the tail on the hind wing. This is subspecies *ligatus*, photographed on a leaf in rain forest beside the research station at Wau in New Guinea. This has the shortest tail of any of the subspecies, barely visible as such in this specimen. The pattern of green spots on the upper side is much as on the underside seen here, the main difference being the absence of the red and black eyespot on the hind wing.

DATA

Scientific name: *Graphium agamemnon*

Family: Papilionidae

Wingspan: About 2.8 in (7 cm).

Flight period: All year.

Larval food plants: Members of the custard apple family (Annonaceae).

Range: Over much of tropical Asia and Australasia.

Five-bar Swordtail

Visit almost any damp, sandy, forested riverbank over a vast area of Asia and this is probably the first butterfly you will see, busily sucking up water through its proboscis and expelling it regularly and forcibly from its rear end. The presence of only five black bars across the forewing distinguishes it instantly from other similar whitish species, such as *Graphium glycerion* and *G. sikkimica*, which both have more than five bars. The upper side is more or less identical to the underside seen here on an individual photographed in Thale Ban National Park, southern Thailand.

DATA

Scientific name: *Graphium agetes*

Family: Papilionidae

Wingspan: About 2.4 in (6 cm).

Flight period: All year.

Larval food plants: Members of the custard apple family (Annonaceae).

Range: Over most of the warmer parts of Asia.

Broadwinged Five-bar Swordtail

DATA

Scientific name: *Graphium antiphates*

Family: Papilionidae

Wingspan: About 3 in (7.5 cm).

Flight period: All year.

Larval food plants: Members of the custard apple family (Annonaceae).

Range: Over most of tropical Asia.

This is the butterfly most likely to be found drinking alongside the Five-bar Swordtail *(Graphium agetes)* on almost any sandy forested riverbank in tropical Asia. On its upper side it is not unlike the previous species, being a translucent whitish color, with five black bars on the forewing and black wing tips. However, the wings are much broader and more rounded, and the underside is very different, being an attractive mix of green, black, yellow, and blue, as on this specimen seen puddling in Thale Ban National Park in Thailand. As with many species of *Graphium,* there is a very long tail on the hind wing, hence the common name of swordtail.

Malagasy Tail-less Jay

The presence of trees seems to be the only requirement for this species, which is widespread in Madagascar both in the dry western forests and the eastern rain forests. As with most members of the genus, the adult males spend much of their time drinking from sandy riverbanks—this individual was seen in rain forest in Ranomafana National Park. The upper side is blackish brown with a pattern of large and small greenish yellow spots. The underside is reddish brown, and the spots are a pale, almost silvery green color.

DATA

Scientific name: *Graphium cyrnus*

Family: Papilionidae

Wingspan: About 2.8 in (7 cm).

Flight period: All year.

Larval food plants: Members of the custard apple family (Annonaceae).

Range: Madagascar.

Malayan Zebra

Of the papilionids most likely to be found puddling on sandy riversides in tropical Asia, the Malayan Zebra is by far the most common of the tail-less species. The large yellow spot near the tip of the hind wing makes it easy to recognize. The male, as pictured here in rain forest in Thale Ban National Park in Thailand, is pale bluish gray with black spots. The female is slightly larger and lacks the blue tones, her whitish coloration making her a passable mimic of the unpalatable danaid *Ideopsis gaura*.

DATA

Scientific name: *Graphium delessertii*

Family: Papilionidae

Wingspan: About 3.5 in (9 cm).

Flight period: All year.

Larval food plants: Members of the custard apple family (Annonaceae).

Range: Thailand, Malaysia, and much of Indonesia.

Common Jay

Pictured here drinking on a sunny riverbank in dense rain forest in Malaysia's Taman Negara National Park, the Common Jay is another papilionid commonly encountered in this habitat. The basic color is black with many pale blue semitranslucent spots, which are slightly paler on the underside than above. The four red spots on the hind wing are only present on the underside. A single red spot is just visible on the rear margin of the forewing. This is absent in the very similar *Graphium evemon.*

DATA

Scientific name: *Graphium doson*

Family: Papilionidae

Wingspan: About 2.8 in (7 cm).

Flight period: All year.

Larval food plants: Members of the custard apple family (Annonaceae).

Range: Over much of tropical Asia, from India to the Philippines.

Malagasy Red-spotted Jay

Although widespread on the island of Madagascar, the Malagasy Red-spotted Jay does not seem to be a particularly common species. The specimen pictured below, photographed in the spectacular Kirindy Forest, was the only one seen by the author in six months spent looking almost continuously for insects and other wildlife on Madagascar. The upper side is very similar to the underside seen here, both being brown with a pattern of semi-translucent bluish spots. However, the red spots are not present on the upper side. The sides of the body are also spotted with red.

DATA

Scientific name: *Graphium evombar*

Family: Papilionidae

Wingspan: About 2.6 in (6.5 cm).

Flight period: All year.

Larval food plants: Unknown, probably members of the custard apple family (Annonaceae).

Range: Madagascar.

Eastern White Lady

The specimen pictured here was one of about 50 individuals that formed a dense cluster as they drank from the bottom of a dried-up pond in Sokoke Forest on the coast of Kenya. Most of them flew off as the author carefully stalked them, but fortunately this one was so absorbed in its drinking that it stayed put. With its black-and-white pattern, repeated on both sides, it is a convincing mimic of such unpalatable species as the Friar *(Amauris niavius)*. However, the red wing bases on the Eastern White Lady, evident in the photograph, are an immediate giveaway.

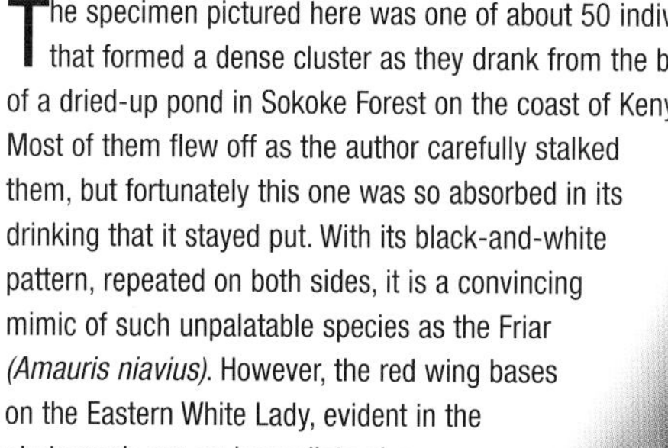

DATA

Scientific name: *Graphium philonoe*

Family: Papilionidae

Wingspan: About 2.8 in (7 cm).

Flight period: All year.

Larval food plants: Members of the custard apple family (Annonaceae).

Range: Africa (Ethiopia, Sudan, Kenya, Uganda, Malawi, Mozambique).

Common Striped Swordtail

The very wide distribution displayed by this common species is made possible by its wide ecological tolerance. Although always most abundant in wooded habitats, as here in Ghana's Bobiri Forest, the Common Striped Swordtail is also common in open areas such as agricultural land and savanna. Large clusters of males are often seen drinking along the edges of streams, especially when these are used by local people for washing clothes or bathing. Both sides of the wings are similar, having green bands and whitish spots, but with only a single red spot on the upper-side margin of the hind wing. The long tails are tipped with white.

DATA

Scientific name: *Graphium policines*

Family: Papilionidae

Wingspan: About 3 in (7.5 cm).

Flight period: All year.

Larval food plants: Various Annonaceae and *Landolphia* in the family Apocynaceae.

Range: Over most of sub-Saharan Africa except for very dry or temperate areas.

Common Bluebottle

During the author's brief stay in the ancient rain forest of Malaysia's Taman Negara National Park clusters of this species were constantly present on some sandy banks in a broad river, as depicted here. The open river was far less gloomy than the dense forest, in which few butterflies were seen. With its bright bluish green translucent windows cutting across its black wings, this is a striking species. The red markings seen here on the underside are not repeated on the upper side. One of the reasons for the success of this common and widespread butterfly must be its use of a wider range of food plants than is typical in *Graphium*.

DATA

Scientific name: *Graphium sarpedon*

Family: Papilionidae

Wingspan: About 3.5 in (9 cm).

Flight period: All year.

Larval food plants: In at least five families, including Lauraceae, Sapotaceae, and Myrtaceae.

Range: Over much of tropical Asia, from India to the Philippines.

Green-spotted Triangle

DATA

Scientific name: *Graphium weiskei*

Family: Papilionidae

Wingspan: About 3.2 in (8 cm).

Flight period: All year.

Larval food plants: Unknown.

Range: New Guinea.

The males of this mainly mountain species are among the most spectacularly colored members of the genus. The basic brown coloration of the wings is adorned with a series of green, pink, and purple patches. On the underside, as seen above, the pattern is far more subdued, consisting largely of brown with some patches of white and green. This cryptic combination enables the butterfly to blend in with its surroundings when drinking on damp ground, as seen here on a mountainside near Wau. The female is brown.

Scarce Swallowtail

DATA

Scientific name: *Iphiclides podalirius*

Family: Papilionidae

Wingspan: About 3 in (7.5 cm).

Flight period: Mostly May–June and August–September, in two broods.

Larval food plants: Sloe *(Prunus spinosa)*, cultivated apples, and other trees in the rose family (Rosaceae).

Range: From North Africa across Europe and temperate Asia to China.

Because of its penchant for breeding on cultivated fruit trees in orchards, this species is often found around towns and villages, as seen here in Portugal. With its long, slender, hind-wing tails it is more akin to *Graphium* or *Eurytides* than *Papilio*. Its basic coloration is white with a hint of cream, this being darker and more pronounced in the first brood. In subspecies *feisthamelii* the wings are grayish white. There is a series of dark bands across the wings, repeated on the underside. Toward the tip of each hind wing there is an eyespot that gives a decided "false head" impression, the purpose of which may be defensive.

Crimson Rose

DATA

Scientific name: *Pachliopta hector*

Other common name: Common Rose

Family: Papilionidae

Wingspan: About 3.5 in (8.5 cm).

Flight period: All year.

Larval food plant: *Aristolochia indica* in the family Aristolochiaceae.

Range: India and Sri Lanka.

The author's sole visit to India took place in the long dry season, when few butterflies are on the wing. The Crimson Rose seen here briefly perched on a leaf in the Periyar Sanctuary in the Western Ghats in Kerala State, was one of the few butterflies present. It is one of the characteristic papilionids of southern India, and after rain it can be very common in forests and leafy backyards. The upper side is velvety black with white markings on the forewing and numerous red spots on the hind wing. The head and the tip of the abdomen are also red.

Orchard Butterfly

Because its caterpillar eats the leaves of citrus trees, such as cultivated oranges and lemons, this butterfly is often considered as a pest in backyards and orchards. It is also found in native forests, as seen below, photographed on the edge of rain forest in Lamington National Park in the state of Queensland, Australia. The sexes differ considerably. In the female (illustrated) the forewings are unmarked, but the hind wings bear a striking array of red and blue spots next to a large white patch. In the rather smaller male the forewings bear a row of white spots, and the hind wings have a single red spot, but no blue markings.

DATA

Scientific name: *Papilio aegeus*

Family: Papilionidae

Wingspan: About 4.1 in (10.5 cm).

Flight period: January–March in south; all year in north.

Larval food plants: Citrus trees (Rutaceae).

Range: Eastern Australia and on New Guinea and nearby islands.

Giant African Swallowtail

As well as being the largest butterfly in Africa, the males of this species are one of the world's largest flying insects. Found mainly in the rain-forest canopy, this huge butterfly is rarely seen, so the author was fortunate to see the specimen illustrated. Every day for over a week it spent most of the day puddling in the same spot on the muddy logging road in Ghana's Bobiri Forest. It was completely unperturbed by close human presence, probably because it contains a huge dose of poison, sufficient to kill five cats. Its orange and black coloration therefore serves a warning function, as in the similar-looking *Acraea* legionnaires.

DATA

Scientific name: *Papilio antimachus*

Family: Papilionidae

Wingspan: Males about 9.5 in (24 cm); females much smaller.

Flight period: All year.

Larval food plants: Unknown.

Range: Africa (Sierra Leone to Uganda).

Common White-banded Swallowtail

Usually seen flying rapidly down a rain-forest track or logging road, this large black-and-white butterfly will sometimes stop to perch on a leaf. This is exactly the scenario that allowed this photograph to be taken, in Ghana's Bobiri Forest. The wings are velvety black with a whitish cream band down each wing and some white spots spaced out around the margin of the hind wing. The underside is light brown with a white band and conspicuous black veins. Both sexes are fond of flowers; but while they feed—in common with many species of *Papilio*—their wings are constantly fluttered, making photography difficult.

DATA

Scientific name: *Papilio cyproeofila*

Family: Papilionidae

Wingspan: About 4.3 in (11 cm).

Flight period: All year.

Larval food plants: Peppers *(Piper)* in the family Piperaceae.

Range: Africa (Sierra Leone to the Congo region and Angola).

Mocker Swallowtail

DATA

Scientific name: *Papilio dardanus*

Family: Papilionidae

Wingspan: About 3.7 in (9.5 cm).

Flight period: October–April in South Africa; all year elsewhere.

Larval food plants: *Calodendron*, *Citrus*, *Teclea*, etc. (Rutaceae).

Range: Over most of sub-Saharan Africa.

Because of its complex pattern of mimicry this species has been dubbed "world's most interesting butterfly." The male is a fairly normal cream butterfly with black-bordered forewings and tailed, black-spotted hind wings. In Madagascar this also sums up the females, but over the rest of the range they are mimics of various unpalatable danaids and are tail-less, except in Ethiopia. Some mimic the Common Tiger *(Danaus chrysippus)*, while for others, such as the one seen here, the model is some species of black-and-white *Amauris*. These days the main habitat is often backyards, but the female shown below is in semidry forest in the Boabeng-Fiema Sanctuary in Ghana, fluttering her wings as she visits a flower.

Citrus Swallowtail

DATA

Scientific name: *Papilio demodocus*

Family: Papilionidae

Wingspan: About 3.9 in (10 cm).

Flight period: All year.

Larval food plants: Mainly citrus trees (Rutaceae).

Range: Over most of sub-Saharan Africa and on Madagascar.

With its habit of breeding on cultivated citrus trees it is hardly surprising that this is the commonest swallowtail in Africa, and it is often abundant in the centers of large cities. In Gambia the author once watched a female laying eggs on an isolated lemon tree in the concrete courtyard of a restaurant, complete with tables busy with diners. However, it is also found in forest, especially those that are not too wet, as here in the Berenty Reserve in Madagascar. The upper side is deep brown, heavily dusted with gold. There are numerous pale yellow spots and a pale yellow band across the hind wing, which has a single blue and red eyespot and no tails. There are three blue and red eyespots on the underside.

Eastern Tiger Swallowtail

DATA

Scientific name: *Papilio glaucus*

Family: Papilionidae

Wingspan: 2.5–4.9 in (6.3–12.5 cm).

Flight period: March–November in south; May–August in New York; June–July farther north and in the mountains.

Larval food plants: Many trees, including wild cherry, tulip tree, birch, and cottonwood.

Range: Alaska and Canada, through the eastern United States to Mexico.

Found in every kind of habitat that has some trees, the males (and most of the females) of this common swallowtail can be recognized by their pattern of black tiger stripes on a pale yellow background. There is one long tail and one very short tail on each hind wing. This form is similar to the Two-tailed Tiger Swallowtail *(Papilio multicaudata)* pictured on page 402, but the latter has narrower bands and its second tail is much longer. The female illustrated here is of the form that mimics the Pipevine Swallowtail *(Battus philenor)*, with blue and black wings. It is pictured on *Lantana camara* in a backyard in South Carolina.

Jackson's Swallowtail

DATA

Scientific name: *Papilio jacksoni*

Family: Papilionidae

Wingspan: About 3.2 in (8 cm).

Flight period: All year.

Larval food plants: *Citrus*, etc. (Rutaceae).

Range: Africa (Uganda, Kenya, and eastern Congo region).

Favoring the dark rain-forest understory, as seen here in Kenya's Kakamega Forest, this species is also found in drier forest types, especially in upland areas. For example, it is common in the forests around Nairobi in Kenya. In the male the upper side is blackish brown with a white band on each wing; this band is reduced to unconnected spots on the forewing. The female has broader wings with scattered white spots on the forewing and a broad white patch on the hind wing, in addition to a row of white spots set in from the margin.

Old-world Swallowtail

DATA

Scientific name: *Papilio machaon*

Family: Papilionidae

Wingspan: About 3 in (7.5 cm).

Flight period: April–September in south; July–August in north.

Larval food plants: Members of the sunflower family (Asteraceae) in North America; carrot family (Apiaceae) elsewhere.

Range: North America, from Alaska through central Canada to western United States. Also from Europe and North Africa across temperate Asia to Japan.

Within its European range this species is distinctive enough to identify at first sight, but in North America there are several confusingly similar swallowtails. These can be separated only by a detailed examination of the pattern of markings on the side of the abdomen and the structure of the hind-wing eyespots. In general terms, this is a typical black-and-yellow swallowtail with fairly long hind-wing tails. In common with several other species, there is a row of blue spots inward from the margin of the hind wing. In North America it is mostly a northern species of meadows and tundra, restricted mainly to high mountains in the south of its range.

Mechow's Swallowtail

DATA

Scientific name: *Papilio mechowi*

Family: Papilionidae

Wingspan: About 3.9 in (10 cm).

Flight period: All year.

Larval food plants: Unknown.

Range: Africa (Cameroon to Angola, southern Sudan and Uganda).

The specimen illustrated here was photographed in Budongo Forest in Uganda, the only place in that country where this large rain-forest butterfly is likely to be seen, since it is reasonably common there. It is most easily distinguished from several similar species by the sharply angled hind wing on which the white marginal spots are shaped somewhat like teeth. The ground color is a rich velvety blackish brown with pale cream wing bands, split up into individual spots on the forewing.

Great Mormon Swallowtail

This large swallowtail, divided into at least 13 subspecies, is unusual in occurring not only in tropical regions of Asia but also in temperate countries such as Korea and Japan. It is found in most habitats that have some trees and is often common in backyards, especially where citrus trees are planted. Both sexes feed at flowers, but the males also come down to puddle on sandy riverbanks, as seen here in Thale Ban National Park in Thailand. The males never have tails and are mainly black. The females can be with or without tails and occur in a wide range of forms, each of which mimics a different species of unpalatable swallowtail. In all cases black is the preponderant color.

DATA

Scientific name: *Papilio memnon*

Family: Papilionidae

Wingspan: About 5.1 in (13 cm).

Flight period: All year in the tropics; only in summer in temperate areas.

Larval food plants: Citrus trees (Rutaceae).

Range: Over most of Asia.

Western Emperor Swallowtail

Only a few minutes before this picture was taken in Ghana's Bobiri Forest, a heavily loaded logging truck had to be towed out of the spot where this large and splendid butterfly was peacefully drinking. The Western Emperor Swallowtail is a common species in suitable habitats—mainly rain forest in which the canopy is still reasonably intact. Both sexes visit flowers, fluttering their wings in typical swallowtail fashion as they feed. The ground color is blackish brown, with cream wing bands and a long hind-wing tail. This tail distinguishes it instantly from the otherwise similar and also very common Citrus Swallowtail *(Papilio demodocus)*.

DATA

Scientific name: *Papilio menestheus*

Family: Papilionidae

Wingspan: About 4.7 in (12 cm).

Flight period: All year.

Larval food plants: Mainly on *Fagara macrophylla*; also on *Citrus* (Rutaceae).

Range: Africa (Sierra Leone to Cameroon).

Two-tailed Tiger Swallowtail

This typical black-and-yellow swallowtail can be distinguished from the Eastern Tiger Swallowtail *(Papilio glaucus)* by the narrow black wing bands and the presence of two tails—one long and one short. (In *P. glaucus* the second one is just a stump.) The Two-tailed Swallowtail is likely to crop up in a variety of habitats, including moist valleys, streamsides, parks, backyards, roadsides, and desert. It is seen here in the Chiricahua Mountains in Arizona. Males spend most of the day patrolling for females but also puddle on mud, while both sexes visit flowers.

DATA

Scientific name: *Papilio multicaudata*

Family: Papilionidae

Wingspan: About 4.1 in (10.5 cm).

Flight period: May–June, August–September.

Larval food plants: Ash, wild cherry, serviceberry, hoptree, and others.

Range: Mainly western North America from British Columbia southward through the Rockies to Mexico and Guatemala.

Yellow Helen

The Yellow Helen is a rather variable butterfly that occurs in a number of subspecies. In most of them the band of spots on the forewing (not always present) and the large patch on the hind wing are bright yellow. In other subspecies, such as *albolineatus*, seen here puddling beside the river at Bukit Lawang in Sumatra, the markings are white rather than yellow. In all cases the ground color is a rich velvety black, overlaid in fresh specimens (as seen below) by a pattern of golden spots. This form is often known as the Black-and-white Helen. Although rain forest is the main habitat, this species also occurs in disturbed areas.

DATA

Scientific name: *Papilio nephelus*

Family: Papilionidae

Wingspan: About 4.5 in (11.5 cm).

Flight period: All year.

Larval food plants: Citrus family (Rutaceae).

Range: Much of tropical Asia, from India to Indonesia.

Green-patch Swallowtail

DATA

Scientific name: *Papilio phorcas*

Family: Papilionidae

Wingspan: About 3.5 in (9 cm).

Flight period: All year.

Larval food plants: *Calodendron, Clausena, Citrus, Fagara, Teclea, Toddalia* (Rutaceae).

Range: Over most of sub-Saharan Africa except for Ethiopia and southern Africa.

Green is generally a rare color in butterflies, and the beautiful shade of apple green seen in this species is particularly attractive. The distribution of this species, which is found only in rain forest of reasonably good quality, is relatively patchy. However, adults were common enough when the author visited Kenya's Kakamega Forest, where the accompanying photograph was taken of a basking adult. Several specimens were also puddling, wings closed, on the muddy paths. They looked a little like partially dead leaves, since the green on their undersides is very pale and almost restricted to a large patch at the base of the black hind wing.

Common Mormon

DATA

Scientific name: *Papilio polytes*

Family: Papilionidae

Wingspan: About 3.5 in (9 cm).

Flight period: All year.

Larval food plants: *Citrus, Clausena, Fortunella, Glycosmis, Zanthoxylum,* etc. (Rutaceae).

Range: Over most of tropical Asia.

As with the much larger Yellow Helen *(Papilio nephelus),* the males of this species occur in a single form, while the females are variable and mimic various unpalatable swallowtails. The ground color of the wings is velvety black, overlaid with a shimmer of golden spots, extremely evident on the forewings of the very fresh male illustrated here. He was photographed in the Botanic Gardens at Bogor, on the Indonesian island of Java. This is subspecies *javanus*, in which the hind-wing tails present in other subspecies are reduced to stumps. The creamy whitish spots along the edge of the forewing, which form a band on the hind wing, are always present in males. Female coloration depends on which butterfly she is mimicking.

King Swallowtail

DATA

Scientific name: *Papilio thoas*

Family: Papilionidae

Wingspan: About 4.5 in (11.5 cm).

Flight period: All year.

Larval food plants: Mainly citrus trees (Rutaceae); also peppers *(Piper)* in the family Piperaceae.

Range: Mexico to Argentina and on Cuba, Jamaica, and Trinidad.

If you see a butterfly resembling the one above anywhere in North America, it is probable that you are looking at a Giant Swallowtail *(Papilio cresphontes)*. This is a common species in North America, while the almost identical King Swallowtail is a tropical species that only rarely strays into southern Texas. The basic pattern of yellow bands on a blackish background is fairly simple, and, unlike some reasonably similar species, there are no blue spots around the margin of the hind wing. The King Swallowtail is most often seen puddling, as here in rain forest in Venezuela's Guatopo National Park.

Zenobia Swallowtail

Although superficially very similar to the Common White-banded Swallowtail *(Papilio cyproeofila)*, and likewise seen here puddling in Bobiri Forest, the Zenobia Swallowtail is easily distinguished by the absence of any white spots around the margin of the hind wing. Also, the forewing of this rain-forest butterfly is rather shorter and broader, and the band on both wings is broader and a deeper shade of yellowish cream. In this respect it differs from another species that lacks the hind-wing spots, the Volta Swallowtail *(P. nobicea)*, a local species found only in the hills of the Ghana–Togo border area. It differs mainly in having pure white wing bands.

DATA

Scientific name: *Papilio zenobia*

Family: Papilionidae

Wingspan: About 4.1 in (10.5 cm).

Flight period: All year.

Larval food plants: *Piper umbellatum* (Piperaceae).

Range: Africa (Sierra Leone to Uganda).

Common Cattleheart

This is a genus of unpalatable butterflies that generally have a black ground color to the wings. Males typically have a green patch on each forewing, while both sexes have a red patch on the hind wings. They are mimicked by a number of butterflies in other families and are most often seen visiting flowers along forest edges. Rain forest is the normal habitat, but the specimen illustrated here was photographed in gallery forest along a small river. This ran through the savanna-like *campo cerrado* near Brazil's capital city, Brasilia.

DATA

Scientific name: *Parides anchises*

Family: Papilionidae

Wingspan: About 1.8 in (7 cm).

Flight period: All year.

Larval food plants: Pipevines *(Aristolochia)* in the family Aristolochiaceae.

Range: Over the whole of tropical South America and on Trinidad.

Apollo

Found only on flowery mountain slopes in the south of its range, as seen here in the French Alps, farther north this species occurs down to sea level. It seems to be decreasing generally and has recently gone extinct in a number of areas. Its most noticeable features are the very plump, hairy body and semitransparent wings, which are only sparsely covered with whitish scales. The number of black spots is variable, as is the number of red spots on the underside of the hind wing. In North America the Small Apollo *(Parnassius phoebus)* and the American Apollo *(P. clodius)* are not unlike the butterfly pictured here.

DATA

Scientific name: *Parnassius apollo*

Family: Papilionidae

Wingspan: About 3 in (7.5 cm).

Flight period: July–August.

Larval food plants: Stonecrops *(Sedum)* and houseleeks *(Sempervivum)* in the family Crassulaceae.

Range: Europe, then eastward to central Asia.

Malagasy Clubtail

DATA

Scientific name: *Pharmacophagus antenor*

Family: Papilionidae

Wingspan: About 3.5 in (9 cm).

Flight period: All year.

Larval food plants: Aristolochiaceae.

Range: Madagascar.

Perhaps more commonly known as *Atrophaneura antenor*, this large, robust butterfly is a powerful flier. The author once watched a lone individual flying strongly out to sea from the beach at Morondava on the west coast of Madagascar. Its main habitat is forest, both the rain forests of the east and the seasonally dry forests of the west, as seen here in this mating pair, photographed in the Forest Reserve at Ampijoroa. The upper side and underside are very similar except for a row of bright red spots around the rear margin of the hind wing in the male. These spots are only pale pinkish orange on the underside.

Ghost Brimstone

Although common enough in the tropical parts of its vast range, this species is only a stray in the far south of the United States, usually in southern Texas, but migrating occasionally as far north as Colorado. It is easily identified by its unusually large size and its white coloration. In males there is invariably a yellow ultraviolet-reflecting band on the forewing. Females also sometimes have this band, but it does not reflect ultraviolet light. The band contains a black dot on one edge. When feeding on flowers, as seen here on a roadside in Veracruz State in Mexico, the wings are usually held partly open.

DATA

Scientific name: *Anteos clorinde*

Family: Pieridae

Wingspan: About 3.2 in (8 cm).

Flight period: All year in south; May–December in north.

Larval food plants: *Cassia spectabilis* and other plants in the pea family (Fabaceae).

Range: United States to Argentina and in the West Indies.

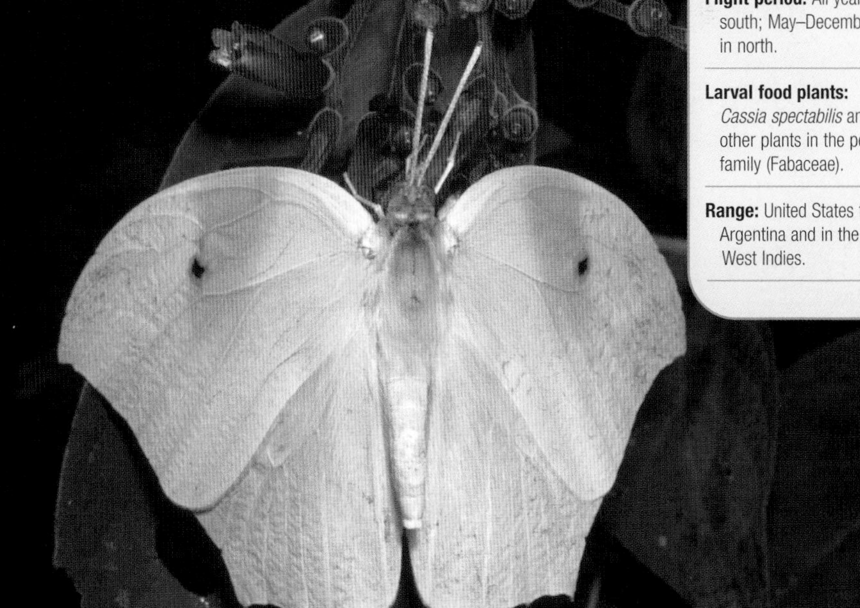

Orange Tip

DATA

Scientific name: *Anthocharis cardamines*

Family: Pieridae

Wingspan: About 1.6 in (4 cm).

Flight period: April–June in a single brood.

Larval food plants: *Cardamine, Sisymbrium,* etc., in the cabbage family (Brassicaceae).

Range: From Europe through temperate Asia to China.

Only males of this species have the bright orange wing tips seen in the photograph, which was taken in England. In the female the forewing is white except for a narrow black patch on the tip and a single black spot. In both sexes the underside of the hind wing is mottled with a dense pattern of black and yellow spots. From a distance they give the impression of a green pattern, which blends in perfectly with the surroundings when the butterfly is at rest among leaves with its wings closed. Woodland edges, flowery meadows, and roadsides are the typical habitat. The North American *Anthocharis sara* and *A. cethura* look similar.

Orange Albatross

The flamboyantly colored males of this common butterfly are often seen in dense throngs on sandbanks in rain-forest rivers, as seen here in Malaysia's Taman Negara National Park. The color of the wings varies from bright orange to brick red. The females are not often seen, spending most of their time in the rain-forest canopy and seldom coming down to the ground. Their color is highly variable and can be brown, white, yellow, orange, red, or bluish gray.

DATA

Scientific name: *Appias nero*

Family: Pieridae

Wingspan: About 2.8 in (7 cm).

Flight period: All year.

Larval food plants: Capparaceae.

Range: Over much of tropical Asia from India to the Philippines and Sulawesi.

Dark Mocker White

The five species of *Archonias* all mimic noxious butterflies belonging to other families. This species mimics *Heliconius xanthocles mellitus*, and a day-flying moth *Pericopis phyleis* in the family Arctiidae. The upper side and the underside of the wings are similar. The forewing is black with a pale yellow patch. The hind wings are black with a varying amount of orange plus a few small cream flecks and some red at the extreme bases. This is a rain-forest species, usually seen puddling on the ground, as here in Peru's Tingo Maria National Park.

DATA

Scientific name: *Archonias negrina*

Family: Pieridae

Wingspan: About 2.2 in (5.5 cm).

Flight period: All year.

Larval food plants: Unknown.

Range: Colombia, Ecuador, and Peru.

Sharp-veined White

The Sharp-veined White is found in a variety of habitats, especially in backyards and agricultural areas, but also in natural habitats, such as the woodland edge in England, where the accompanying picture of a mating pair was taken. As can be seen, the greenish veins that give this species its common name in Britain are very prominent on the underside, particularly on the yellowish hind wing. The forewing is white with a yellowish tip. Above, both wings are pure white, sometimes with the veins lined in gray, with or without one or two small black spots.

DATA

Scientific name: *Artogeia napi*

Other common names: Veined White, Mustard White, Green-veined White (in Britain)

Family: Pieridae

Wingspan: About 1.6 in (4 cm).

Flight period: April–September, in two or more broods.

Larval food plants: Mostly cabbages and related plants (Brassicaceae).

Range: From North Africa across Europe to Asia and Japan, and in North America.

Small White

DATA

Scientific name: *Artogeia rapae*

Other common name: Cabbage Butterfly

Family: Pieridae

Wingspan: About 2 in (5 cm).

Flight period: April–September in two or more broods.

Larval food plants: Mostly cabbages and other related plants (Brassicaceae).

Range: From North Africa across Europe to Asia and Japan. Introduced in North America and Australia.

The green caterpillars of this very common species can be a pest on cultivated cabbages, boring into their centers. The adults are found in most kinds of habitats from backyards, cabbage fields, and open woodland to windy coasts where wild cabbage *(Brassica oleracea)* grows on the spray-drenched cliff faces. They also visit flowers for nectar, particularly members of the thistle family (Asteraceae), as seen here in England. The upper side is mostly white with a black tip to the forewing, which bears one or two black spots. Below, the forewing is white with two black spots and a yellowish tip; the hind wing is yellowish.

Brown-veined White

DATA

Scientific name: *Belenois aurota*

Family: Pieridae

Wingspan: About 1.7 in (4.3 cm).

Flight period: All year.

Larval food plants: Bush cherry *(Maerua cafra)*, bastard shepherd's tree *(Boscia oleoides)*, and other Capparaceae.

Range: Over most of Africa and the Middle East, eastward to India.

Countless millions of these very common butterflies often make migrations across the drier parts of Africa. The author encountered a small migration in the Kalahari Desert in South Africa, where the butterflies pictured below paused to drink on damp sand around a water hole. Mainly a butterfly of savanna and semidesert, this is a rare species in the forest zone, where it is found only in large cleared areas. In the male the underside is extensively covered with a network of brown veins. The female's underside is similar but has in addition a number of yellow spots. In both sexes the upper side is mainly white with black wing tips.

Calypso White

DATA

Scientific name: *Belenois calypso*

Family: Pieridae

Wingspan: About 2.2 in (5.5 cm).

Flight period: All year.

Larval food plants: *Cadaba, Maerua, Ritchiea, Capparis* (Capparaceae).

Range: West Africa to Zambia, Malawi, and Angola.

Although mainly a butterfly of rather dense, semiwooded savanna, the Calypso White is also found in relatively undisturbed rain forest—the small group shown above was seen puddling on a path in Kenya's Kakamega Forest. There is a certain amount of variation, this being subspecies *minor*, restricted to Uganda and western Kenya. The upper side is mainly white with black tips to the forewings and large black spots around the margin of the hind wing. The female is similar but has more black. The underside is variable, especially the hind wing, which can be yellow or white with a variable number of black spots.

Caper White

DATA

Scientific name: *Belenois java*

Family: Pieridae

Wingspan: About 2.2 in (5.5 cm).

Larval food plants: Various capers (Capparaceae).

Range: New Guinea, Australia, and on numerous Pacific islands.

Formerly included in the genus *Anaphaeis*, the Caper White is a noted migrant, pictured here feeding on a flower of bugle *(Ajuga)* in Wyperfeld National Park in the state of Victoria, Australia. Here the habitat is rather dry and known locally as mallee bush, named for the rather small species of eucalyptus trees that grow there. As can be seen, the underside of this attractive butterfly is strikingly marked with black, white, and yellow. The upper side is less impressive, being mainly white with black wing tips. This is subspecies *teutonia*.

Yellow-banded Dart White

DATA

Scientific name: *Catasticta sisamnus*

Family: Pieridae

Wingspan: About 2.4 in (6 cm).

Flight period: All year.

Larval food plants: Probably mistletoes (Loranthaceae).

Range: Honduras to Bolivia and Peru.

The genus *Catasticta* contains more than 100 species of rather colorful butterflies that are closely related to the jezebels *(Delias)* from Asia and Australasia. In all cases where the food plant is known it is in the Loranthaceae. Both sexes of this rain-forest butterfly feed at flowers, but the males also puddle, as seen here in Peru's Tingo Maria National Park. The male is whitish above with broad black wing borders, while the more attractive female is similar but yellow. In both sexes the underside is black with variable yellow and white spotting.

Small Mocker White

Often included in *Archonias*, the two species in this genus both resemble members of the tiger-striped grouping of ithomiids and heliconiids and are probably Batesian mimics of these unpalatable species. The fact that this specimen is puddling on a muddy track in Peru's Tingo Maria National Park is something of a giveaway. Puddling is common in pierids, but rarely if ever seen in the tiger-striped ithomiids and heliconiids. The wings, similar on both sides, are black with yellow spots on the forewing, which has an orange patch toward the hind margin. There is a much bigger orange patch on the hind wing, which is bordered with white spots.

DATA

Scientific name: *Charonias theano*

Family: Pieridae

Wingspan: About 2.4 in (6 cm).

Flight period: All year.

Larval food plants: Unknown.

Range: Over most of tropical South America.

Clouded Yellow

In the south of its range this species breeds for much of the year, attaining high population levels that explode northward in summer, reaching northern areas such as the British Isles as early as late March. Successive invasions may take place through the summer, but the onset of the northern winter spells death for all stages of this warmth-loving butterfly. The migrating adults are strongly attracted to members of the thistle family (Asteraceae), especially knapweeds *(Centaurea).* This male was seen on a grassy slope in England. Females are paler yellow or even grayish white.

DATA

Scientific name: *Colias crocea*

Family: Pieridae

Wingspan: About 2 in (5 cm).

Flight period: April–October.

Larval food plants: Vetches *(Vicia)* and other small members of the pea family (Fabaceae).

Range: North Africa and south and central Europe, eastward to Iran.

Common Sulfur

Often common in alfalfa fields, this species is found in a wide variety of mainly open habitats, including open woodland, fencerows, roadsides, vacant lots in cities, urban parks, and backyards, as seen here in South Carolina. In both sexes the upper side is a bright lemon yellow, edged with black, and with an orange spot near the border of the hind wings. On the underside of the hind wing there is a silver spot with two red rings around it and usually a smaller spot nearby. The Orange Sulfur *(Colias eurytheme)* is very similar but is more orange than yellow.

DATA

Scientific name: *Colias philodice*

Family: Pieridae

Wingspan: About 2 in (5 cm).

Flight period: June–August.

Larval food plants: Many members of the pea family (Fabaceae).

Range: Most of North America, excluding eastern and central Canada and a few other areas.

Scarlet Tip

DATA

Scientific name: *Colotis danae*

Family: Pieridae

Wingspan: About 1.6 in (4 cm).

Flight period: All year.

Larval food plants: Mainly *Cadaba* (Capparaceae).

Range: Sub-Saharan Africa, Arabian Peninsula, India, Sri Lanka.

In Africa this is a butterfly of open savanna, as seen here on a campsite in Kenya's Masai Mara, photographed during the rainy season when butterflies and other insects are far more abundant. This is subspecies *pseudacaste*, found from Tanzania to Ethiopia. The nominate subspecies *danae* is from India and Sri Lanka, while subspecies *annae* occupies southern Africa. In both sexes the wing tips are usually a bright scarlet, of a shade otherwise seen only in *Colotis euippe*, which can be distinguished by its more rounded forewing. In some females the scarlet tips are absent.

Veined Yellow

DATA

Scientific name: *Colotis protomedia*

Other common name: Yellow Splendor

Family: Pieridae

Wingspan: About 2.4 in (6 cm).

Flight period: All year.

Larval food plants: *Maerua* (Capparaceae).

Range: Nigeria to East Africa and the Arabian Peninsula.

Although mainly a butterfly of savanna grasslands, this distinctive species is also found in scrubby areas, backyards, and in open dry forest. It is pictured here in a small remnant stand of forest north of Mombasa in Kenya. In both sexes the upper side is pale lemon yellow with black wing borders in which there are widely spaced yellow spots. The tip of the forewing is black and contains a variable number of pale yellow spots. The underside is unmistakable, because the wing veins are picked out in broad greenish gold bands.

Northern Jezebel

DATA

Scientific name: *Delias argenthona*

Family: Pieridae

Wingspan: About 2 in (5.5 cm).

Flight period: All year.

Larval food plants: Mistletoes (Loranthaceae).

Range: Australia and New Guinea.

The genus *Delias* contains some 170 species, most of which are noted for their strikingly colored undersides. In Australia the Northern Jezebel is almost restricted to a mainly coastal belt of subtropical and tropical habitat from northern New South Wales northward to Cape York and the Northern Territory. Its main habitat is in the rain-forest understory—it is seen here in Lake Barrine National Park in Queensland—but it also visits flowers in backyards. As in most jezebels, the upper side is rather drab, being mainly pale white in the male and white with black borders, spotted with yellow, in the female. The area of the forewing's underside that cannot be seen in the illustration is mainly white.

Painted Jezebel

DATA

Scientific name: *Delias hyparete*

Family: Pieridae

Wingspan: About 2.4 in (6 cm).

Flight period: All year.

Larval food plants: Mistletoe *(Dendrophthoë pentandra)* in the Loranthaceae.

Range: India, southern China, Thailand to Indonesia and the Philippines.

Over its wide range this lovely butterfly occurs in a number of subspecies, of which this is *metarete*. Often found now in backyards, it was originally a forest butterfly. In fact, after the author had experienced several days of leech-infested walking in the rain-forest understory of Malaysia's Taman Negara National Park, the Painted Jezebel pictured here was the only butterfly seen. All other butterflies found were in more open spots along the rivers or around the park buildings. As with other jezebels, the upper side is an anticlimax, being mainly white, but the combination of red, yellow, and white on the underside is quite something.

Gold-flecked Jezebel

During the author's single visit to New Guinea it was hoped that numerous species of Jezebels could be photographed. However, fate dictated otherwise, for a typhoon had swept through the area only days before, leaving few butterflies of any kind to be seen. This was the only Jezebel photographed, puddling on the ground near Wau. It serves to illustrate that not all *Delias* are brilliantly colored, this species being one of the darker ones, with black wings. The underside of the hind wing bears just a few yellow spots, but these are much larger on the forewing (only the edges being visible in the illustration).

DATA

Scientific name: *Delias microsticha*

Family: Pieridae

Wingspan: About 1.6 in (4 cm).

Flight period: All year.

Larval food plants: Mistletoes (Loranthaceae).

Range: New Guinea.

Common Jezebel

The range of this species extends from Sydney in the southeast of Australia northward to Cape York. Although often found in backyards and parks, this is mainly a rain-forest butterfly, pictured here in the deep shade of the understory in Lake Barrine National Park in Queensland. As in the Gold-flecked Jezebel *(Delias microsticha)*, the basic wing color is black, but in the Common Jezebel the markings on the underside are striking, particularly the narrow red band that zigzags its way down the hind wing. As can be seen in the accompanying photograph, the tip of the forewing is yellow but the rest is black except for a dusting of gray near the base.

DATA

Scientific name: *Delias nigrina*

Family: Pieridae

Wingspan: About 1.6 in (4 cm).

Flight period: All year.

Larval food plants: Mistletoes (Loranthaceae).

Range: Australia.

Tiger-mimic White

DATA

Scientific name: *Dismorphia amphione*

Family: Pieridae

Wingspan: About 2.8 in (7 cm).

Flight period: All year.

Larval food plants: *Inga* trees in the pea family (Fabaceae).

Range: Mexico to Argentina and on Trinidad.

About 40 species are included in the genus *Dismorphia.* Most of them have longish narrow wings and are mimics of various unpalatable tiger-striped species of heliconiids and ithomiids. Whether or not the *Dismorphia* species themselves are also unpalatable has yet to be adequately tested. The Tiger-mimic White—by far the commonest and most widespread member of the genus—is found in all kinds of forested habitats as long as they are not too dry. This photograph was taken on a flowery roadside in the Northern Range of Trinidad. The upper side is similar to the underside but paler.

Variable Tiger-mimic White

Anyone glancing quickly at the illustration below might think that it simply shows a tiger-striped ithomiid feeding on a bird dropping, a very common phenomenon. However, look again and count the number of legs. The total comes to six. Ithomiids have only four functional legs, but pierids have six, giving a quick and easy clue to the true identity of this species. Taken in rain forest at Rancho Grande in Venezuela, the photograph shows subspecies *theucharila*. Farther north there is a gradual transition to transparent wings in subspecies *fortunata* of Central America, which mimics clear-winged ithomiids.

DATA

Scientific name: *Dismorphia theucharila*

Family: Pieridae

Wingspan: About 2 in (5 cm).

Flight period: All year.

Larval food plants: Unknown.

Range: Mexico to Brazil.

Nonconformist Mimic White

Unlike the Tiger-mimic White *(Dismorphia amphione)* and the Variable Tiger-mimic White *(D. theucharila)*, this *Dismorphia* does not have long narrow wings—it exhibits something more closely approaching the normal pierid wing shape, especially in the hind wings. In its underside coloration it resembles a species of *Catasticta* or *Leodonta*. The underside of the hind wings is boldly patterned in black and yellow but the forewing, which is much narrower, is white except for a black tip. This rain-forest butterfly is seen puddling on the ground in Peru's Tingo Maria National Park.

DATA

Scientific name: *Dismorphia lygdamis*

Family: Pieridae

Wingspan: About 2 in (5 cm).

Flight period: All year.

Larval food plants: Unknown.

Range: Colombia, Ecuador, Peru.

Barred Sulfur

Found in backyards, fields, and other open areas, this species occurs in wet- and dry-season forms. In the male the yellow area on the forewing is greater in the dry-season form, and the black margin around the hind wing is reduced. The wet-season female is usually white with black tips to the forewings and a black hind-wing margin. In the dry-season female there is always some yellow on the forewing. In the photograph below, taken in Mexico, two males are sitting beside a female and "saluting" her with one forewing in courtship.

DATA

Scientific name: *Eurema daira*

Family: Pieridae

Wingspan: About 1.6 in (4 cm).

Flight period: All year.

Larval food plants: Various members of the pea family (Fabaceae).

Range: From the extreme southern United States to Brazil; also in the West Indies.

Common Grass Yellow

DATA

Scientific name: *Eurema hecabe*

Family: Pieridae

Wingspan: About 1.4 in (3.5 cm).

Flight period: All year.

Larval food plants: Mostly members of the pea family (Fabaceae).

Range: Africa, Madagascar, and through the Arabian Peninsula and Asia to Australia.

Despite not being present in the Americas, this is probably the world's most common and abundant butterfly, often occurring in huge yellow clouds on the African savanna. The subspecies pictured below *(solifera)* is found almost throughout Africa, being absent only from the driest deserts and the wettest and most intact rain forests. Wherever these have been opened up by humans, the Common Grass Yellow is sure to be present, as evidenced by this group puddling in Ghana's Bobiri Forest. The cleared areas here are covered with the introduced sensitive plant *(Mimosa pudica)*, a favorite larval food. The upper side is yellow with black margins, but there is wide variability, and several other species are very similar.

Brimstone

DATA

Scientific name: *Gonepteryx rhamni*

Family: Pieridae

Wingspan: About 2.2 in (5.5 cm).

Flight period: March–May and July–August.

Larval food plants: Buckthorns *(Rhamnus)* in the family Rhamnaceae.

Range: From Europe and North Africa to Asia Minor and Siberia.

Since it passes the winters as an adult, this species is often on the wing on warm days as early as March. The bright yellow males will be seen flying along some hedgerow, dipping down at intervals to inspect anything that resembles the pale greenish white, leaflike females. After mating, the overwintered individuals die off, to be succeeded in July by their offspring. They avidly search out flowers such as thistles, as seen here in England. Except when in flight the wings, which are similar on both sides, are always kept closed. In the male the head and antennae are a very attractive shade of pink.

Latticed Tile White

DATA

Scientific name: *Hesperocharis nereina*

Family: Pieridae

Wingspan: About 2.4 in (6 cm).

Flight period: All year.

Larval food plants: Unknown.

Range: Ecuador, Peru, and Bolivia.

The genus *Hesperocharis* has 10 species, in three of which the hind-wing underside is similar to that of the species illustrated here, seen puddling in rain forest in Peru's Tingo Maria National Park. In *H. marchalii* the tip of the hind wing is much more angled, while in *H. graphites* it is conspicuously scalloped, with two short "tails." In *H. nereina* and *H. marchalii* the forewing underside is white with a patterned tip, but in *H. graphites* it is cream with a large yellow patch along the front margin. In all three species the upper side is mainly white.

Brown-bordered White

DATA

Scientific name: *Itaballia pandosia*

Family: Pieridae

Wingspan: About 2 in (5 cm).

Flight period: All year.

Larval food plants: Unknown.

Range: Honduras to Brazil and Peru.

Pictured here mating in the Tambopata National Reserve, Peru, the Brown-bordered White is a species of the perpetual twilight zone of the understory of dense, intact rain forest. As can be seen here, the sexes are similar on the underside, with a bold pattern of black and white and an orange line inward from the margin of the hind wing. The upper side is similar but lacks the orange hind-wing line, and the female is yellowish rather than white. This is subspecies *pisonis*, restricted to Colombia and Peru, and considered by some to be a distinct species.

Dyson's Ensign

DATA

Scientific name: *Leodonta dysoni*

Family: Pieridae

Wingspan: About 2.4 in (6 cm).

Flight period: All year.

Larval food plants: Unknown.

Range: Costa Rica to Peru.

Both sexes of this attractive butterfly are attracted to flowers such as *Cephaelus*, *Fuchsia*, and *Eupatorium*, but the males also puddle on damp ground, as seen here in rain forest in Peru's Tingo Maria National Park. They also perch on leaves and engage in long chases of other butterflies, almost always returning to the same perch time after time. The ground color on both sides is white, and very broad black margins occupy about half the wing area on the upper side. The underside of the forewing is white on its basal half but black with yellow spots at the tip, as on much of the hind wing.

Common Dotted Border

Originally a butterfly of open woodland and savanna, this species has taken advantage of the interference of humans to spread into a far wider range of habitats. It is now common in cleared areas within the main rain-forest zone—this individual was seen puddling on a logging road in Ghana's Bobiri Forest. It has also invaded agricultural areas and city backyards. In both sexes the upper side is mainly white with black tips to the forewings, but in the female half of the hind wing is black. Below, the yellow hind wing with its broad black border is diagnostic for this species.

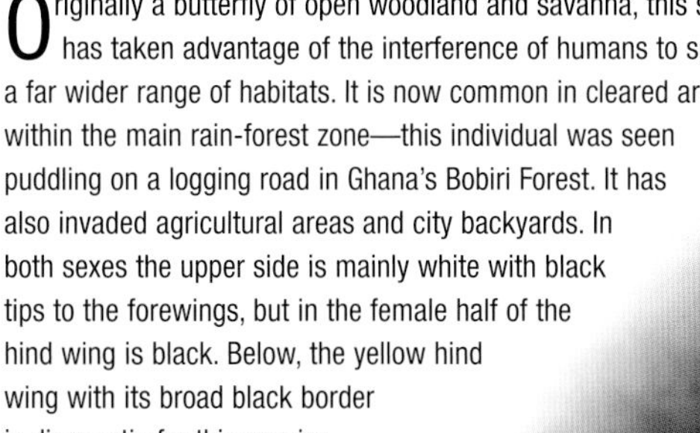

DATA

Scientific name: *Mylothris chloris*

Family: Pieridae

Wingspan: About 2.2 in (5.5 cm).

Flight period: All year.

Larval food plants: Mainly mistletoes (Loranthaceae), e.g., *Englerina gabonensis*.

Range: Over most of sub-Saharan Africa.

Blue Vagrant

DATA

Scientific name: *Nepheronia thalassina*

Other common name: Cambridge Vagrant

Family: Pieridae

Wingspan: About 2.6 in (6.5 cm).

Flight period: All year.

Larval food plants: *Hippocratea* (Celastraceae).

Range: Over most of sub-Saharan Africa.

The blue shade typical of the males is extremely subtle and difficult to record on camera. Even to the naked eye it tends to come and go as the butterfly moves and changes its angle relative to the observer. The female lacks any hint of blue and is white with a dark border on the forewings and black dots on the hind wing. Both sexes are very fond of flowers—the male pictured here was one of many feeding on a large stand of *Eupatorium* flowers that had colonized a cleared area beside the logging road in Ghana's Bobiri Forest. Within the rain-forest zone such an open area is a typical habitat for this butterfly of dry forest and the transition zone to savanna.

Pamela's Tiger-mimic White

The members of this genus are noted for the striking difference between the sexes. The males are relatively normal white or yellow pierids, while most of the females are mimics of various ithomiids and heliconiids in the so-called tiger-striped mimicry grouping. Tests with caged birds indicate that *Perrhybris* females are as noxious as their models, thus making them Muellerian rather than Batesian mimics. Like the female shown here perched on a *Lantana camara* flower in Peru's Tingo Maria National Park, both sexes visit flowers. The male is white with black wing tips.

DATA

Scientific name: *Perrhybris pamela*

Family: Pieridae

Wingspan: About 3 in (7.5 cm).

Flight period: All year.

Larval food plants: *Capparis* (Capparaceae).

Range: Over most of tropical South America.

Apricot Sulfur

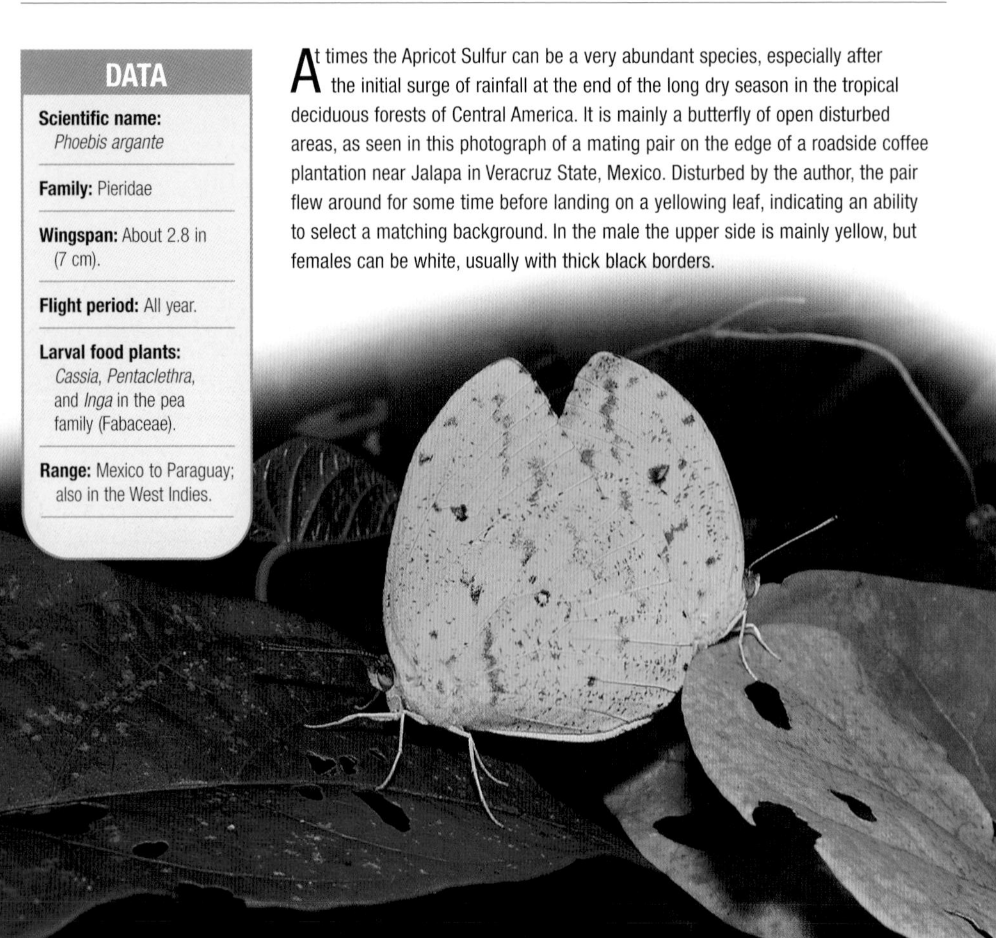

DATA

Scientific name: *Phoebis argante*

Family: Pieridae

Wingspan: About 2.8 in (7 cm).

Flight period: All year.

Larval food plants: *Cassia*, *Pentaclethra*, and *Inga* in the pea family (Fabaceae).

Range: Mexico to Paraguay; also in the West Indies.

At times the Apricot Sulfur can be a very abundant species, especially after the initial surge of rainfall at the end of the long dry season in the tropical deciduous forests of Central America. It is mainly a butterfly of open disturbed areas, as seen in this photograph of a mating pair on the edge of a roadside coffee plantation near Jalapa in Veracruz State, Mexico. Disturbed by the author, the pair flew around for some time before landing on a yellowing leaf, indicating an ability to select a matching background. In the male the upper side is mainly yellow, but females can be white, usually with thick black borders.

Tailed Sulfur

DATA

Scientific name: *Phoebis rurina*

Family: Pieridae

Wingspan: About 3.2 in (8 cm).

Flight period: All year.

Larval food plants: *Cassia fruticosa* in the pea family (Fabaceae).

Range: Mexico to Brazil.

This species is easily distinguished by the hind wings, which extend outward into a sort of tail. This is slightly longer in the male, pictured here puddling in tropical dry forest in Santa Rosa National Park in Costa Rica. The male is plain yellow above, and its underside is as seen here. The females are more variable and may be white with a black spot on each forewing or yellow with a reddish orange band along the margin of the hind wing. Both sexes visit flowers, but only the males puddle. Most habitats are used, including pastures and open spots in lowland rain forest.

Cloudless Sulfur

DATA

Scientific name: *Phoebis sennae*

Family: Pieridae

Wingspan: About 2.6 in (6.5 cm).

Flight period: All year in south; May–September in north.

Larval food plants: Senna *(Cassia)* in the pea family (Fabaceae).

Range: United States to Patagonia; also in the West Indies.

On the wing throughout the year in the tropics and in the southern United States, in summer this species migrates northward as far as Maine and Montana. It mainly inhabits open or brushy areas but also occurs in rain forest, especially on riverbanks, and is seen here in the Tambopata National Reserve in Peru. The photograph shows a male of subspecies *marcellina*, in which the underside is more or less unmarked. In the other subspecies the hind wing in particular is adorned with many brown and white blotches that make it look like a dying leaf. The upper side is pale yellow in the male and pale yellow, yellowish orange, or white in the female, usually with some dark dots on the borders.

Large White

DATA

Scientific name: *Pieris brassicae*

Family: Pieridae

Wingspan: About 2.4 in (6 cm).

Flight period: April–May and July–August.

Larval food plants: Mainly cabbages and related plants in the Brassicaceae; also nasturtiums *(Tropaeolum)* in the Tropaeolaceae.

Range: North Africa and Europe across Asia to the Himalayas.

This is one of the most familiar butterflies in backyards across Europe. The adults are often seen on flowers such as lavender and buddleia, while large groups of caterpillars are an all too familiar sight on cultivated cabbages, which are often reduced to skeletons. The adults appear in two broods, differing in various small details of coloration. In the first-brood females the tip of the forewing is dusted with black, but in those of the second brood it is deep black. In both sexes the underside of the hind wing is plain yellow, while the forewing bears two large black dots and a dusted black tip.

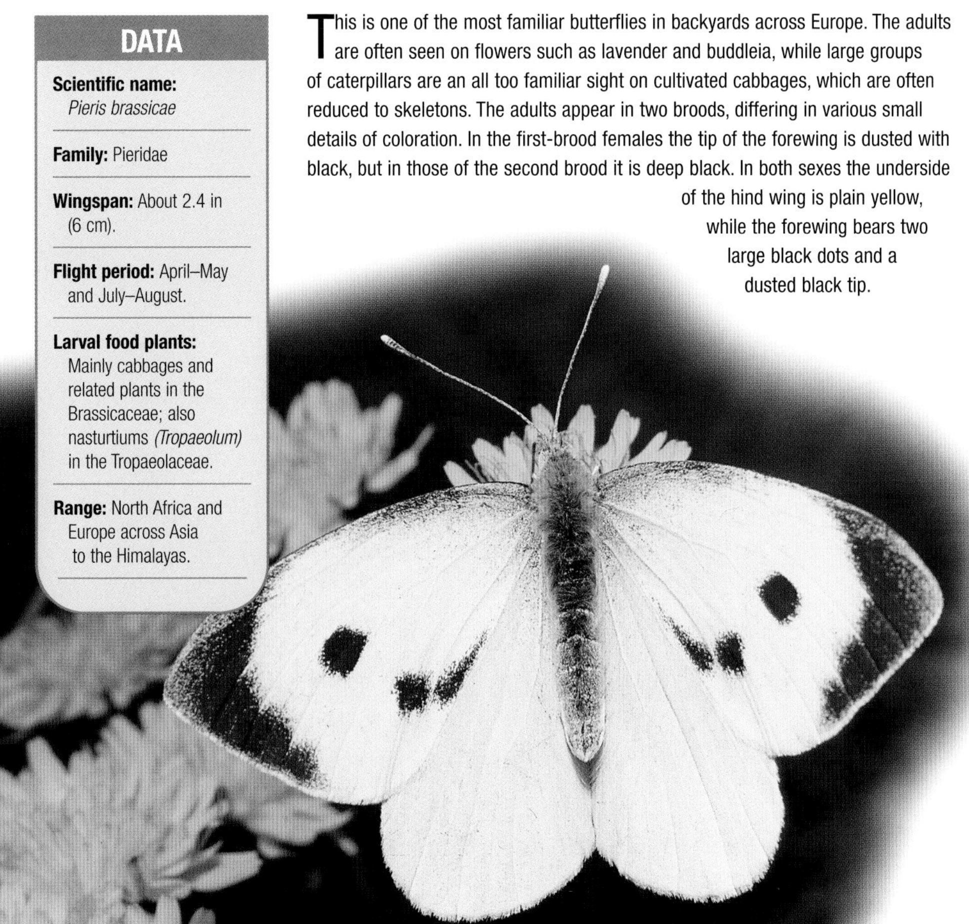

Malaysian Albatross

DATA

Scientific name: *Saletara panda*

Family: Pieridae

Wingspan: About 1.6 in (4 cm).

Flight period: All year.

Larval food plants: Various.

Range: Malaysia and Indonesia to the Philippines.

This species was long known as *Saletara liberia*. Often seen drinking alongside groups of the Orange Albatross *(Appias nero)*, the Malaysian Albatross is a familiar sight on sandbanks in rain-forest rivers, as seen here in Malaysia's Taman Negara National Park. The underside is cream or pale yellow. The upper side is whitish yellow with a narrow black margin to the forewings (except for the trailing margin), a broad black tip to the forewings, and a row of small white dots around the hind-wing margin. The puddling butterflies seen here belong to subspecies *distanti*.

Veined Southern White

The genus *Tatochila* comprises some 16 species of butterflies that inhabit the temperate zones of South America. Several of them, including the species shown below, are adapted to surviving in the harsh and often arid environment of the high Andes. This specimen was photographed as it roosted in the late afternoon on a rocky, cactus-studded slope near Iscayache in Bolivia. Its main distinguishing feature is the way in which the network of veins on the underside of both wings is picked out in black against the yellow of the wings. The upper side is mainly white.

DATA

Scientific name: *Tatochila xanthodice*

Family: Pieridae

Wingspan: About 1.8 in (4.5 cm).

Flight period: Mainly October–April.

Larval food plants: Unknown.

Range: Colombia, Ecuador, Bolivia, and Peru.

Dog-face

The common name of this butterfly comes from the pattern on the upper side of the male, comprising a broad brown patch on each forewing, scalloped on its inner edge to give a doglike impression, aided by a single brown spot near the top of each forewing. The hind wings are yellow with a partial brown border. The female is pale yellow to white with a plain hind wing and sparsely patterned forewing. The underside of the male is as seen here (at Oruro in the Bolivian Andes), with the brown "dog face" on the forewing just showing through. This species is common in open places, especially in pastures where its clover and alfalfa food plants are promoted by the ranchers.

DATA

Scientific name: *Zerene cesonia*

Family: Pieridae

Wingspan: About 2.6 in (6.5 cm).

Larval food plants: *Indigofera*, *Trifolium*, *Medicago* in the pea family (Fabaceae).

Range: Mexico to Argentina, Cuba, Hispaniola, and Puerto Rico.

Neave's Banded Judy

The 12 African species of *Abisara* are the only members of the large family Riodinidae that are present in Africa. They fall into two groups, one with a brown ground color and violet markings, the other—as seen here—with white bands on the wings. This is one of several species that are difficult to tell apart. They all have a pair of eyespots on the tailed hind wing, forming a false head. Males sit with wings partly open; on first landing they do an abrupt about-face, placing the false head where the real head has just been. This is a rain-forest species, photographed here in Kenya's Kakamega Forest.

DATA

Scientific name: *Abisara neavei*

Family: Riodinidae

Wingspan: About 1.6 in (4 cm).

Flight period: All year.

Larval food plants: *Maesa lanceolata* (Myrsinaceae).

Range: Africa (Nigeria to Kenya, Tanzania, and Zambia).

Amarynth Metalmark

DATA

Scientific name: *Amarynthis meneria*

Family: Riodinidae

Wingspan: About 1.2 in (3 cm).

Flight period: All year.

Larval food plants: Unknown.

Range: Venezuela to Colombia, Peru, and Bolivia.

This sole representative of the genus *Amarynthis* is seen here feeding on a typically small, drab rain-forest flower on the edge of a track in Tingo Maria National Park, Peru. This is just the place to find metalmarks, rather than deep inside the gloomy forest interior. The Amarynth Metalmark is one of a number of similar black-and-red species from different genera. There is a single narrow red band parallel to the margin of each wing, and a broken band near the forewing's front margin (costa). There is a scatter of tiny white dots on each wing, and a series of red spots is present on the body.

Toreador Beautymark

DATA

Scientific name: *Ancyluris meliboeus*

Family: Riodinidae

Wingspan: 1.8 in (4.5 cm).

Flight period: All year.

Larval food plants: Unknown.

Range: Amazon region of South America.

The 20 or so members of this genus are some of the most striking of the South American riodinids. However, it is probable that many of the described species are really just forms of others, and the real number could be as low as six to 10. This species, for example, is very similar to *Ancyluris colubra*. It is depicted here puddling in rain forest near Satipo in Peru. The ground color is deep velvety black. There is a single red band on the forewing and two on the hind wing, which has a number of small white spots along its hind margin.

Mormon Metalmark

DATA

Scientific name: *Apodemia mormo*

Family: Riodinidae

Wingspan: About 1 in (2.5 cm).

Flight period: March–October in south; July–September farther north.

Larval food plants: Wild buckwheat *(Eriogonum)* in the Polygonaceae.

Range: United States (from Washington State through the Rockies to California and Arizona); southward to Sinaloa in Mexico.

This is by far the most widespread of the 20 species of Riodinidae that occur in the United States. Compared with the brilliant array of spectacular species farther south in Central and South America, they are rather a drab bunch, of which this is probably the best. The basic pattern of silvery white spots on a reddish brown background, broad grayish black margins dotted with white, and white fringes is variable, and there are numerous subspecies that show minor variations on this theme. Shown above is subspecies *mejicanus*, photographed in April in desert near Tombstone, Arizona.

Snappy Metalmark

This little butterfly seems to be associated with tropical deciduous forests, and the specimen illustrated here was photographed in such a habitat in Oaxaca State in Mexico. In the male (illustrated) the wings are black, each one having a silvery translucent spot. There is a broad red margin to the front of the hind wing, where it is overlapped by the rear edge of the forewing. The female is a mosaic of various shades of brown with some small silvery spots. This species is often found on various kinds of small white flowers, exactly as seen here.

DATA

Scientific name: *Calydna sturnula*

Family: Riodinidae

Wingspan: About 1 in (2.5 cm).

Flight period: All year.

Larval food plants: Unknown.

Range: Mexico to Brazil.

Mantinea Green Metalmark

DATA

Scientific name: *Caria mantinea*

Family: Riodinidae

Wingspan: About 1.2 in (3 cm).

Flight period: All year.

Larval food plants: Unknown.

Range: Peru, Brazil, Ecuador, and Bolivia.

The butterflies in this genus are distinguished by their brilliant iridescent upper sides and the way in which the front of the forewing (the costa) is bowed. Both of these features are clearly visible in this little jewel seen perched on a leaf on the side of a track in rain forest in Peru's Tingo Maria National Park. The forewings are rather a dull brown, but there is an iridescent green patch at the base and across each wing toward the tip. The hind wings are mostly iridescent green.

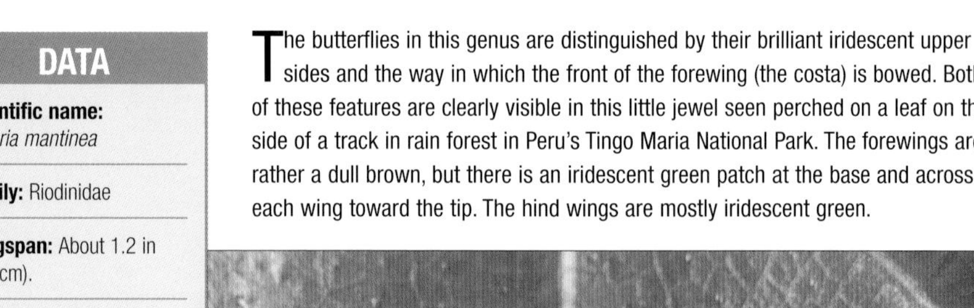

Theodora Metalmark

DATA

Scientific name: *Chalodeta theodora*

Family: Riodinidae

Wingspan: About 0.9 in (2.2 cm).

Larval food plants: Unknown.

Range: Amazon region of South America to Paraguay.

The eight or so species in *Chalodeta* are often included in the genus *Charis*, but they have short hairs arising from between the facets of the eyes. The caterpillars are covered in a dense pile of short hairs, with long tufts around the sides. They are all rain-forest butterflies, although often relatively common in second-growth or disturbed areas. The specimen illustrated above was puddling on damp ground in Peru's Tingo Maria National Park. The wings are velvety black with an iridescent golden line and a thinner, slightly broken line near the margins.

Six-tailed Brushfoot

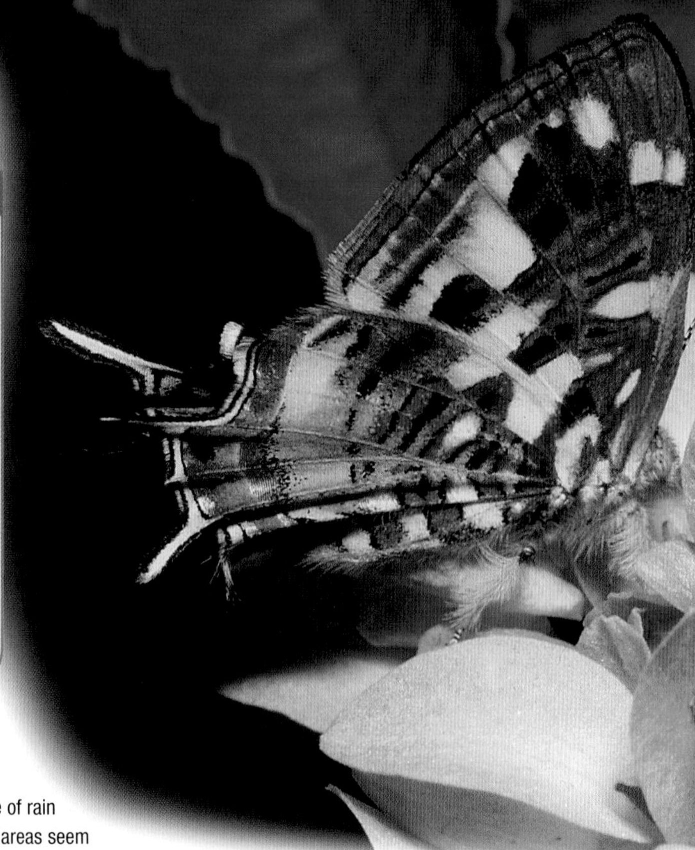

DATA

Scientific name: *Charis chrysus*

Family: Riodinidae

Wingspan: About 1 in (2.5 cm).

Flight period: All year.

Larval food plants: Dead leaves on the ground.

Range: Over much of tropical South America and in Trinidad.

Open parkland on the edge of rain forest or second-growth areas seem to be as good a place as any to find this little butterfly, seen here on a flowering vine in the backyard of the Simla research facility in Trinidad's Northern Range. As is typical for the genus, the upper side is a somber shade of brown, but the underside is an attractive checkerboard of reddish brown, white, black, and blue. There are three tails on each hind wing, and the legs are densely hairy.

Actoris Metalmark

DATA

Scientific name: *Cremna actoris*

Family: Riodinidae

Wingspan: About 1.2 in (3 cm).

Flight period: All year.

Larval food plants: Unknown.

Range: Over most of tropical South America.

The genus *Cremna* contains about four species of rain-forest butterflies. The males—like this one near Satipo in Peru—are usually seen perched on foliage in the rain-forest understory. The black wings are covered in an intricate pattern of blue spots with a few white spots around the borders. The abdomen is ringed in silvery white. Some species in the genus are seldom seen, apparently because they spend most of their time high up in the rain-forest canopy. Known larval food plants for other members of the genus include orchids and bromeliads.

Mourning Metalmark

DATA

Scientific name: *Crocozona coecias*

Family: Riodinidae

Wingspan: About 1 in (2.5 cm).

Flight period: All year.

Larval food plants: Unknown.

Range: Ecuador, Peru, and Bolivia.

The genus *Crocozona* is a small genus of just four species, all of which are found mainly in good-quality rain forest. The specimen illustrated here was drinking on a deeply shaded rock face over which there was a constant seepage of water, in Tingo Maria National Park in Peru. The wings are a particularly deep velvety black, each with a narrow red bar, and there are a few small white spots down the wing margins. *Crocozona fasciata* from Peru and Bolivia is larger, deep brown rather than black, and has a broad red patch on each forewing.

Chiricahua Tanmark

Apart from the fact that its forewings are rounded at the tip, rather than being slightly hooked, this species is very close to the Arizona Tanmark *(Emesis zela)* and may simply be an extreme seasonal form of it. Intermediate forms have been noted. On the upper side the ground color is brownish gray with numerous small black flecks and an orange patch on each hind wing. The fringes are white. The underside is brownish orange with lines of small black dots. Seen here in the Chiricahua Mountains in Arizona, this butterfly's habitat is mainly among oaks along streams in desert.

DATA

Scientific name: *Emesis ares*

Other common names: Ares Tanmark, Ares Metalmark

Family: Riodinidae

Wingspan: About 1.4 in (3.5 cm).

Flight period: July–September.

Larval food plants: Oaks *(Quercus)* in the family Fagaceae.

Range: Southern Arizona and adjacent Mexico.

Orange Tanmark

DATA

Scientific name: *Emesis fatimella*

Family: Riodinidae

Wingspan: About 1.6 in (4 cm).

Flight period: All year.

Larval food plants: Unknown.

Range: Costa Rica to Brazil and Bolivia; also in Trinidad.

Formerly known as *Emesis fatima*, the Orange Tanmark is one of the more attractive members of the genus. It is typically found in light gaps in rain forest, such as along streams, or as here, in the backyard of the Simla research facility in Trinidad, which is bordered by rain forest and old semiforested cocoa plantations. The bright orange coloration indicates that this is a male. He is feeding on a small *Bidens* flower. These seem to be popular with a range of butterflies. The female is more yellowish orange and has slightly broader tips to the forewings.

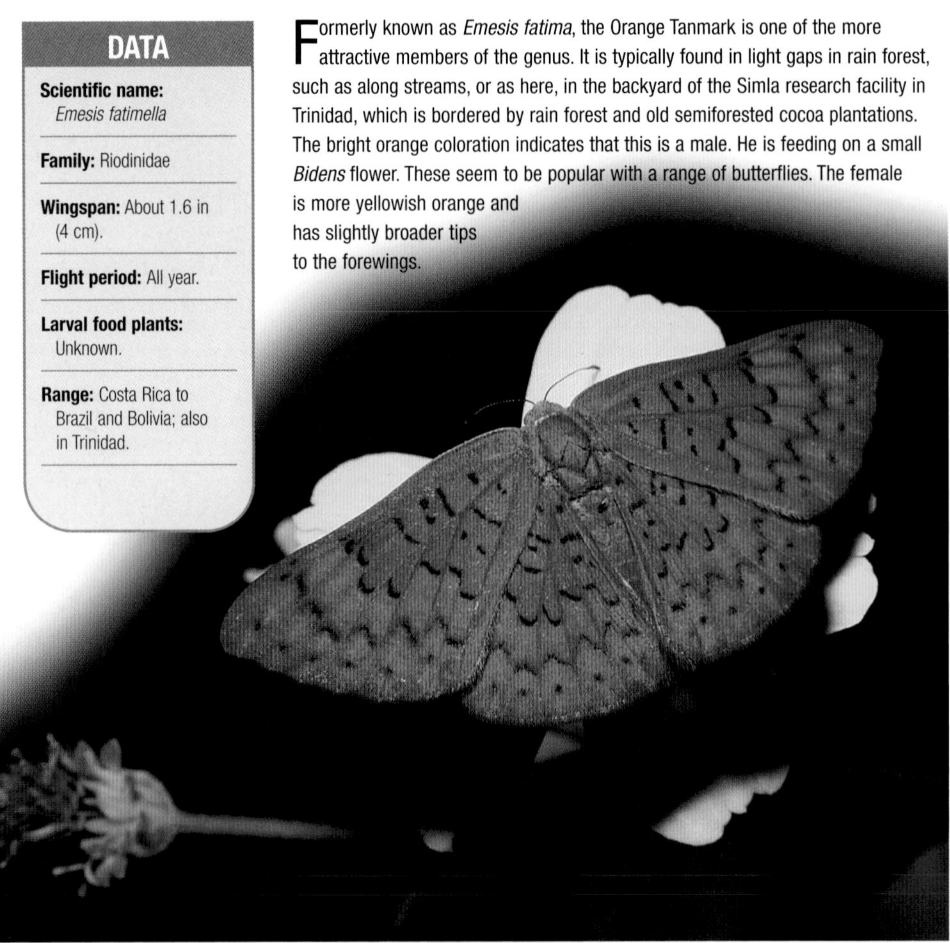

Lucinda Tanmark

DATA

Scientific name: *Emesis lucinda*

Family: Riodinidae

Wingspan: About 2 in (5 cm).

Flight period: All year.

Larval food plants: *Neea laetevirens* and *N. amplifolia* in the four-o'clock family (Nyctaginaceae).

Range: Mexico to Bolivia and Brazil.

As with the Orange Tanmark *(Emesis fatimella)*, the specimen illustrated here is visiting a *Bidens* flower at Simla in Trinidad. Although originally a rain-forest butterfly, the Lucinda Tanmark is probably now more common in disturbed and second-growth habitats than in primary rain forest. The female (illustrated) is gray with a network of black lines and a white patch near the tip of each forewing. This patch is absent in the otherwise similar male, although the tips of the forewings are lighter gray than the rest. In both sexes the underside is brownish.

Great Tanmark

DATA

Scientific name: *Emesis mandana*

Family: Riodinidae

Wingspan: About 2 in (5 cm).

Flight period: All year.

Larval food plants: Members of the Euphorbiaceae, Rhizophoraceae, Sterculiaceae, and Anacardiaceae.

Range: Mexico to Brazil.

The common name recently given to this species is not particularly appropriate, since several other tanmark species have a greater wingspan, although this is one of the larger species. It can be recognized by its size and warm reddish brown coloration. The pattern of short dark lines is much the same as in several other members of the genus. The underside is yellowish brown. *Emesis tegula* is similar but smaller and it is a duller shade of brown. The Great Tanmark is found in a variety of mainly disturbed habitats. It is seen here on the edge of a roadside coffee plantation in Veracruz State, Mexico.

Duke of Burgundy Fritillary

A fritillary only in name and appearance, this is the sole European representative of the large family Riodinidae. It is found in woodland clearings and in flowery meadows and is seen here in England. The upper side is remarkably like some of the smaller European fritillaries, being dark brown to almost black with a pattern of brownish orange spots. The underside is reddish brown with some dark markings on the forewing and a line of white spots on the hind wing. Again, the pattern is not unlike that seen in a number of true fritillaries.

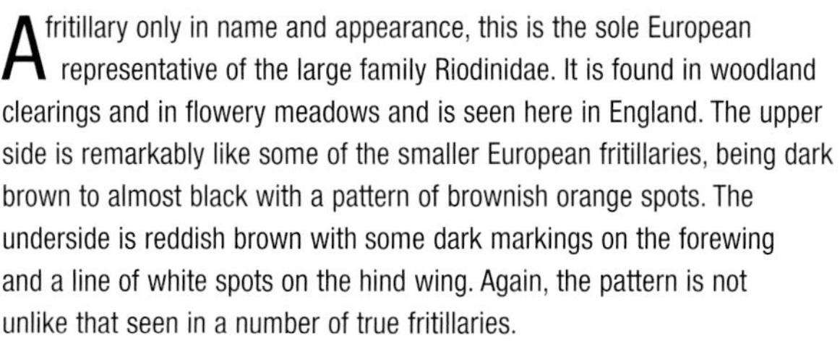

DATA

Scientific name: *Hamearis lucina*

Family: Riodinidae

Wingspan: About 1.2 in (3 cm).

Flight period: May–August in two broods in south; May–June in single brood in north.

Larval food plants: Primroses and cowslips *(Primula)* in the Primulaceae.

Range: Over most of Europe.

Black-spotted Bluemark

Most often seen visiting small white flowers or damp sand, this butterfly is associated with a wide range of forested habitats. The specimen illustrated here was puddling on a semiforested roadside in the Chapada de Guimarães in Brazil. Its bright blue coloration and pattern of small black spots indicate that it is a male. The females are a dull grayish brown, mottled with black. In both sexes the underside is whitish, covered with numerous black spots and zigzag lines.

DATA

Scientific name: *Lasaia agesilas*

Family: Riodinidae

Wingspan: About 1.2 in (3 cm).

Flight period: All year.

Larval food plants: Unknown.

Range: Mexico to Colombia and Brazil.

Bespectacled Eyemark

DATA

Scientific name: *Mesosemia jeziela*

Family: Riodinidae

Wingspan: About 1.4 in (3.5 cm).

Flight period: All year.

Larval food plants: Members of the madder family (Rubiaceae).

Range: Ecuador and Peru.

The 100 or so members of this genus are renowned for their jerky gait. They walk around on leaves in the rain-forest shrub layer, looking like little clockwork toys. They can be identified by the squarish wing shape and, typically, an eyespot on each forewing. In most species the underside bears a pattern of dark and light lines with an eyespot on the forewing. In the Bespectacled Eyemark the combination of black wings, each with a blue and white band, and the eyespot gives the impression of a little face peering out, especially when the wings are held only partly open, as is the norm. The specimen in the photograph was seen in Tingo Maria National Park, Peru.

Common Mimic Metalmark

DATA

Scientific name: *Panara thymele*

Family: Riodinidae

Wingspan: About 1.3 in (3.3 cm).

Flight period: All year.

Larval food plants: Unknown.

Range: Widespread in tropical South America.

The four species in the genus *Panara* resemble certain warningly colored day-flying moths in the families Arctiidae and Geometridae. They are also very similar to some other riodinids, such as the Small Dancer *(Riodina lysippoides)*, although the latter is much smaller and has a short tail on each hind wing. In all four species the ground color is dark velvety black. There are red bands on the forewings or on all four wings, as seen in this species, which was photographed in rain forest in the Rancho Grande reserve in Brazilian Amazonia.

Sword-tailed Beautymark

DATA

Scientific name: *Rhetus arcius*

Family: Riodinidae

Wingspan: About 1.4 in (3.5 cm).

Flight period: All year.

Larval food plants: *Terminalia amazonica* (Combretaceae) and *Mabea occidentalis* (Euphorbiaceae).

Range: Mexico to Brazil and Bolivia.

Plants with small white flowers seem to be the type most often visited by this species, exemplified in this female feeding on a member of the parsley family (Apiaceae) on the edge of a coffee plantation in Veracruz State in Mexico. This is a typical habitat for a butterfly that is usually seen in light gaps in rain forest or in second-growth areas with forest nearby. In both sexes the wings are black with white bands, and there is also a red band toward the tip of the hind wing, which is drawn out into a long tail. In the male, however, the hind wing band only starts out white before changing to bright blue as it continues down the wing to the tip of the tail.

Variable Beautymark

Both sexes of this stunningly beautiful little butterfly visit flowers, but the males can also be found on damp sand, as seen here in rain forest in Peru's Tingo Maria National Park. When not feeding, the males perch beneath leaves and dash out to intercept passing butterflies. They are bright blue with black wing tips and three red spots near the tip of the hind wings, which bear a short tail. The female is brownish with two white bands down the forewing and one on the hind wing; this is similar to the pattern found on the underside in both sexes.

DATA

Scientific name: *Rhetus periander*

Other common name: Blue Doctor (in Trinidad)

Family: Riodinidae

Wingspan: About 1.8 in (4.5 cm).

Flight period: All year.

Larval food plants: Unknown.

Range: Mexico to Argentina and on Trinidad.

Small Dancer

DATA

Scientific name: *Riodina lysippoides*

Family: Riodinidae

Wingspan: About 0.9 in (2.3 cm).

Flight period: All year.

Larval food plants: Unknown.

Range: Argentina and Uruguay.

The six members of this genus can be recognized by the way in which the hind wings are angled. This sometimes produces a short tail, as in the species illustrated here, photographed in semideciduous rain forest in Finca El Rey National Park in Salta Province, Argentina. The forewings are black with a faint brown tinge, the hind wings are pure black, and each wing is crossed by a narrow orange bar. There is just a suggestion of a white tip to the forewing.

Tailed Sally

The three species in this genus are restricted to forests on the island of Madagascar. The butterfly illustrated here was photographed in rain forest in the Ranomafana National Park on the eastern side of the island. The upper side is dark brown. The underside is much paler with a few white lines. There are two small eyespots near the tip of the forewing and two much bigger ones near the tip of the hind wing. That has three tails, arising near a red patch. The combination of tails, eyespots, and red patch adds up to a classic false head, designed to lure the attention of enemies away from the real head.

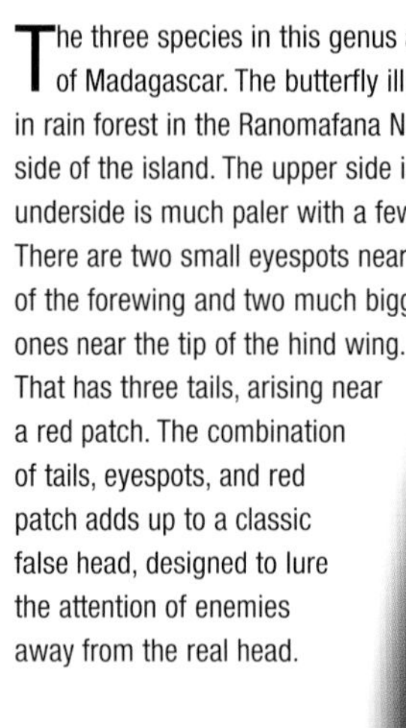

DATA

Scientific name: *Saribia tepahi*

Family: Riodinidae

Wingspan: About 1.5 in (3.8 cm).

Flight period: All year.

Larval food plants: Unknown.

Range: Madagascar.

Gyas Jewelmark

The caterpillars of these tiny butterflies graze on the mosses and liverworts (known as epiphylls) that often coat the surface of long-lived rain-forest leaves. The adults are not often seen, and the specimen illustrated here was spotted on a leaf beside a stream running through rather gloomy rain forest in Corcovado National Park in Costa Rica. The upper side is a drab dark brown. The underside is a far more attractive shade of reddish brown with a series of metallic blue lines. The legs are densely covered in long hairs.

DATA

Scientific name: *Sarota gyas*

Family: Riodinidae

Wingspan: About 0.8 in (2 cm).

Flight period: All year.

Larval food plants: Mosses and liverworts.

Range: Honduras to Colombia and Brazil.

Fan-striped Metalmark

Scientific name: *Siseme neurodes*

Family: Riodinidae

Wingspan: About 1.2 in (3 cm).

Flight period: All year.

Larval food plants: Unknown.

Range: Colombia to Bolivia and Peru.

The 10 or so members of this genus are sometimes mistaken for specimens of *Ancyluris*. In this species the upper side and underside are more or less identical. The wings are grayish white with a broad whitish bar down each, bordered on its outer side by a black bar that is connected to the wing border by a series of black lines, rather like the bars of a cage. The hind wings have an orange patch near the slightly tailed tips. The specimen illustrated here is puddling in rain forest in Peru's Tingo Maria National Park.

Dog-faced Metalmark

DATA

Scientific name: *Thisbe lycorias*

Family: Riodinidae

Wingspan: About 2 in (5 cm).

Flight period: All year.

Larval food plants: *Cassia alata* in the pea family (Fabaceae).

Range: Mexico to Panama.

In common with many other riodinids, this species habitually perches on the underside of a leaf, as seen here in rain forest in Corcovado National Park in Costa Rica. A broad white bar runs across each of the brown wings. There is a small white patch near the tip of the forewing and a few reddish spots, mostly near the front edge of the forewing (known as the costa). The tip of each hind wing is slightly tailed and has a black spot beside a small red patch, giving the butterfly the appearance of having a head at the rear end when viewed from above.

Mountain Beauty

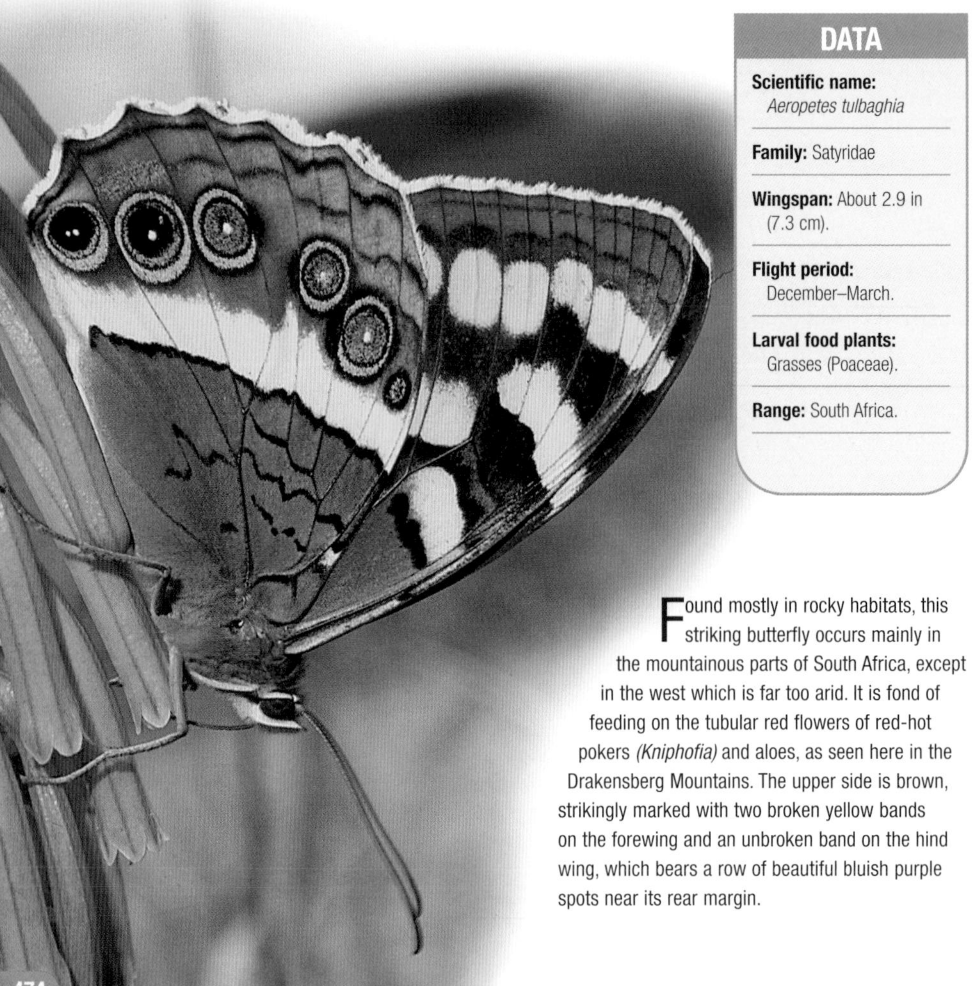

DATA

Scientific name: *Aeropetes tulbaghia*

Family: Satyridae

Wingspan: About 2.9 in (7.3 cm).

Flight period: December–March.

Larval food plants: Grasses (Poaceae).

Range: South Africa.

Found mostly in rocky habitats, this striking butterfly occurs mainly in the mountainous parts of South Africa, except in the west which is far too arid. It is fond of feeding on the tubular red flowers of red-hot pokers *(Kniphofia)* and aloes, as seen here in the Drakensberg Mountains. The upper side is brown, strikingly marked with two broken yellow bands on the forewing and an unbroken band on the hind wing, which bears a row of beautiful bluish purple spots near its rear margin.

Ringlet

DATA

Scientific name: *Aphantopus hyperantus*

Family: Satyridae

Wingspan: About 1.7 in (4.3 cm).

Flight period: June–July.

Larval food plants: Grasses (Poaceae) and sedges *(Carex)* in the family Cyperaceae.

Range: Western Europe.

Anywhere with some long grass is likely to be home to a colony of Ringlets, including the author's backyard, in which a small area of grass is kept unmown for their larvae. A damp woodland edge with plenty of brambles *(Rubus fruticosus)* is also a good place because the adults love to feed on bramble flowers. As seen on this mating pair in England, the underside of the wings is very distinctive with its pattern of three eyespots on the forewing and five on the hind wing. The upper side is a much darker shade of brown with just one or two inconspicuous eyespots on each wing, although even these may be absent.

Dentate Bush Brown

DATA

Scientific name: *Bicyclus dentata*

Family: Satyridae

Wingspan: About 1.7 in (4.3 cm).

Flight period: All year.

Larval food plants: Grasses (Poaceae).

Range: Africa (Congo region, Uganda, Rwanda, Burundi, Kenya, and Tanzania).

A purely tropical African genus, *Bicyclus* has more than 90 species of seasonally variable butterflies in which the eyespots on the underside are better developed in the wet-season forms than in the dry-season forms. The specimen illustrated here is in a typical pose, perched on dead leaves on the rain-forest floor in Kenya's Kakamega Forest. The upper side is dark brown with inconspicuous eyespots on the forewing. The underside is far more attractive—it has three eyespots on the forewing and eight on the hind wing.

Stately Bush Brown

Like other members of its genus, the Stately Bush Brown is usually found on the ground in shady spots in rain forest, as seen here near Kpalimé in Togo. However, this species has also been trapped high in the forest canopy. In the male (illustrated) the underside is light brown with two eyespots on the forewing and seven on the hind wing, three of which are very small. The female is similar but has a white band on the apex of the forewing. In both sexes the upper side is dark brown.

DATA

Scientific name: *Bicyclus xeneas*

Family: Satyridae

Wingspan: About 2 in (5 cm).

Flight period: All year.

Larval food plants: Unknown.

Range: Africa (Sierra Leone to the Congo region).

Hesione Satyr

In the old abandoned cocoa plantations around the Simla research facility in Trinidad this was the one butterfly that was almost guaranteed to be seen on the ground in the most deeply shaded spots. The females could be found laying their eggs on isolated grasses growing near the bases of trees. *Cissia* is one of the genera that were once included in a very wide concept of *Euptychia*. This species can be recognized by its distinctive underside, on which two white bands cross both wings. The upper side is brown.

DATA

Scientific name: *Cissia hesione*

Family: Satyridae

Wingspan: About 1.6 in (4 cm).

Flight period: All year.

Larval food plants: Grasses (Poaceae).

Range: Mexico to Brazil; also on Trinidad.

Pink-tipped Glasswing Satyr

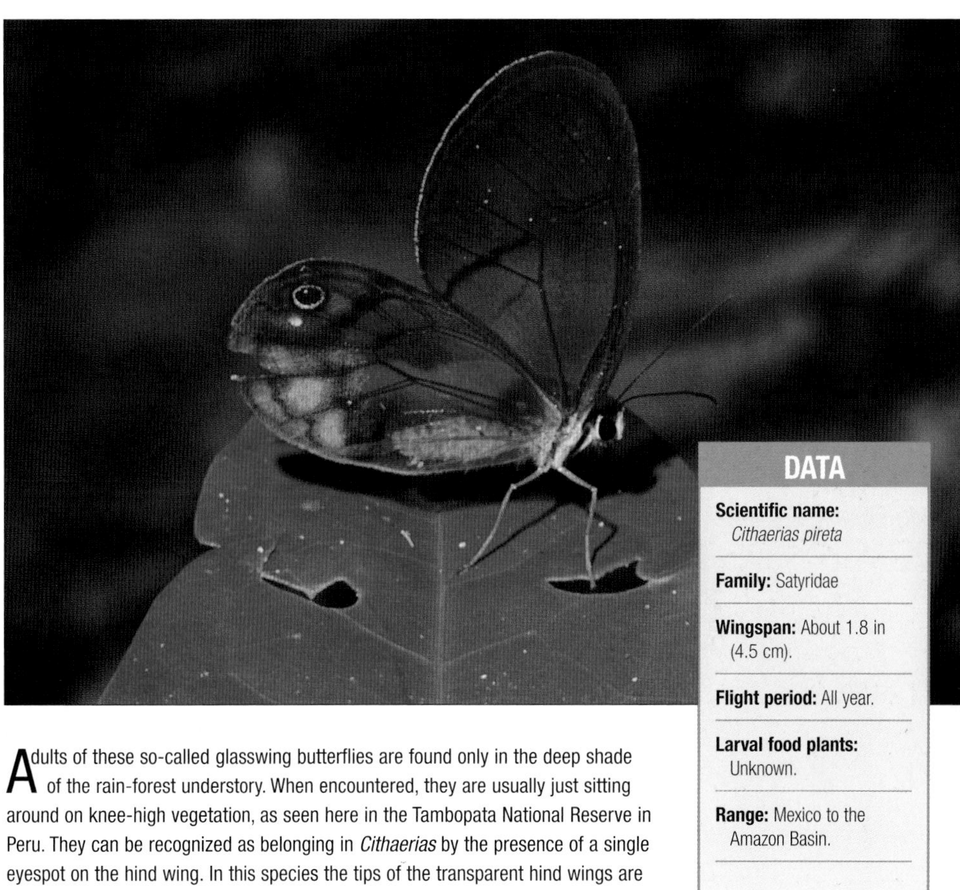

DATA

Scientific name: *Cithaerias pireta*

Family: Satyridae

Wingspan: About 1.8 in (4.5 cm).

Flight period: All year.

Larval food plants: Unknown.

Range: Mexico to the Amazon Basin.

Adults of these so-called glasswing butterflies are found only in the deep shade of the rain-forest understory. When encountered, they are usually just sitting around on knee-high vegetation, as seen here in the Tambopata National Reserve in Peru. They can be recognized as belonging in *Cithaerias* by the presence of a single eyespot on the hind wing. In this species the tips of the transparent hind wings are flushed with red. In other species this flush can be bluish violet or yellowish. Both sexes are attracted to decomposing fruit on the forest floor.

Small Heath

DATA

Scientific name: *Coenonympha pamphilus*

Family: Satyridae

Wingspan: About 1.2 in (3 cm).

Flight period: May–September, in several broods.

Larval food plants: Grasses (Poaceae).

Range: From North Africa and Europe eastward to Iran and Turkestan.

The Small Heath is found in open grassy places such as heaths, moors, and mountainsides. Like this individual, photographed in England, it invariably perches with its wings closed. The underside is mainly pale orange on the forewing, with a single ocellus, and pale brownish on the hind wing. The upper side is pale orange with a small and rather obscure eyespot near the tip of the forewing. It never seems to be a particularly active butterfly, apparently spending much of its time perched among grass on or near the ground, although it often feeds on flowers.

Autumn Widow

The four species of *Dira* are restricted to southern Africa, where they occur mainly in mountainous or desert areas. The specimen illustrated here was photographed in semidesert in Mountain Zebra National Park in Cape Province. As can be seen, when at rest on stony ground the Autumn Widow blends in very well with its surroundings. The author had great difficulty in obtaining this picture because the butterfly simply disappeared every time it landed. The upper side of the wings is brown. A yellow patch near the tip of the forewing contains two eyespots, and there are three eyespots on the hind wing.

DATA

Scientific name: *Dira clytus*

Family: Satyridae

Wingspan: About 1.8 in (4.5 cm).

Flight period: March–May.

Larval food plants: Grasses (Poaceae).

Range: South Africa.

Black-veined Clearwing Satyr

The single species in the genus *Dulcedo* can be distinguished from other similar glasswing butterflies by the absence of any red or purple flush on the hind wing and by the rounded wing shape. The wings are transparent with an open network of blackish lines, and there is a single small eyespot on the hind wing. This species is mainly associated with rain-forest swamps in which there are numerous palms. It was in just this kind of situation that the specimen illustrated below was photographed, feeding on a fallen palm fruit at Finca La Selva in Costa Rica.

DATA

Scientific name: *Dulcedo polita*

Family: Satyridae

Wingspan: About 2.8 in (7 cm).

Flight period: All year.

Larval food plants: Palms *(Geonoma, Welfia)* in the family Arecaceae.

Range: Nicaragua to Colombia.

African Palmfly

DATA

Scientific name: *Elymniopsis bammakoo*

Family: Satyridae

Wingspan: About 3 in (7.5 cm).

Flight period: All year.

Larval food plants: Palms *(Elaeis guineensis, Phoenix reclinata, Raphia hookeri)* in the family Arecaceae.

Range: West Africa to Uganda and northwestern Tanzania.

Formerly included in the Asian genus *Elymnias*, this distinctive species has now been split off into a new genus. Mainly a rain-forest insect, it can survive in quite degraded habitats and even in leafy backyards. Adults often feed on fallen fruit but may puddle, as seen here in Ghana's Bobiri Forest. The coloration is similar to that of *Acraea epaea*, of which the African Palmfly appears to be a mimic. The upper side is black with two white or orange patches on the forewing and one on the hind wing.

Water Ringlet

DATA

Scientific name: *Erebia pronoe*

Family: Satyridae

Wingspan: About 1.6 in (4 cm).

Flight period: July–September.

Larval food plants: Grasses (Poaceae).

Range: Europe.

Mountainous, subarctic, and arctic tundra in Europe, temperate Asia, and North America is where the 80 or so species of *Erebia* are to be found. It is a notoriously difficult genus, and there are considerable problems in defining the species, some of which occur very locally. They all have at least two eyespots on the forewing. This species, photographed on a flowery slope in the Pyrenees Mountains in France, is recognized by the reddish band on the forewing, which contains three eyespots, and by the hind-wing underside, which is silvery gray with a brown band near the margin.

Blue Satyr

Photographed on the ground in rain forest in the Tambopata National Reserve in Peru, this is one of a number of beautiful blue species that have been split away from *Euptychia* and placed in the genus *Caeruleuptychia*. They generally have brilliant blue upper sides as well as the blue underside seen here, although the upper side would normally be visible only when the butterfly is in flight. When at rest, all species of *Euptychia* (in the broad sense) generally close their wings. As illustrated below, the presence of six small eyespots on the hind wing and four even smaller ones on the forewing is diagnostic for this species.

DATA

Scientific name: *Caeruleuptychia glauca*

Family: Satyridae

Wingspan: About 1.6 in (4 cm).

Flight period: All year.

Larval food plants: Unknown.

Range: Peru, Brazil, and Ecuador.

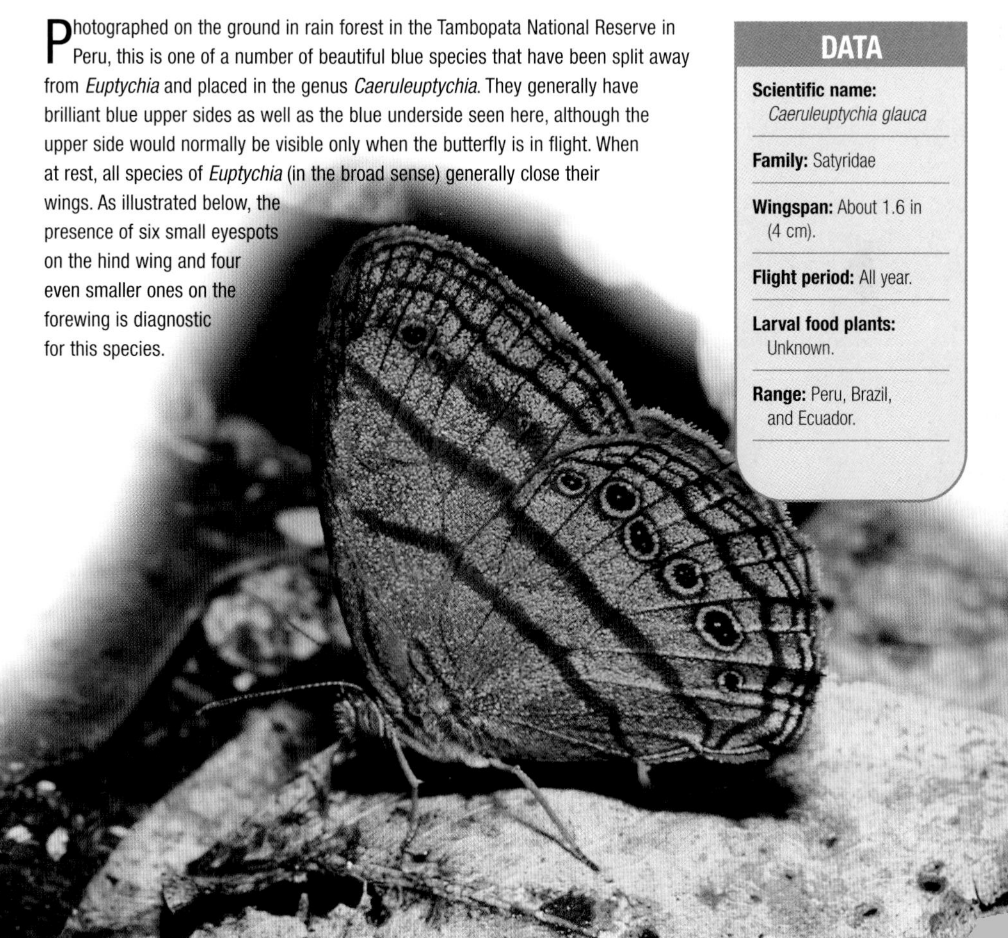

Southwestern Xenica

The genus *Geitoneura* contains just three species, all of which are restricted to the southern half of Australia. They occur mostly in open woodlands of gum trees *(Eucalyptus)*, often resting on the ground among fallen leaves, as seen here at Granite Rock near Perth. The upper side is mottled brown and orange with a small eyespot on each wing. The underside is paler, and—as seen here—the underside of the hind wing is a little like a dead leaf, making the butterfly hard to spot when it is on the ground.

DATA

Scientific name: *Geitoneura klugii*

Family: Satyridae

Wingspan: About 1.6 in (4 cm).

Flight period: September–December.

Larval food plants: Grasses (Poaceae).

Range: Southwestern Australia.

Yellow-banded Evening Brown

DATA

Scientific name: *Gnophodes betsimena*

Family: Satyridae

Wingspan: About 2.6 in (6.5 cm).

Flight period: All year.

Larval food plants: Grasses (Poaceae).

Range: Over most of sub-Saharan Africa and on Madagascar.

This widespread butterfly occurs in three subspecies. Madagascar is home to subspecies *betsimena*, while *diversa* is from east of the Rift Valley to South Africa, and *parmeno* (illustrated) covers the rest of Africa. Although found in gallery forest along rivers and in wooded savanna, this is mainly a forest species, and is seen here in Ghana's Bobiri Forest. The adult butterfly spends most of the day on the ground in deep shade, where it resembles a dead fallen leaf. It becomes active only in late afternoon. The upper side is brown with a yellow band across the apex of the forewing (poorly defined in the male).

Clearwing Satyr

The presence of two eyespots on each hind wing is the main diagnostic character used to recognize the three species of glasswing butterflies in this genus. As in *Dulcedo* and *Cithaerias*, the adults are found sitting around on low vegetation in the shadiest parts of the rain forest, as here in Atlantic coast rain forest at Fazenda Montes Claros in the state of Minas Gerais, Brazil. Apart from the eyespots, the only markings on this species are a narrow reddish band at the apex of the hind wing, which also bears a broadly Y-shaped blackish band.

DATA

Scientific name: *Haetera piera*

Family: Satyridae

Wingspan: About 2.4 in (6 cm).

Flight period: All year.

Larval food plants: Unknown.

Range: Over most of tropical South America.

Southern Satyr

This is another genus that is still included in *Euptychia* by some workers, such as d'Abrera. the Southern Satyr is found in open grassy places and in woods, and is seen here in Georgia. The upper side is brown. The underside, shown here, is silvery brown with a narrow dark wavy line across each wing. On the underside of the hind wing there are six eyespots, three of which are well defined, and there are five rather indistinct eyespots on the forewing. The adults have been seen feeding on sap, fermenting fruit, and mud but never apparently on flowers.

DATA

Scientific name: *Hermeuptychia hermes*

Family: Satyridae

Wingspan: About 1.2 in (3 cm).

Flight period: April–October in north; all year in south.

Larval food plants: Grasses (Poaceae).

Range: United States (New Jersey to Florida and Texas).

Common Brown

Scientific name: *Heteronympha merope*

Family: Satyridae

Wingspan: About 2.4 in (6 cm).

Flight period: November–April.

Larval food plants: Grasses (Poaceae).

Range: Australia.

The most frequently seen butterfly in southern Australia, the Common Brown flies mainly in dry forests of gum trees *(Eucalyptus)*. As depicted here in the Grampian Mountains near Melbourne in the state of Victoria, this species can be very hard to see when sitting on the ground among a carpet of dead gum leaves. The males and females are very different. Above, the male is a mixture of orange and dark brown, vaguely reminiscent of the Wall Brown *(Lasiommata megera)*, but with only a single eyespot on each wing. The female is larger and mainly pale orange with partial black tips to the forewings.

Grayling

DATA

Scientific name: *Hipparchia semele*

Family: Satyridae

Wingspan: About 1.8 in (4.5 cm).

Flight period: July–August.

Larval food plants: Grasses (Poaceae).

Range: Europe to Armenia.

The Grayling is very much a butterfly of open ground, such as heathlands, moorlands, hillsides, and windswept grassy clifftops. It is very fond of settling on bare ground, when with wings closed and often slightly tilted over to one side, it is extremely difficult to spot. A typical pose is shown here, on heathland in England. The upper side is brown with a pale orange patch on the forewing containing two eyespots, and one on the hind wing with a single small eyespot. The underside of the forewing also bears an orange patch and two eyespots, but these are covered when the wings are closed.

Common Brown Ringlet

DATA

Scientific name: *Hypocysta metirius*

Family: Satyridae

Wingspan: About 1.3 in (3.2 cm).

Flight period: All year in north; August–May in south.

Larval food plants: Grasses (Poaceae).

Range: Australia.

This is a common species, ranging along a broad coastal strip in Queensland and New South Wales. It is found in a variety of wooded habitats, and the specimen illustrated above was photographed in rain forest on the Atherton Tableland in Queensland. This butterfly has a jerky and rather slow mode of flight and settles frequently, usually with its wings open. In this pose it exposes the rather facelike topside, with the eyespots on the hind wings resembling two staring eyes. The underside is light orange, and the apices of the forewings are shaded in light gray.

Large Wall Brown

Found mainly in rocky places in hills and mountains, the Large Wall Brown is particularly fond of sitting open-winged on bare paths or rocks, as seen here in the Pyrenees Mountains in France. Where it occurs in two broods, the first brood is larger than the second, while in the latter, as seen here, the upper side is almost entirely a warm brownish orange. In the first brood at least half the forewing is dull brown. On the underside the forewing is orange with a black eyespot which has two white "pupils." The hind wing is mottled pale brown with seven small eyespots.

DATA

Scientific name: *Lasiommata maera*

Family: Satyridae

Wingspan: About 2 in (5 cm).

Flight period: June–July in north; in two broods in south (May–June and August–September).

Larval food plants: Grasses (Poaceae).

Range: From North Africa and western Europe across Asia Minor to the Himalayas.

Wall Brown

DATA

Scientific name: *Lasiommata megera*

Family: Satyridae

Wingspan: About 1.8 in (4.5 cm).

Flight period: April–August (two broods in north, three in south).

Larval food plants: Grasses (Poaceae).

Range: From North Africa and Europe to Syria and Iran.

Although it spends much of its time basking on walls, rocks, paths, or other warm bare places, the Wall Brown is also fond of certain types of flowers, especially knapweeds *(Centaurea)*, as seen here in England. The ground color of the upper side is yellowish orange with a latticework of blackish markings. There is a single conspicuous eyespot on the forewing and four on the hind wing, one of these being very small. The underside is mainly orange on the forewing with one large eyespot and mottled brownish on the hind wing, where there are seven small eyespots.

Meadow Brown

DATA

Scientific name: *Maniola jurtina*

Family: Satyridae

Wingspan: About 2 in (5 cm).

Flight period: June–August.

Larval food plants: Grasses (Poaceae).

Range: Canary Islands and North Africa to Europe, Asia Minor, and Iran.

Just about any area that has some long grass and is not too shaded will be suitable for this very common butterfly, although it disappears at higher elevations on mountains. Although often seen basking open-winged, as illustrated here in England, this species is also fond of flowers. The upper side of the female (illustrated) is brown. There is a conspicuous orange patch on the forewing, containing a single eyespot, and a less intense orange patch on the hind wing. The male is plain brown with a single small eyespot. In both sexes the forewing underside is mostly orange with one eyespot, while the hind wing is brown.

Marbled White

This is by far the most common of several very similar butterflies in Europe, some of which are highly localized in occurrence. The favored habitat is open slopes with long grasses, although highly acid soils seem to be avoided, at least in England. The basic coloration is white, broken up by patches of black to give a marbled effect. The underside is more cream than white with one or two tiny eyespots on the forewing and six on the hind wing. In subspecies *lacheses* the black markings are rather sparse, while in subspecies *lucasi* they are very heavy.

DATA

Scientific name: *Melanargia galathea*

Family: Satyridae

Wingspan: About 2 in (5 cm).

Flight period: June–July.

Larval food plants: Grasses (Poaceae).

Range: From western Europe through southern Russia to Iran.

White-barred Evening Brown

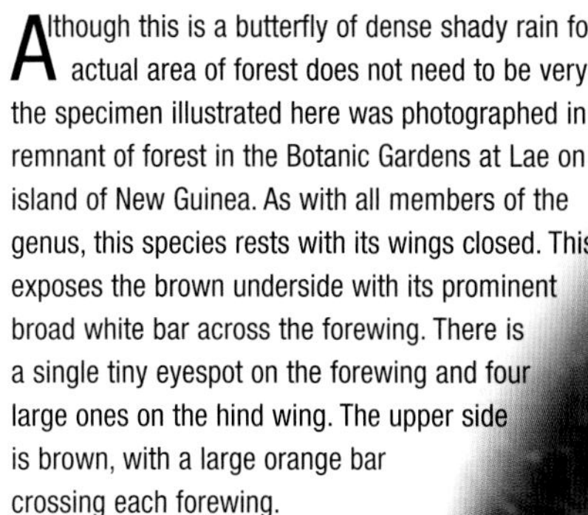

Although this is a butterfly of dense shady rain forest, the actual area of forest does not need to be very large, and the specimen illustrated here was photographed in a tiny remnant of forest in the Botanic Gardens at Lae on the island of New Guinea. As with all members of the genus, this species rests with its wings closed. This exposes the brown underside with its prominent broad white bar across the forewing. There is a single tiny eyespot on the forewing and four large ones on the hind wing. The upper side is brown, with a large orange bar crossing each forewing.

DATA

Scientific name: *Melanitis amabilis*

Family: Satyridae

Wingspan: About 2.8 in (7 cm).

Flight period: All year.

Larval food plants: Grasses (Poaceae).

Range: Buru and Moluccas, the island of New Guinea, Bismarck Archipelago, Bougainville, and the Solomon Islands.

Common Evening Brown

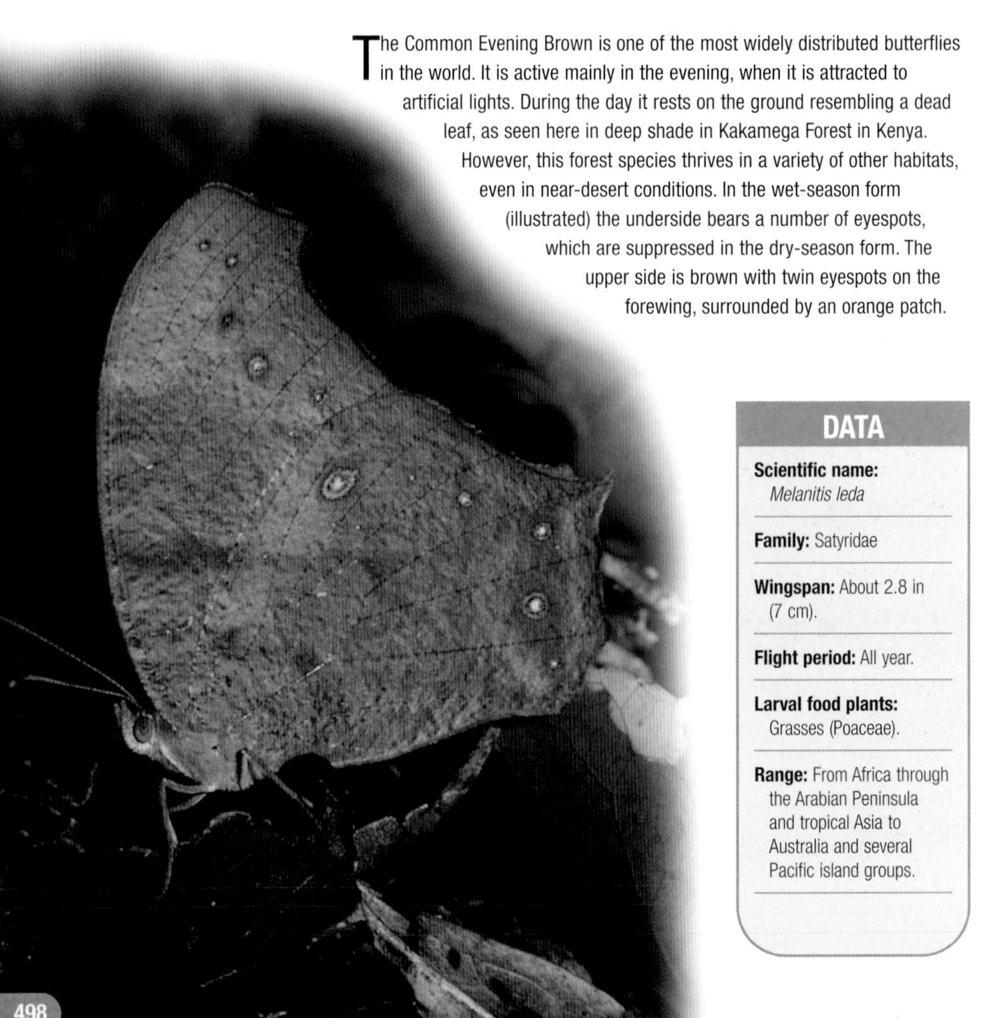

The Common Evening Brown is one of the most widely distributed butterflies in the world. It is active mainly in the evening, when it is attracted to artificial lights. During the day it rests on the ground resembling a dead leaf, as seen here in deep shade in Kakamega Forest in Kenya. However, this forest species thrives in a variety of other habitats, even in near-desert conditions. In the wet-season form (illustrated) the underside bears a number of eyespots, which are suppressed in the dry-season form. The upper side is brown with twin eyespots on the forewing, surrounded by an orange patch.

DATA

Scientific name: *Melanitis leda*

Family: Satyridae

Wingspan: About 2.8 in (7 cm).

Flight period: All year.

Larval food plants: Grasses (Poaceae).

Range: From Africa through the Arabian Peninsula and tropical Asia to Australia and several Pacific island groups.

Dark Evening Brown

Although the underside of this species is usually rather dark, paler forms also exist, particularly in the dry-season form, seen here on a carpet of pale dead leaves in woodland at Periyar in southern India. Such a cryptic insect is usually impossible to see until it flies, and even then it may take several attempts before it can be located again. Found in backyards, woodland, and along shady roadsides, this relatively common species usually skulks in deep shade during the day. The upper side is dark brown with a large eyespot on each forewing, partly surrounded by a small orange patch.

DATA

Scientific name: *Melanitis phedina*

Family: Satyridae

Wingspan: About 2.4 in (6 cm).

Flight period: All year.

Larval food plants: Grasses (Poaceae).

Range: From India and Sri Lanka to China, Myanmar (Burma), and Japan.

Gladeye Bush Brown

DATA

Scientific name: *Mycalesis patnia*

Family: Satyridae

Wingspan: About 1.5 in (3.8 cm).

Flight period: All year.

Larval food plants: Grasses (Poaceae).

Range: Southern India and Sri Lanka.

One of the world's most entertainingly named butterflies, the Gladeye Bush Brown is found in the tropical forests of southern India and Sri Lanka. These regions experience a prolonged dry season, during which the dead leaves that cover the ground crunch underfoot, followed by a long monsoon season of heavy rain. The butterfly seen here was photographed in the dry season at Periyar in Kerala State in southern India and was one of very few butterflies present during the period of drought. The upper side is brown with a single large eyespot on each forewing.

Elegant Bush Brown

Photographed in rain forest in the Varirata National Park near Port Moresby on the great island of New Guinea, the specimen illustrated here was in a particularly shady part of the forest. The underside is especially attractive, with its ground color of bright yellowish orange. There are two eyespots on the forewing and six on the hind wing—two large and four small. The upper side is much drabber, being dingy dark brown with a single eyespot on the forewing and three on the hind wing.

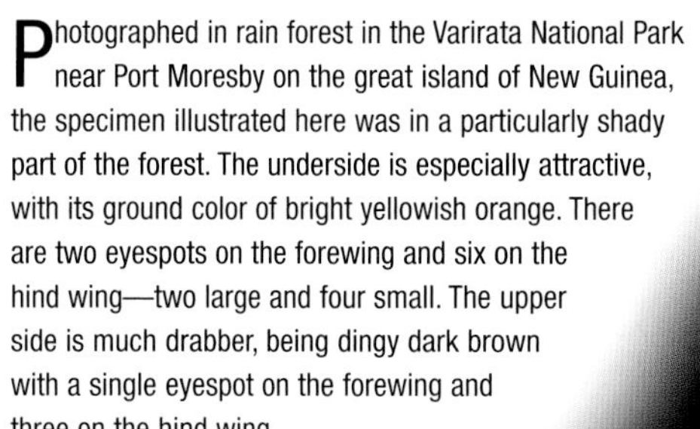

DATA

Scientific name: *Mycalesis phidon*

Family: Satyridae

Wingspan: About 1.6 in (4 cm).

Flight period: All year.

Larval food plants: Grasses (Poaceae).

Range: Aru and Waigeu, across the island of New Guinea to the Bismarck Archipelago.

Orange Bush Brown

DATA

Scientific name: *Mycalesis terminus*

Family: Satyridae

Wingspan: About 1.6 in (4 cm).

Flight period: All year.

Larval food plants: Grasses (Poaceae).

Range: Buru, Moluccas, Misool, Waigeu, the island of New Guinea to the Bismarck Archipelago; also Australia.

The mating pair illustrated here was photographed in rain forest in Lake Barrine National Park in the Australian state of Queensland. This is the only Australian state that has the year-around tropical climate needed by this species. The upper side is brown with an orange patch on the forewing, which has a blackish tip. There are four eyespots on each wing, two of them always being very tiny. The eyespots are larger and better developed in the male. The underside is brown, and a cream band divides the rest of each wing from a row of eyespots.

Brown Arctic

DATA

Scientific name: *Oeneis chryxus*

Family: Satyridae

Wingspan: About 2 in (5 cm).

Flight period: May–July.

Larval food plants: Grasses (Poaceae).

Range: From Southern Alaska to Quebec and Michigan, southward through the Rockies to New Mexico.

Photographed here on a mountainside in the Rockies in Wyoming, the Brown Arctic is very much a butterfly of cool climates, as are the nine other members of the genus found in North America. Some of them are very similar to the species shown here, which is found in open woodland and alpine tundra in dry, sandy, or rocky places. The upper side, normally seen only when the butterfly is in flight, is tawny brown. The hind-wing underside bears a mottled cryptic pattern, making the butterfly hard to see when at rest on the ground. The forewing is pale orange with either one or two small eyespots.

Speckled Wood

DATA

Scientific name: *Pararge aegeria*

Family: Satyridae

Wingspan: About 1.6 in (4 cm).

Flight period: March–October.

Larval food plants: Grasses (Poaceae).

Range: North Africa, Europe, and Asia Minor to central Asia.

The butterfly featured here belongs to subspecies *tircis* and is found in northern, central, and eastern Europe. The photograph was taken in the author's backyard in England. In this form the ground color is creamy white, with brown markings covering most of the wings. There is a single eyespot on the forewing and three on the hind wing. The underside is similar but paler. In subspecies *aegeria* the ground color is orange. Mostly associated with light gaps in woodland, the Speckled Wood also occurs in more open habitats—even on exposed, almost treeless coastal cliffs— and is fairly common in backyards.

Dark-webbed Ringlet

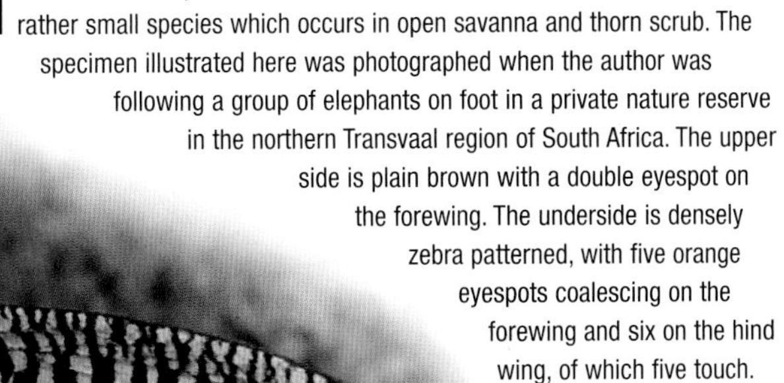

There are few satyrids with a more attractive underside pattern than this rather small species which occurs in open savanna and thorn scrub. The specimen illustrated here was photographed when the author was following a group of elephants on foot in a private nature reserve in the northern Transvaal region of South Africa. The upper side is plain brown with a double eyespot on the forewing. The underside is densely zebra patterned, with five orange eyespots coalescing on the forewing and six on the hind wing, of which five touch.

DATA

Scientific name: *Physcaenura panda*

Family: Satyridae

Wingspan: About 1.2 in (3 cm).

Flight period: All year in north; November–April in south.

Larval food plants: Grasses (Poaceae).

Range: Southern Africa, northward to Zimbabwe.

Lady Slipper

DATA

Scientific name: *Pierella hyalinus*

Family: Satyridae

Wingspan: About 2.2 in (5.5 cm).

Flight period: All year.

Larval food plants: Crab's claws *(Heliconia)*. in the Heliconiaceae.

Range: Trinidad, Guianas, and Amazon Basin.

In the rather narrow, elongate shape of the forewing the butterflies in *Pierella* are similar to *Cithaerias* but do not have transparent wings. During the author's stay at Simla in Trinidad the Lady Slipper was relatively common, fluttering low across the ground in deep shade in the old abandoned cocoa plantations, where the accompanying photograph was taken. The forewings are a rather drab shade of brown, but the hind wings are a lovely iridescent blue. The underside is pale brown with a silvery sheen, and there are two eyespots on each hind wing.

Gatekeeper

Fond of basking open-winged on fences and gateposts (hence its common name), this species is found in a wide variety of habitats, such as roadsides, open woodland, and backyards. It seems to be especially common around bramble bushes *(Rubus fruticosus)* and is very partial to their flowers. The large area of brownish orange on the upper side makes this one of the most attractive European satyrids. The underside of the forewing is similar to the upper side but paler, but the hind-wing underside is mainly pale brown.

DATA

Scientific name: *Pyronia tithonus*

Family: Satyridae

Wingspan: About 1.4 in (3.6 cm).

Flight period: July–August.

Larval food plants: Grasses (Poaceae).

Range: Europe to Asia Minor and the Caucasus.

Clio Satyr

DATA

Scientific name: *Rareuptychia clio*

Family: Satyridae

Wingspan: About 1.6 in (4 cm).

Flight period: All year.

Larval food plants: Probably *Selaginella* club mosses.

Range: Peru, Ecuador, and Brazil.

The genus *Euptychia* used to contain some 200 often rather confused species, but many have now been split off into separate genera (although these are not accepted by some lepidopterists). The underside is generally of most interest—the upper side being mainly plain brown, as in this species. These butterflies are all denizens of the shady rain-forest understory. The individual illustrated here, for example, was photographed in Peru's Tambopata National Reserve and is feeding on sap bleeding from a stem wounded by an insect larva within. The white band and elongate eyespots on the underside of the hind wing are distinctive.

Black Satyr

Photographed here in southern France, the Black Satyr is a butterfly of open, dry, stony slopes. It spends much of the time on the ground, where its cryptic coloring makes it hard to spot. The underside of the wings is blackish brown—down the hind wing there are two jagged-edged bands that are a little paler, and on the forewing there is a single eyespot. The upper side is dark brown with a single inconspicuous eyespot (sometimes two) on the forewing. Several other species are similar.

DATA

Scientific name: *Satyrus actaea*

Family: Satyridae

Wingspan: About 2 in (5 cm).

Flight period: July–August.

Larval food plants: Grasses (Poaceae).

Range: Southwest Europe, Asia Minor, Syria, and Iran.

Bates's Malagasy Brown

DATA

Scientific name: *Strabena batesii*

Family: Satyridae

Wingspan: About 1.2 in (3 cm).

Flight period: All year.

Larval food plants: Unknown.

Range: Madagascar.

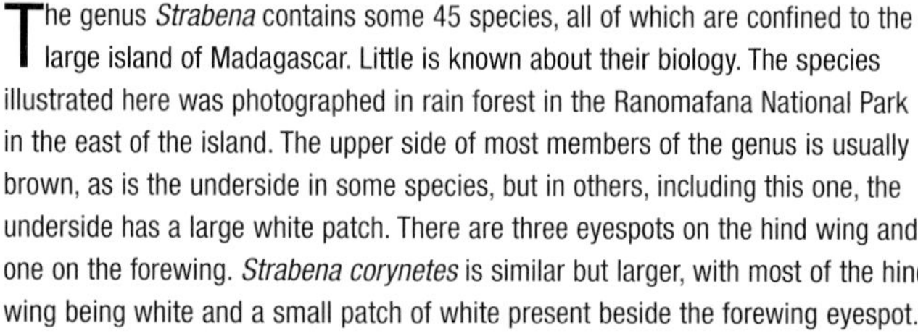

The genus *Strabena* contains some 45 species, all of which are confined to the large island of Madagascar. Little is known about their biology. The species illustrated here was photographed in rain forest in the Ranomafana National Park in the east of the island. The upper side of most members of the genus is usually brown, as is the underside in some species, but in others, including this one, the underside has a large white patch. There are three eyespots on the hind wing and one on the forewing. *Strabena corynetes* is similar but larger, with most of the hind wing being white and a small patch of white present beside the forewing eyespot.

Northern Sword-grass Brown

DATA

Scientific name: *Tisiphone helena*

Family: Satyridae

Wingspan: About 2 in (5 cm).

Flight period: All year.

Larval food plants: Sword grasses *(Gahnia)* in the sedge family (Cyperaceae).

Range: Australia.

This species is restricted to rain forest on the Atherton Tableland near Cairns in Queensland, Australia, where the accompanying picture was taken. This individual is feeding on the introduced plant *Lantana camara*, which is now a widespread pest but is often a favorite with tropical butterflies. The forewing upper side is mostly pale orange, with black tips and two eyespots. The hind wing is mainly brown, also with two eyespots. The underside is like a pale version of the upper side, with four black spots on the hind wing.

Penelea Satyr

DATA

Scientific name: *Taygetis penelea*

Family: Satyridae

Wingspan: About 2.2 in (5.5 cm).

Flight period: All year.

Larval food plants: Grasses (Poaceae).

Range: Costa Rica to the Amazon Basin and in Trinidad.

The Penelea Satyr is yet another of those satyrids that seek out the gloomiest spots in rain forest and spend most of the day on the forest floor, becoming active toward dusk. This species was common in the deep shade of the old abandoned cocoa trees at Simla in Trinidad, where the accompanying picture was taken. The upper side is dull brown, as with most other members of the genus. The underside is mostly light brown with a cream stripe across the hind wing. The hind wing also bears four eyespots, one of which is very tiny.

Yellow-barred Brown

One of the most common butterflies of the region, this species is found in rain forest, disturbed areas, plantations of rubber and oil palm, parks, and backyards. It was photographed here in rain forest at Bukit Lawang in Sumatra. The underside of the forewing is light brown with a cream band and a single small eyespot. The hind wing is also pale brown but has a beautiful purplish blue flush, visible in the picture. There are three properly developed eyespots and five that are small and imperfect. The upper side is brown.

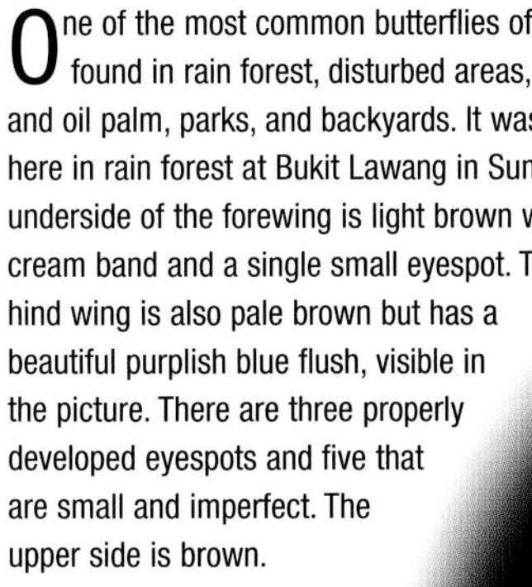

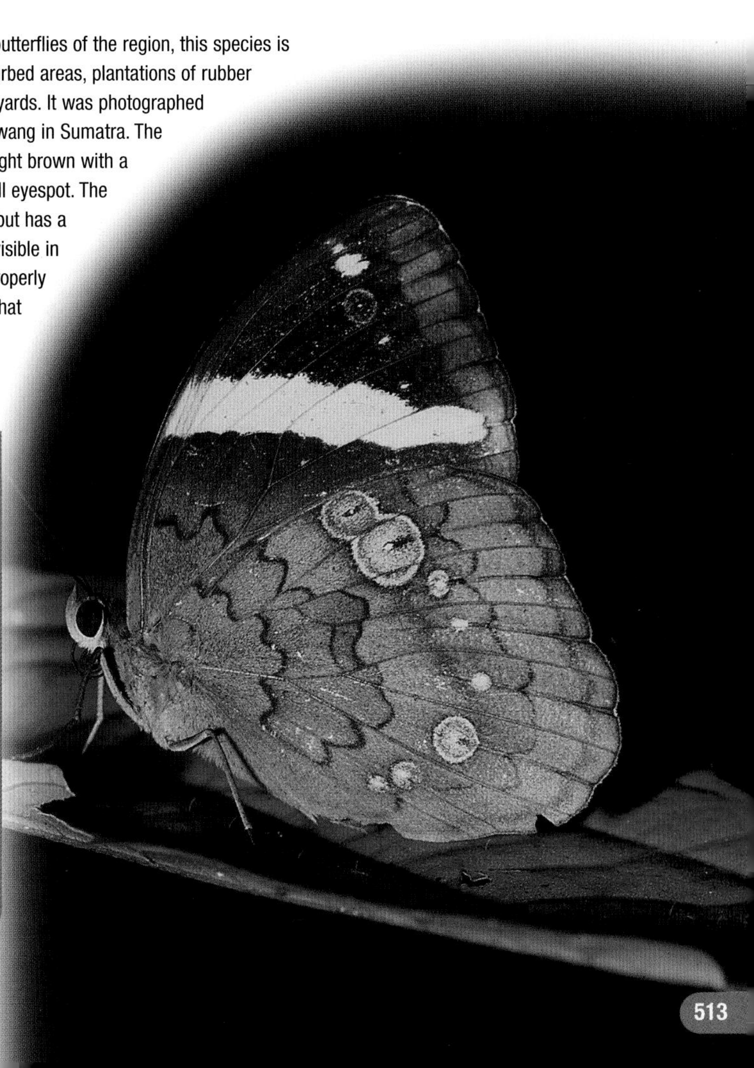

DATA

Scientific name: *Xanthotaenia busiris*

Family: Satyridae

Wingspan: About 2.4 in (6 cm).

Flight period: All year.

Larval food plants: *Calamus* in the palm family (Arecaceae).

Range: Myanmar (Burma) to Malaysia and Indonesia.

Common Ringlet

DATA

Scientific name: *Ypthima doleta*

Family: Satyridae

Wingspan: About 1.4 in (3.5 cm).

Flight period: All year.

Larval food plants: Grasses (Poaceae).

Range: Africa (Senegal to Sudan and Uganda).

This is one of the more distinctive members of a genus of butterflies that are often extremely hard to tell apart. They are mainly butterflies of grassy savanna, and the Common Ringlet is one of the few that can be found in open areas in the forest zone. The one seen here was photographed in the garden behind the author's room in Ghana's Bobiri Forest. The upper side is brown, with a large eyespot on the forewing and three smaller ones on the hind wing. The antennae are brown, ringed with white above and with a white line running along below. The underside is similar but mottled.

Gray Ringlet

Photographed in savanna on a campsite in Meru National Park in Kenya, this individual is feeding on a flower belonging to the sunflower family (Asteraceae), which is always popular with nectar-seeking butterflies. However, species of *Ypthima* do not seem to be attracted to sap, dung, or fermenting fruit. On the upper side this is a rather shiny gray butterfly with a large eyespot on the forewing and two (one very tiny) on the hind wing. The underside bears a very fine zebralike pattern of extremely narrow wavy stripes (irrorations).

DATA

Scientific name: *Ypthima granulosa*

Family: Satyridae

Wingspan: About 1.3 in (3.3 cm).

Flight period: All year.

Larval food plants: Grasses (Poaceae).

Range: East Africa to Malawi and Mozambique.

Glossary

Words in SMALL CAPITALS refer to other entries in the Glossary.

Amazonia The tropical area around the Amazon River in South America, mainly in Brazil but also including areas of Peru, Bolivia, and Ecuador.

antennae Twin feelers on a butterfly's head.

apex The tip of the wing (usually forewing).

apical At the tip (of the wing, usually forewing).

Batesian mimic An edible butterfly (or other insect) that mimics the color and pattern of a species that is not edible.

campo cerrado A vast region of savannalike vegetation in central Brazil, now largely destroyed for the pursuit of agriculture, resulting in an enormous loss of biodiversity. *See also* SAVANNA.

eyespot a distinct eyelike pattern on a butterfly's wing; the rim and center ("pupil") often have contrasting colors.

falcate With an incurved margin, resulting in a more or less hooked tip.

forewings The front pair of a butterfly's four wings.

frass Debris or excrement produced by the caterpillar.

hind wings The rear pair of a butterfly's four wings.

mimicry The phenomenon of one species of insect imitating another. The insect being mimicked is called the model; the copycat is called the mimic. *See also* BATESIAN MIMIC and MUELLERIAN MIMIC.

morph Form or phase of an insect (or other animal).

Muellerian mimic A butterfly (or other insect) that is itself inedible and mimics the color and pattern of another (usually more numerous) inedible species.

nectaring The practice of visiting flowers to drink the nectar they contain.

puddling Drinking on the ground, often on mud soaked with mammal urine.

savanna Area of open grassland with scattered trees (usually thorn trees); the term is mainly used for African habitats.

sex brand A thick patch of sex cells or scent scales on a butterfly's wing that produce scent hormones, or pheromones, which attract mates and aid in sex recognition.

tiger-striped mimicry grouping/complex A group of butterflies (and also moths) that all bear a yellow and black or yellow and brown pattern of stripes, which confers protection for the whole group from enemies such as birds. From bitter experience the latter quickly learn to recognize the "tiger-striped" uniform (and other color combinations that have the same function) and subsequently avoid all butterflies that wear it.

tundra Treeless area in the Arctic region.

underside The underneath of a butterfly when viewed with its wings open flat.

upper side The topmost side of a butterfly when viewed from above with its wings open flat.

vein One of the supporting structures in a butterfly's wing.

warning coloration An easily recognized pattern (e.g., black and white or black and red), which warns an enemy that the butterfly (or other insect) so adorned is poisonous or distasteful and should not be eaten.

Page numbers in **bold** type refer to main entries; *italic* page numbers refer to illustrations in the introductory section.

A

D

T

U

V

W

X

Y

Z

Further Reading

d'Abrera, B., *The Concise Atlas of Butterflies of the World*, Hill House Publishers, Ossining, NY, 2001.

Braby, M. F., *The Complete Field Guide to Butterflies of Australia*, CSIRO Publishing, Collingwood, Australia, 2004.

Cech, R., and G. Tudor, *Butterflies of the East Coast: An Observer's Guide*, Princeton University Press, Princeton, NJ, 2007.

DeVries, P. J., *The Butterflies of Costa Rica and their Natural History* (2 volumes), Princeton University Press, Princeton, NJ, 1997.

Heppner, J. B., *The Monarch*, Scientific Publishers, Gainesville, FL, 2005.

Hernández, L. R., and P. L. Veitía, *Field Guide of Cuban–West Indies Butterflies*, Zulia University, Maracaibo, Venezuela, 2004.

Lafranchis, T., *Butterflies of Europe*, Diatheo, Paris, 2004.

Larsen, T. B., *Butterflies of West Africa* (2 volumes), Apollo Books, Stenstrup, Denmark, 2005.

Larsen, T. B., *Hazards of Butterfly Collecting*, Cravitz Printing, Brentwood, UK, 2004.

Monastyrskii, A., and A. Devyatkin, *Common Butterflies of Vietnam*, Labour and Social Affairs Publishers, Hanoi, 2005.

Preston-Mafham, R., and K. Preston-Mafham, *Butterflies of the World*, Facts On File, New York, 2004.

Scott, J. A., *The Butterflies of North America*, Stanford University Press, Palo Alto, CA, 1992.

Tilden, J. W., and A. C. Smith, *Western Butterflies* (a Peterson Field Guide), Houghton Mifflin, Boston, MA, 1986.

Tolman, T., and R. Lewington, *Butterflies of Britain and Europe*, Collins, London, 2004.

Tomlinson, D., and R. Still, *Britain's Butterflies*, WILDGuides, Maidenhead, UK, 2002.

Tyler, H., Brown, K., and K. Wilson, *Swallowtail Butterflies of the Americas*, Scientific Publishers, Gainesville, FL, 1994.

Vane-Wright, R. I., *Butterflies*, Smithsonian Institution Press, Washington, DC, 2003.

Warren, A. D., *Butterflies of Oregon*, University Press of Colorado, Boulder, CO, 2005.

Woodhall, S., *Field Guide to Butterflies of South Africa*, C. Struik, Cape Town, 2005.